Developing a Written Voice

Developing a Written Voice

DONA J. HICKEY
University of Richmond

Mayfield Publishing Company
Mountain View, California
London   •   Toronto

For Gordon

Library of Congress Cataloging-in-Publication Data
Hickey, Dona J.
    Developing a written voice / Dona J. Hickey
        p.   cm.
    Includes bibliographical references and index.
    ISBN 1-55934-049-5
    1. English language—Rhetoric.   2. College readers.   I. Title.
PE1408.H4786   1992
808'.042—dc20   92-14928
                                                                  CIP

Manufactured in the United States of America
10 9 8 7 6 5 4 3 2 1

Mayfield Publishing Company
1240 Villa Street
Mountain View, CA 94041

Sponsoring editor, Janet M. Beatty; managing editor, Linda Toy; production
editor, April Wells-Hayes; copyeditor, Carol I. Beal; text and cover designer,
David Bullen; art director, Jeanne M. Schreiber; manufacturing manager,
Martha Branch. The text was set in 10½/12 Bembo and printed on 50# Finch
Opaque by Malloy Lithographing.

Acknowledgments and copyrights appear at the back of the book on pages
259–260, which constitute an extension of the copyright page.

Preface

Voice is an important quality of good writing, and yet composition textbooks that openly address the subject devote a chapter or less to it. More often, the subject comes up in style manuals intended primarily as supplementary material to a writing course. One problem has been that as much as voice is important, it is also elusive. It's just plain hard to talk about. It's hard to define, it's hard to explain its features, and it's hard to find an organized way of introducing and teaching it to others. Still, we all know it when we hear it. And we talk about voice in all three areas of English studies—composition, creative writing, and literature—because we value it highly and recognize voice as the one quality, hard as it may be to pin down, that separates merely competent writing from good writing.

APPROACH

This book is my honest attempt to make voice the center of classroom discussion in a writing course. It is not a rulebook; it is, by nature and necessity, exploratory. It is a dialog that roots students in traditional rhetoric while encouraging them to explore important stylistic issues that have an impact on voice. This is a student-centered, process-oriented writing text, offering multiple drafts of student and professional work within a collaborative setting. It aims at the subtleties of style and voice within the humanistic framework of social interaction. Ultimately, this is a book about self-definition and of consciously taking responsibility for one's words.

Because of that approach, I have avoided the usual format of style books. That is, individual chapters are not devoted to particular stylistic features. Instead, they are organized by levels of discourse—colloquial, formal, and informal. My belief is that we make stylistic choices (which affect voice) based on the rhetorical situation in which we find ourselves. Although there is no one set of stylistic features that belongs exclusively to informal or formal discourse, it is impossible to talk about voice outside a rhetorical framework except in the most limited way.

Voice is always heard within a rhetorical framework: who's talking to whom, about what, where. Consequently, you will find overlap from chapter to chapter, and you will hear me repeat that there are no specific rules for creating informal or formal voices. There are, however, touchstones. And these we can explore as we listen to various ways writers create speech melodies (pitch, stress, and duration) within and across levels of discourse, paragraphs, and sentences.

One major concern among those who talk about voice is the question of whether we have one voice uniquely ours or multiple voices. My own answer to this question is that both positions are valid, depending on the writer. Some writers like to use many voices, all of them authentic; some prefer one voice, modifying it only as necessary to suit the subject, audience, and occasion. In this book, therefore, you'll find nods in both directions. I've left wiggle room—space to discuss this issue in the classroom.

ORGANIZATION

Every chapter has writing activities, including collaborative work and peer response. Some activities are short exercises; others involve longer, more developed pieces of writing. Because of the nature of the subject, the focus is on personal writing, but not exclusively so. There are opportunities for practicing academic discourse or other forms of critical writing, and there are samples of these styles in Chapters 5, 6, and 9. Chapter 9 includes a student sample of critical analysis. Every chapter includes samples of professional and student writing.

Briefly, I'd like to outline the chapters according to specific topics of discussion.

Chapter 1: Voice and the Writer

Here I set the parameters of the text, introducing the notion of voice, the importance of intonation, speech rhythms, and the interplay between stylistic features and discourse occasions. The core of this chapter is the discursive nature of reading and writing, the social nature of communication, and the importance of choice in individual expression. The chapter concludes by urging a spirit of experimentation rather than exhorting writers to follow a prescribed set of formal structures.

Chapter 2: Colloquial Voices: Discovering Sounds of Speech

Voice is described in relationship to audiences and distances from them. Writers inductively explore their assumptions about style and the subsequent influence on voice. Exercises are designed to teach that forms and structures can liberate as well as constrict.

Chapter 3: Toward a Developed Essay: Sustaining a Colloquial Voice

The chapter begins with several samples of classroom and professional writing, with commentary and questions for discussion. Suggestions for imitation follow the professional samples. Chapter 3 concludes with an essay assignment, focusing on process and peer response.

Chapter 4: Formal Voices, Part I: Pattern Play

Beginning with colloquial voices and moving to the far end of the continuum—formal voices—allows writers to understand the concept of vocal registers. This chapter offers more than a compendium of tropes and schemes. It offers exercises to explore what various forms and structures are good for as writers consider effects of particular stylistic choices. Chapter 4 prepares the way for the weaving of rhetorical and current writing theory presented in Chapter 5.

Chapter 5: Formal Voices, Part II: From Pattern to Product

Here writers learn that no rules apply for producing levels of discourse, that rhetorical choices are always relative, and that revision is worth the pain it often demands. The early exercises extend work at imitation into self-reflection and analysis. These exercises encourage writers to make unconscious knowledge conscious, thereby strengthening the scaffolds necessary for writing growth. The chapter leads to creating a developed piece of formal writing, again with emphasis on process, revision, and peer response. A student essay concludes the chapter, with excerpts from planning, drafting, and revising.

Chapter 6: Informal Voices: The Middle Ground

This chapter builds on the preceding ones, emphasizing the rhetorical nature of voice. It treats different levels of informality, beginning with the high-middle range, one often associated with academic discourse. Writers are asked to bring in a text that excludes them. This exercise focuses on the barriers students often perceive in texts, the points at which they abandon reading. By emphasizing the effects of choices on audiences, the exercise prepares for the discussion of the features of informal voices. The later imitation exercises ("in the manner of") are freer than those in Chapter 5 and encourage greater exploration. The chapter ends with an essay assignment and a sample student essay.

Chapter 7: Informal Voices:
Special Effects of the Wild Mix

Chapter 7 focuses on a special brand of informality in which the speaker intentionally draws from the extreme ends of the continuum (low to high informality). Three professional models begin the chapter, illustrating the effects of stylistic disjunction. An essay assignment follows, again an imitation "in the manner of" one of the samples provided in the chapter. Sample student essays conclude the chapter.

Chapter 8: The Voice of the Paragraph:
The Organizing Power of Intonation Patterns

Here the emphasis shifts from the aesthetic to the practical. Chapter 8 concerns voice as connective tissue between sentences and across chunks of discourse. It begins by focusing on three possibilities a paragraph can have: sense without sound of sense, sound of sense without sense, and both sense and sound of sense. Several exercises follow to show that intonation, as well as structure, carries information. The chapter's discussion and exercises offer a possible cure for disconnectedness at the paragraph level.

Chapter 9: Your Voice and Your Audience

Chapter 9 concludes the text. It offers a summary of previous discussion and suggests a synthesis of information. Multiple texts from several authors illustrate the point of preceding chapters: that verbal habits are conscious choices and that voice and style are inseparable. Writers observe voice in context with occasion, purpose, and audience. Two writing activities follow: The first is critical analysis followed by a student example of the assignment; the second is an exercise in modifying voice for different audiences.

Appendix: Applications: Practice in Problem Solving

The appendix offers 15 suggested assignments, a sample of one student writing the same exposition for two different audiences, and a series of exercises deriving from *Tough, Sweet, and Stuffy* by Walker Gibson.

ACKNOWLEDGMENTS

In this text, I recognize all my teachers, particularly Justin Replogle of the University of Wisconsin—Milwaukee, who taught me the music of printed voices. My best writing reflects his teaching. He and Bill Smith of Western Washington University read the manuscript in all of its stages. Their encouragement and help were invaluable.

Mary Blewett of Cardinal Stritch College and Julie O'Neill generously contributed their own writing and support to this project. Their voices, as well as the many student voices in this text, provide lessons in harmony and grace.

Without Jan Beatty, *Developing a Written Voice* would not exist. My best fortune was meeting her at the Conference on College Composition and Communication in Chicago. She is the kind of editor writers hope for but seldom find. (All the more troubling to think I almost ran her down in the campus parking lot.) To her and to the editing and production staff at Mayfield Publishing, I am especially indebted.

My reviewers responded with interest and care. Their detailed commentary gave shape to the final version. Thanks to Wendy Bishop, Florida State University; Mary Edge Blewett, Cardinal Stritch College; Kathleen Shine Cain, Merrimack College; James V. Catano, Louisiana State University; Carolyn Channell, Southern Methodist University; Shirley Morahan, Northeast Missouri State University; Justin Replogle, University of Wisconsin—Milwaukee; William E. Smith, Western Washington University; Jennifer Wolfe Thompson, University of Kansas; and Molly Abel Travis, Tulane University.

The University of Richmond strongly supported my work on this project; thanks to all my colleagues here, particularly Barbara Griffin, whose counsel has never failed me.

Contents

Introduction

Voice and the Writer

This book is about voice. By voice, I mean the writer's relationship to subject, audience, and occasion as it is revealed through the particular blend of speech patterns you hear as you read.

Voice is the sum effect of all the stylistic choices a writer makes to communicate not only information about a subject but also information about himself or herself to a particular audience. In that sense, all writing can be said to be expressive—except for highly technical discourse, in which the convention is the absence of voice. To the audiences of technical discourse, the felt presence of the writer is undesirable. That is not to say that the technical writer does not have a "style." Rather, the style—a writer's habitual language choices—is not voiced. We don't hear the strong intonation patterns of personal speech. We don't hear the person behind the information.

This chapter sets the parameters of the text, focusing, in part, on the importance of intonation, speech rhythms, and the interplay between stylistic features and discourse occasions. At the heart of the chapter is the discursive nature of reading and writing, the social nature of communication, and the importance of choice in individual expression. At the end of this overview, the general structure of the text as well as its spirit is described: This is a book not about rules but about experiments. It's about discovering written voices and, in that discovery, the links between language and ideas. Voice, finally, is not only a way of speaking but also a way of knowing.

OUR DUAL ROLE AS READERS

Reading is an act in which we perform two roles simultaneously: that of the speaker and that of the audience. As we transform written sentences into speech, we reproduce the speaking personality of the writer. We become part of the cultural, social, and psychological world represented by the writer's speech habits. In short, we perform the writer's role, and by doing so, we make black squiggles on the page become the voice of a particular person in a particular place at a particular time.

As we read, we are the audience to the voice we hear. Not only do we take in information about the world, but we also meet the person delivering information. In all but purely technical or scientific writing, we hear not only what the writer knows but also who he or she is. The personality we hear determines the level at which we respond as one interested, sympathetic human being to another. In expressive writing, the stronger the personality, the more active our reading is. That is, if we hear the sound of a lively, distinct personality while we're reading, we listen harder and we feel we can talk back. We enter a conversation of a sort—we might smile, nod, frown, even argue, as if the words we give voice to were intended for our ears only. The degree to which each of us feels like an invited, well-cared-for guest determines our listening pleasure. The degree to which we make our own readers feel the same way determines theirs.

SPEECH MELODY

"Listening pleasure" is significant, because in a very real sense, voice is music. It is the verbal tune we create when we talk in earnest about our interests, beliefs, joys, sorrows, and fears to someone who matters. The tunes of conversation (intonation) are determined by the rise and fall, timbre, rhythm, and pace of our voices. Getting readers to hear tunes is what good writing is all about. The writers we admire most are those whose sentences, one after the other, become the sound pattern of a distinct, engaging, human personality. In writing, that sound is directed by printed cues. From them, we make the music of speech heard, if only in our heads; and we respond to its special qualities intellectually, socially, and emotionally.

Naturally, the voice we hear in our heads cannot replicate all the tonal richness of real talk. And it is tonal richness—the writer's feeling about the information, heard in the verbal tune running across phrases and sentences—that we want to capture, not the imprecision and discursiveness of speech. Robert Frost said, "There are moments that we actually touch in talk what the best writing can only come near." He meant the melody and rhythm of speech, those lively vocal runs that put us in touch with another person but are impossibly hard to suggest in print. Although we lose a lot in going from the spoken word to the written word, what we gain from trying to capture the tunes of speech marks the difference between writing that's heard and writing that's viewed. This difference is vital. Frost says, "Good writing is good speaking caught alive" (Thompson 180).

Here's a short example from one of Frost's narrative poems, "The Pauper Witch of Grafton":

All is, if I'd a-known when I was young
And full of it, that this would be the end,
It doesn't seem as if I'd had the courage
To make so free and kick up in folks' faces.
I might have, but it doesn't seem as if.

The vitality Frost captures here is not in the vocabulary of the speech but in the melody. It's the intonation pattern running across the lines that we hear in our heads and to which we respond as one sympathetic human being to another. The emotional appeal is in the music. Here is the passage without the melodic interest of real talk:

If I'd a-known this would be the end
When I was full of it and young,
It doesn't seem as if I'd had the courage
To kick up in folks' faces and make so free.
I might have done it, but it doesn't seem as if I would.

Can you hear how the tune fades? It's there to some degree; but gone are the sharp pitch changes, heavy stresses, and pauses created by the original construction and by ellipsis (the omissions in "I might have, but it doesn't seem as if"). Frost's printed cues help us hear a stronger, more engaging voice.

THE IMPORTANCE OF INTONATION TO MEANING

To understand a bit more about the nature of our quarry—the sound of spoken expression—let's consider the importance intonation has for meaning. The sound of a sentence often carries more meaning than the words themselves. Your response to "How are you?" depends almost entirely on the sound of the question. Generally, the intonation suggests only polite acknowledgment of your presence. So you respond with a ritualistic, "Fine. How are you?" But sometimes you hear sincerity and respond accordingly.

In some cases, intonation patterns carry all the meaning; the words, little or none. For example, the phrase "Nice haircut" can be spoken to express praise or insult. As an insult, the word *nice* means its opposite. Two other phrases like it are "Some party" and the simple word "Sure." Consider the common commands "Search me" or "Come on." They can be spoken to indicate an earnest expression of the literal meaning, as in "I really don't have your keys. Search me." Or they can be used to indicate tone, as in "I have no idea what she means. Do you?" "Search me." In reading these examples, you place sharp stress on either *search* or *me,* depending on the context of meaning. The context of meaning determines the intonation you use. "Come on" can literally mean "Come on—we're in a hurry. Move." Or it can mean "I don't believe you." The message is entirely dependent on the sound pattern. And the sound pattern depends on the context of meaning.

There are also occasions where meaning is conveyed only by intonation or intonation and gesture; no words are used at all. An example is the sound we make to indicate "I don't know," accompanied usually by a shrug. In this instance, the sentence sound is formulaic—we all use the same down-up-down tonal glide to indicate "I don't know."

Robert Frost believed sentence tones (which he called the "sound of sense") are "already there—living in the cave of the mouth." He considered them "real cave things: they were before words were" (Thompson 191). To write a "vital sentence," he believed, "we must write with the ear on the speaking voice" (Thompson 159). "The ear is the only true writer and the only true reader. Eye readers miss the best part. The sentence sound often says more than the words" (Thompson 113). According to Frost:

> Only when we are making sentences so shaped [by spoken sentence tones] are we truly writing. A sentence must convey a meaning by tone of voice and it must be the particular meaning the writer intended. The reader must have no choice in the matter. The tone of voice and its meaning must be in black and white on the page. (Thompson 204)

Frost wasn't the only poet to make such claims. Marianne Moore did too: "The better the artist, moreover, the more determined will he be to set down words in such a way as to admit of no interpretation of the accent but the one intended . . ." (96).

I'd like to stop here a moment to explain why I've brought Frost and Moore into this text. After all, this is not a book about writing poetry. Nevertheless, poets—especially poets like Frost, who also happened to write intelligently in plain language about the art of writing—have been some of our greatest teachers. Poetry is the art of sound. And in modern poetry, many poets of Frost's generation and of later generations were (and are) committed to bringing into print the vitality and beauty of speaking intonation. Although they arrange sound patterns in inventive, unusual ways, they are primarily hunters and gatherers. "Sentence sounds," Frost says, "are gathered by the ear from the vernacular and brought into books. No writer invents them. The most original writer only catches them fresh from talk, where they grow spontaneously" (Thompson 111).

If one pleasure of spoken conversation is the sound of someone's voice rising and falling, quickening and slowing, growing louder and softer, if part of what we enjoy is the curious blend of sounds that makes us recognize a particular personality even if we can't hear her words but only her music, then poets have a lot to teach us about how to get at least some of that listening pleasure into our own writing. So I plan to call on them in this text as well as other kinds of writers who have a poet's ear for the best of talk.

"The best of talk" is information plus the speaker's feeling about that information. In speech, feeling is communicated by gesture, body language, and intonation. And as some of the foregoing examples show, the real information—that is, the meaning—is often not in the words themselves but in the music of the words, the gestures, and the body language. In writing, we can't indicate body language, but we can control how sentences are heard. And it is through our arrangement of words into sentences, one after another, that we can approximate some of the intonation in speech that tells our readers not only information about the world but also how we feel about it, who we are in relationship to it, and who we think our readers are in relationship to us and the message we want to deliver.

THE SOCIAL NATURE OF COMMUNICATION

By extension, the best of talk is civilizing behavior. In speaking to each other, we are always moving between our private selves and our public selves. In that movement, Richard Lanham believes, we become part of, transmit, and renew our culture (246). When we write, we try to capture some of that humanizing act of speech. Lanham puts it this way: "In written, literate cultures, prose inherits this central task of transmission and renewal [of culture]. It must not only do the work of the world but tell us in what spirit that work is done" (246). Our speech, oral or written, Lanham says, "provides a direct readout of behavior" (246). It's no small wonder, then, that we all are sensitive to criticism of our writing. When we write, we tell people who we are. Writing is a social act even though it feels in the doing like a private one.

If the sound of speech is the vitality we seek in writing, you might think that simply transcribing your voice from tape to page would be the answer. But that won't work. Although Robert Frost is right—"There are moments that we actually touch in talk what the best writing can only come near"—there are lots of forgettable moments before and after the memorable ones. Speech includes lots of stops and false starts, sound fillers, repetitions, general clumsiness, and fog. If you've ever tried reading speech transcriptions or have tried transcribing someone's speech yourself, you know exactly what I mean. Later in this chapter, you'll find an exercise that asks you to try recording, transcribing, and editing.

WRITING THAT SOUNDS LIKE SPONTANEOUS SPEECH
A Sample and Discussion

Sometimes, writing that looks and sounds like spontaneous speech is really the product of artful editing or careful planning.

In the following excerpt from *Treat It Gentle,* Sidney Bechet talks about the nature and development of jazz as he recalls its history within his own personal history, beginning with the memory of his grandfather. Bechet wanted to be close to Africa. "It's a mood, you'd call it, an atmosphere I wanted to put myself into. My grandfather, he was Africa."

His grandfather's history, he claims, "is all so mixed up with the music." He recalls hearing the music as his grandfather was "making it, back in those days when it had just been brought over from Africa and was finding itself in the South. Those pieces of melody, that music . . . it was all for something dear to you, something you couldn't make unhappy. It was a thing to wear away your insides" (45–46). In the following passage Bechet illustrates what he means:

> You take when a high note comes through—lifting and going and then stopping because there's no place else for it to go. That's stepping music—it's got to rush itself right off your voice or your horn because it's so excited. You can feel it. People, they go looking for music, you know, needing it. And the music, it's any damn' thing; it's whatever it is you need. Like when you're sad sometimes, you want to remember something, maybe something you was happy about once, and you find an old hat that your aunt once wore and left in a closet—it's just been left there, and she's dead. She was a beautiful woman and she used to wear this hat. She had it for glad times and she had it for bad times; it went a lot of places with her, and she left it behind. All the music I play is from what was finding itself in my grandfather's time. It was like water moving around a stone, all silent, waiting for the stone to wear away. Because all the strains that went to make up the

spirituals, they were still unformed, still waiting for the heart
of ragtime to grab them up, mix in with them, bring them
out of where only a few people could feel the music and need
it, bring it out to where it could say what it had to say.

It's like the Mississippi. It's got its own story. There's
something it wants to tell. (46)

Sidney Bechet was a popular jazz musician in the thirties and
forties whose personal and musical history was recorded on tape
and later transcribed and edited by Desmond Flower. In the passage just given, we can hear the sound of loose, colloquial
speech as Bechet describes how the history of jazz and the history of people creating it are mutually dependent. Bechet lets us
in on his own thinking process as he constructs images and
ideas. It seems, as we listen, that ideas are unfolding in the immediate act of speech.

But we can also hear control in the voice. Bechet isn't rambling.
He isn't veering from the main road, taking this detour and that,
the way we often do in casual conversation. When one idea trig-
gers another, for example, we sometimes indulge the peculiari-
ties of our own thinking process, forgetting our audience, the
poor traveler behind us without a map who's depending on us
to get him home and fears we're more lost than he is. Instead,
the speaker inspires confidence. He knows where he's going and
is aware of us traveling behind. He glances back, adjusts his
speed, and gives signals. We follow easily enough.

Features That Belong to Speech

Let's first consider how the written passage sounds like spontaneous speech.

1. Casual vocabulary and colloquial idioms, including slang.
   For example, "it's got to," "you take when," "like when,"
   "grab them up," "you know."
2. Clipped constructions (short, almost staccatolike clauses
   or sentences). For instance, "It's like the Mississippi. It's
   got its own story. There's something it wants to tell." Or
   "it's any damn' thing; it's whatever it is you need."
3. Loose sentence patterns, common to conversation. For example, "Like when you're sad sometimes, you want to remember something, maybe something you was happy

about once, and you find an old hat that your aunt once wore and left in a closet—it's just been left there, and she's dead." These patterns show a mind in the act of constructing. And as readers, we are in the immediate presence of the speaker finding his way as he goes.

4. Ungrammatical constructions. For example, the use of a pronoun following a subject: "People, they go looking for music. . . ." Subject-verb agreement errors: "maybe something you was happy about once."

5. Repetition of key words and phrases for emphasis. Note the repetition of pronouns, for instance, in several places. Here's one: "And the music—it's any damn' thing; it's whatever it is you need." And another: "grab them up, mix in with them, bring them out. . . ." The repetition of *them* in the second example puts extra emphasis on the compound verbs because, in this instance, readers stress what's new in the phrase, not what's old.

   Emotional power is often gained from repetition. In the following sentence, excerpted from another passage in *Treat It Gentle,* the repetition of *his face* gives emotional significance to the final clause because of the marked rise in pitch, the added stress, and the pause just before the resolution of the sentence: "And when he looked at you there wasn't anything in his eyes . . . it was like they were missing from his face, and his face, it had just come apart" (86).

   In conversation, repetition also acts as adhesive, holding ideas together as we think our way to a point. Notice all the repetition in Bechet's analogy about the hat, for example.

6. Conversational openers to sentences, such as "You know," "You take," or "Say," to cite a few. These have a built-in formula for melody. We all hear sentences that begin with these words in the same way: "You know, you can't have it all." "You take a guy who wants it all." "Say you want it all." The intonation melody in those sentences begins the same way as Bechet's "You take when a high note comes through. . . ." The openers direct your voice in the same intonational patterns. They're fixed. It's what Frost means when he says, "A sentence is a sound in itself on

which other sounds called words may be strung" (Thompson 110).

The sentence sounds are governed by the openers, "Say," "You know," "You take." These are confined to casual discourse, to be sure, but the generalized point is well taken. The more our words are strung on "recognizable sentence sounds" (Thompson 111), the more tuneful our writing is for our listeners. Of course, all this explanation is lost on those who have never heard sentence melodies in conversation. Frost admits, "You can't read a good sentence with the salt in it unless you have previously heard it spoken" (Thompson 108).

From Speech to Print: Controlling Speech Sounds on the Page

Now that we've considered how the passage captures some of the properties of spontaneous speech, let's see how the same passage demonstrates artful editing and control.

1. Coherence. Despite our feeling that ideas are unfolding in the act of speech, it's fairly clear that Bechet knows where he's going. The terms of the analogy and the point it serves, for example, are clearly made—in contrast to what happens in spontaneous speech, where we tend to gather up ideas loosely, carry them hesitantly, and often drop one to pick up another as we move to our destination.

For example, Bechet uses the water-around-the-stone metaphor to describe the evolution of jazz, the "wearing away" of the stone idea linking itself to Bechet's memory of his grandfather's music—"those pieces of melody . . . all for something dear to you . . . a thing to wear away your insides." He has been trying to link two mutually dependent needs: musical and emotional. The music grew out of the need to tell a particular story. And like the Mississippi, that music—its shape, the history of its development—forms itself slowly over time.

2. Punctuation. Punctuation is a printer's invention. In writing, we follow certain conventions for pauses. These pauses—periods, commas, semicolons, colons—indicate

particular relationships between words and clusters of words. The pauses also tell us where and how long to stop. In speech, we simply rest a thought for a particular time, depending on our own thinking speed, our emotions, and our audience's ability to follow our ideas.

Bechet was speaking into a tape recorder. Desmond Flower punctuated his sentences. Flower decided where to put a period, where a dash, where a semicolon. Had Bechet written his own passage, he probably would not have used semicolons. They belong to a more formal style. Given the very informal sound of the speech, semicolons may look incongruous here. But Flower wasn't concerned with consistency. He most likely was concerned with capturing the rhythm of Bechet's speech. He wanted to capture the qualities of his voice.

Punctuation, as tiny a matter as it may seem when you're trying to write, can make a gigantic difference in how you sound. Flower's editing helps put the right emphasis on important words and the right length of pause between clusters of words; and it ensures, through rhythm, the coherence of ideas. You need a convincing example of this point, and I promise to deliver one shortly.

Sidney Bechet's passage is an artful combination of the rhythms of spontaneous speech and careful editing. Flower has preserved, as well as anyone can, the speaking personality of Bechet. As we read, we can hear a believably genuine voice speaking emphatically about something important, and in that voice we recognize the speaker's interest in our own understanding and appreciation of the truth spoken. I have chosen the Bechet sample first because the voice personality is strong, even though it is, in some of its particulars, the idiom of a particular community of speakers. Still, I don't believe there is anyone who can claim he or she doesn't "hear" a voice in this passage.

However, my purpose has not been to lead you to imitate Bechet's voice or to suggest that voice is a matter of capturing the sounds of casual informality in your writing. What is good about the voice is its liveliness—that is, its melody and its rhythms. What's good about what the voice says is the interest of the analogies—how they make clear a point that might be missed by non-initiates of jazz. Bechet has found a way to make an unfamiliar idea familiar—and to make it memorable.

THE ROLE OF SENTENCE STRUCTURE IN CREATING VOICE AND SENSE

Making ideas memorable has much to do with sentence making. In reading the Bechet passage, you might think that a vernacular vocabulary (the common, everyday language of a certain group of people in a certain locality at a certain time) and relatively simple sentences give rise to a voice, but that's not so. The following revision preserves the vocabulary and general structure but changes the punctuation:

> A high note comes through. It lifts and goes and then stops. There's no place else for it to go. That's stepping music. It's got to rush itself right off your voice or horn. It's excited. You can feel it. People go looking for music. They need it. The music is any damn' thing. It's whatever you need.

Now all the clauses are clipped with full periods between them. How does the punctuation affect the voice you hear?

Here is another version of the same passage in which the clauses are stretched loose instead of clipped:

> You take a high note coming through, lifting and going and then stopping because there's no place else for it to go. That's stepping music that's got to rush itself right off your voice or your horn because it's so excited, and you can feel it. People go looking for music, you know, needing it, and the music is any damn' thing, whatever it is you need.

In both of my versions, the voice weakens. In the first, many short sentences, one after the other, create a staccato effect. The voice makes every point with finality. When everything is emphasized (by virtue of one short sentence after another), nothing is. The stresses do not vary, the pitch remains the same, and the rhythms become monotonous. In the second version, nothing is strongly emphasized either, but for different reasons. Here, the information is diffused across sentences, no piece of it stressed more than any other. The result is the same—rhythms that are monotonous.

When readers can't hear what's important in sentences, they can't follow the sense very well. Coherence suffers. When we listen to someone talking, we pay attention to where the voice rises, where the stress falls most heavily, and where the pauses are. The music and rhythm help us follow and remember. The music of speech is the pattern of pitch changes: down up/down up. Rhythm concerns stress (soft/loud) and length, that is, duration of sound (short/long). When we read, we need similar sound cues, only these cues must be provided by sentence pattern and punctuation.

The living part of any piece of writing is the intonation entangled in the sentence construction (syntax) and across sentences. It all happens at the sentence level. How you make sentences depends on the meaning you want to convey, and the meaning conveyed depends on how the sentence is made. Intonation determines meaning, and meaning determines intonation. The two go hand in hand.

Beyond the single sentence, voice helps connect ideas. Intonation patterns can hold large chunks of discourse together. In the first version of my Bechet revision, for example, you can hear how the sense suffers when the voice weakens. Once a voice is established, matters like organization and coherence often take care of themselves. This cohesive value will be emphasized in Chapter 5. For now, it's important to recognize two virtues of voice: *reading pleasure* (what we derive from hearing a believable, engaging human personality behind the page) and *sense* (the ability of voice to build coherence within and across individual sentences and to control, therefore, the possibilities and significance of meaning). Sir Philip Sidney (a sixteenth-century poet) used the terms *teach* and *delight* for these goals.

THE SOUND OF SIGNIFICANCE

Earlier, I discussed briefly how intonation affects meaning and how meaning affects intonation when I used the examples of "Search me" and "Nice haircut." The possibilities of sense in those examples were controlled by the context of meaning and by the intonation. Now I'd like to discuss more specifically how significance is attached to meaning through intonation. Here is an illustration: In a speech given on May 30, 1884, Oliver Wendell Holmes, Jr., said, ". . . recall what our country has done for each of us and ask ourselves what we can do for our country in return." Sound familiar? In John F. Kennedy's inaugural address in 1961, he said, "Ask not what your country can do for you; ask what you can do for your country."

Both speakers make the same basic point. To be sure, both attach significance to it. But it's Kennedy who gave the point a voice—that is, made it *sound* significant—and therefore, it's Kennedy we quote. It's his expression we remember. The reason is Kennedy's compression of a sentence style both speakers use, one that relies on antithesis (a powerful persuasion tactic) and one that demands that important words be placed closely together. The technique is to keep the phrase of the first part of the sentence but invert the meaning in the second. This construction is called *chiasmus,* a term derived from the Greek word for X, chi.

Here is how the X is formed:

(Ask not) what your country can do for you;

(ask) what you can do for your country.

By keeping the construction parallel and reversing the placement of *you* and *country,* the writer ensures a marked rise in pitch and heavy stress on the second *you* and second *country.* As readers, we stress the reversal, the change, in our urge to get the sense of the sentence. And that's just what the writer is trying to control: He wants us to hear loudest that we, and not an amorphous country, are the true agents of betterment. It's the inversion, the second part of the sentence, that chiasmus is designed to ring loud and forcefully.

Although Holmes also makes use of chiasmus with similar pitch and stress changes, it's compression that makes the biggest difference between the two sentences. Kennedy heightens the pitch and stress of the kernel message by eliminating lesser noise—that is, all the little pitches and stresses competing in Holmes's sentence.

Here's one of my own examples of chiasmus in connection with this topic: "If you don't have power over your sentences, your sentences will have power over you." Or "If you don't own the voice in your sentences, the voice will own you." The voice of your sentences is the only voice your readers hear. If it doesn't represent who you are or the "you" you want to be in relation to your audience and your subject, you have lost control to the printed "you"—a sad state of affairs.

For this reason I have been emphasizing the relationship (rather than the differences) between speaking and writing. Without a hearing imagination (an ear) for the sound of good speech, we cannot write what Frost called a "vital" sentence, a sentence with "the salt in it." Without an ear for the *sound* of sense, we often cannot connect our ideas well, either. Intonation patterns (pitch, stress, duration) are crucial to a reader's perception of who you are and what you are saying.

THE WRITER'S VOICE AND THE RHETORICAL SITUATION

Let's return for a last time to the Bechet passage to consider the issue of who the speaker is in relationship to his subject and audience. Earlier, I praised Bechet's voice. And although I might argue that there are certain intrinsic virtues of his voice—a lively speech melody and rhythm, perhaps—those virtues might well be ignored in another setting by another audience in another time. Suppose Sidney Bechet was not a famous jazz musician but, instead, was a fellow student in your music history class. And suppose Bechet submitted his paragraph as part of an assigned personal essay on jazz—an assignment, let's say, given by a professor who assumed that her students already knew the conventions of personal writing for a professional audience. The professor might find merit in the content, but it might be overshadowed by the demerits accumulated on the professor's style sheet. In other words, the professor wants her students to conform to conventions that, for our hypothetical student, were not made explicit.

Out go slang, ungrammatical constructions, and, in general, a vernacular voice. How can we help Bechet please his music professor, his real audience, without sacrificing entirely the voice he's created? The truth is that there is no one dependable solution. Many revisions are possible, because the compromises are many. But any one compromise depends on the writer's ability to adapt to his or her audience and the language that that audience is familiar with.

Fortunately for Bechet, an editor came to the rescue, and rescue was minimal. Bechet talked; and Flower punctuated, shaped, and organized his speech. Flower didn't have to turn it into formal or even middle-range informal discourse. Bechet didn't need to sound like a music scholar to be persuasive; he had played the saxophone and clarinet brilliantly for years. That sealed his ethical appeal. And he wasn't speaking to an academic audience, though even if he were, that audience would be sympathetic because of Bechet's expertise and influence on the history of jazz.

Revising Bechet:
A Low to Middle Range of Informality

Let's return to our problem of conforming Bechet's passage to the expectations of a particular discourse community. Here is a low-middle-range revision; it represents neither extreme—neither low- nor high-middle informality. It's one possible choice for a personal essay. Consider the passage in context—Bechet has been describing the music his grandfather made and is placing himself within that history: the music of "one foot . . . coming up and going down on the ground when there's something stirring to make it move that way . . . when all the leaves are maybe lying low and the wind is coming through sombre like" (46).

> Let's say, for example, a high note comes through—lifting, going, and then stopping because there's no place else for it to go. That's stepping music. It just has to rush off your voice or horn. You can feel it. That feeling is why people look for music, needing it. Yet the music can be anything. It's whatever you need. Suppose you're sad and you want to remember something that made you happy, and you find an old hat your aunt once wore and left in a closet. She had been a beautiful woman who had worn that hat in good times and bad. It went many places with her, and she left it behind. All the music I play is from what my grandfather left behind, from what had yet to be found, free to tell its story. It was like

water moving around a stone, silent, waiting for the stone to wear away. For the strains that later became spirituals were still unformed. They were waiting for the heart of ragtime to find them and bring them to where more than a few people could feel the music and need it. To where the music could say what it had to say.

It's like the Mississippi. It has its own story. There's something the music wants to tell.

This revision borrows from low and middle levels of informality. The markers of a low style are the use of *you,* verb contractions, relatively short sentences with loose connections between them, fragments, and a vocabulary belonging to the everyday speech of generally educated people. The markers of a middle style can best be seen in comparison to Bechet's original passage:

1. The hesitations and repetitions belonging to spontaneous speech have been removed.
2. Also removed are the colloquial sentence openers and fillers—"You take," "you know."
3. Less acceptable fragments and ungrammatical constructions have disappeared—"You take when," "Like when."
4. Dashes, generally belonging to low informal writing, have been removed.
5. Tighter connections have been made between ideas. In connecting sentences, I have made my own interpretation of sense. Other readers may make different connections based on their interpretations of the original text.

Revising to High-Middle Range

Maybe our hypothetical music professor would not be satisfied with a revision that moves us only a few steps up the formality ladder. Let's say she wants her students to strive for a high-middle range, a level maintained by formal speakers whose audience is distant and critical. Achieving this plane of communication often requires more than meeting a demand for greater precision of thought. It requires a level of overall formality that acknowledges a wider personal distance between speaker and audience. Here, then, is a high-middle version of expressive discourse:

Suppose, for instance, a high note sounds, lifting, running, and then stopping because there is nowhere else for it to go. That is stepping music. It rushes off a musician's voice or horn because it simply must. One can feel it. That feeling, I believe, is why people look for music, needing it. Yet the music itself can be anything. It is whatever people need. To illustrate, suppose someone is unhappy and needs a pleasant memory. She discovers an old hat that her aunt had worn and left in a closet. Her aunt, she remembers, had been a beautiful woman who wore that hat in joy and in sorrow. It had accompanied her to many places, and here it is found in the closet, left behind. All the music I play derives from what my grandfather left behind, from what had yet to be found, to be given its voice. It was, in his time, like water moving around a stone, silent, waiting for the stone to wear away. For the strains that would comprise the spirituals were still unformed. They were waiting for the heart of ragtime to discover them and bring them to where more than a few people could feel the music, could need it. To where the music could say what it had to say.

It's like the Mississippi. It has its own story. There is something the music wants to tell.

In writing this version, I created more distance between speaker and audience by raising the level of vocabulary (register), omitting contractions, substituting the pronoun *one* for the more direct *you,* and further refining ideas based on my interpretation of Bechet's passage. In changing vocabulary, I aimed not only for greater personal distance but also, in some cases, for greater precision of thought. It is the search for precision that generally accounts for a higher register of formality in professional writing. Some writers believe that high-sounding vocabulary for its own sake is demanded in professional prose. However, this belief can lead to obfuscation rather than precision.

Vocal Registers: What the Revisions Tell Us

Two final things should be noticed in the revisions: First, levels of formality are not pure. Experienced writers mix words belonging to different vocabulary registers. Even widely separated levels can be mixed to create certain effects, such as humor (In descending the staircase, Tracey tripped and busted her ulna). Intentional incongruities help achieve particular blends of voice we identify as "wry," "ironic," "faintly spoofing," and the like. In that sense, word choice, or diction, contributes to voice. In general, however, the skill is in maintaining a consistent level of diction so that it is clear who is speaking to whom on what occasion and for what reasons. Unintended, large incongruities can provoke laughter when it's most unwelcome.

Second, as voices aim toward higher degrees of formality, they often lose the wide pitch changes and emphatic stress of speech. If you read Bechet's original text and my two versions in succession, you can hear the changes in melody, rhythm, and tone. Although I did try to preserve life in the often deadly sound of formal discourse, it was difficult, and perhaps other writers would make different choices in revising. There is no one correct way to rewrite Bechet's piece to illustrate different rhetorical contexts.

Exercise: From Spoken to Written Discourse

Here is a classroom exercise to help you discover for yourself what happens as you try to transcribe speech into print and as you try to create different levels of formality. Record a short monolog from a television or radio talk show. Whatever you choose, be sure that it is spontaneous talk—that it is not read from a prepared script.

1. Transcribe from the tape onto the page, trying to preserve as accurately as possible the sentence patterns of the speaker, eliminating, of course, all overly distracting filler (*hmm*s, *uh*s).
2. Rewrite the passage to fit a different rhetorical context (audience and occasion).

This exercise can also be done collaboratively: In groups of three or four, read your transcriptions to each other. Choose one to work with. Together, edit it and then rewrite it for another audience and occasion.

After you have completed the exercise individually or collaboratively, describe the problems you encountered and how you solved them. You might also try to answer what was lost or gained when you rewrote the passage to fit another rhetorical situation.

THE IMPORTANCE OF CHOICE IN INDIVIDUAL EXPRESSION

In completing the preceding exercise (either individually or collectively), you discovered, I'm sure, lots of choices in editing and rewriting. Choices are the biggest concern in this textbook. We have all spent many years in English classrooms learning rules that we see broken all the time in professional writing. And we have learned to judge one kind of writing good and another bad, only to see the judgments reversed in someone else's classroom. Good writing, many believe, is a matter of pleasing the teacher. And to some extent, this is true. Good writing, or, more accurately, successful writing, is that which pleases its audience. Different audiences have different needs and different tastes.

So what can you do? Change your personality every time you face a different audience? You don't need to do anything quite so radical. You need only make adjustments. And in this art, we have all had a wealth of experience.

If you have ever had a minor accident while driving the family car, for example, would you describe the experience in the same way to your mother, father, siblings, friends, police, judge? How might you "adjust" the telling to specific audiences without "adjusting" the truth? More generally, how do you present yourself socially in the classroom versus your living room? To your employer versus your co-workers? And would you make slight adjustments in your speech if you were talking to your employer at a meeting versus at the annual picnic? Finally, if your friend happened to pass by while you were talking to your employer on the other side of the wall, would he or she recognize your voice? Probably so.

Exercise: **Private and Public Voices—**
Judging Distances

Let's test the ideas in the preceding paragraph. Here is another short exercise: Briefly describe the same event to three different audiences. Make the audiences as different as possible from each other in age, occupation, educational level, relationship to you, and so on. In class, read your three versions. Ask the class or members of your group to note what differences and similarities they hear. How do your classmates account for them? How do you?

One Voice or Many?

You may find, to some degree, that although we are multivoiced, we also have particular speech patterns that are recognizably our own. We all blend, yet we remain separate. That is, we have public, yet private, selves. Speaking on different occasions to different audiences, we suppress some parts of our private selves and reveal others. To complicate matters, we also continue to revise our private selves according to our cultural, social, and psychological experiences. Such changes take place over long periods of time, however.

The main point is that no one presents an entirely private or public self, even within the same speech or piece of writing. We waver. We move back and forth across a continuum. How far we move in one direction or another depends on where we are, what we're talking about, and who is listening. Yet we each tend to reveal in our speech an identifiable personality, no matter in what context our voices are heard. Given my own personality, I make certain choices when I speak or write that reflect my understanding of a particular rhetorical situation (subject, occasion, audience). And given your personality, you may make different choices when faced with the same rhetorical situation, even though we may both agree on the nature of adjustments or choices that the context demands.

Let me try to make that last point clearer, because it is crucial. Suppose we are both planning to ask our employers for a raise, and we rehearse our arguments for each other to test our potential success. The subject, we agree, is serious; the general occasion, formal. Our employers, let's say, have similar styles of management. Both are rather informal, almost casual in their relationships with employees. They tend to walk a fine line between the roles of supervisor and peer. While you are comfortable with the ambiguity, I am not. For the sake of argument, let's suppose that I prefer clearer boundaries between management and staff and, consequently, maintain a certain degree of personal distance from my supervisors. In general, you are easygoing by nature, and I am not.

We may both agree that the occasion is formal, yet our audiences demand some tempering of that formality because of their similar management styles. Nevertheless, we make different choices in presentation because of our own differences. You don't want to undercut the seriousness of the occasion by sounding too casual. And I want to sound neither too stuffy, by the employer's standards, nor unnaturally chummy, by my own standards. Our voices will be different, but neither one will be wrong.

To Take or Not To Take Advice:
The Curse of Freedom

So how can we help each other? Won't you always be pushing me to sound more like you, and vice versa? To some degree, yes. I'm afraid we can't help being ourselves even when we try to be very objective. Richard Hugo, a poet, used to make these remarks to his writing students:

> Every moment, I am, without wanting or trying to, telling you to write like me. But I hope you learn to write like you. In a sense, I hope I don't teach you how to write but how to teach yourself how to write. At all times keep your crap detector on. If I say something that helps, good. If what I say is of no help, let it go. Don't start arguments. They are futile and take us away from our purpose. As Yeats noted, your important arguments are with yourself. If you don't agree with me, don't listen. Think about something else. (3)

That's a risky thing for a teacher to say, but it's honest. There are, however, basic rhetorical principles and conventions that inexperienced writers need to learn, so teachers can save their students those years of trying to learn by trial and error. But beyond the basics, there is a universe of choice. Earlier, you've heard me say that good writing is what pleases its audience. Different audiences have different pleasures. That's life. But there are audiences who love language (or jazz). They're the ones most writers want to please. Your job as a writer is to learn when and when not to compromise. No one person can teach you that. There is simply no substitute for lots of reading, lots of writing, and many and varied audiences. And there is no end to the learning. The only difference between inexperienced and experienced writers is that, for the experienced writer, the stakes keep going up. Writing doesn't get any easier. In fact, it gets harder, but only by choice.

STYLE VERSUS VOICE

The first part of this book will focus on discovering and strengthening a voice within particular levels of discourse (vocal registers). The voice you create is the voice that you want a particular audience to hear in a particular place at a particular time. To transfer your voice from the air to the page, you will need to pay close attention to the following stylistic features:

1. Sentence patterns
2. Sentence length
3. Word choice
4. Word placement
5. Punctuation

When people talk about style, they refer to a writer's habits of language use. They describe the preceding features as well as larger issues—point of view, tone, and persona, for example. In some cases, such as tone, you'll find that the larger issue can be settled by attending to the five stylistic features I've listed. A writer can be said to have a style when he or she intentionally and habitually relies on particular verbal patterns. But that writer may not have a voice emerging from his or her style that could be described as tuneful, rhythmical intonation patterns. To have a style is not necessarily to have a voice. You need only read a few government documents, academic articles, and textbooks to recognize that fact. Often, reading these materials is like listening to a dial tone.

But there are occasions where tonal flatness is effective, even desirable. One I've already described on the first page of this chapter: highly technical or scientific writing. There the presence of personality as heard in the intonation patterns is an intrusion, not a pleasure.

Sometimes, a nonvoiced style is desirable in expressive writing. For example, a writer may want an audience to hear the voice accompanying a particular emotion: sadness, fatigue, or cold anger, to name a few. If so, the writer will make certain stylistic choices that suggest the feeling through sound rather than through direct statement. Clauses will be relatively short, and most of them will be of equal length; sentence patterns may be repeated, and sentence openers, too. The general design will be one of parallelism, repetition, and intonation units of similar length, pitch, and stress. The desire is for weighted feeling as transcribed into speech sounds.

Here is an example of an effective flat voice:

A window, two white curtains. Under the window, a window seat with a little cushion. When the window is partly open—it only opens partly—the air can come in and make the curtains move. I can sit in the chair, or on the window seat, hands folded, and watch this. Sunlight comes in through the window too, and falls on the floor, which is made of wood, in narrow strips, highly polished. I can smell the polish. There's a rug on the floor, oval, of braided rags. This is the kind of touch they like: folk art, archaic, made by women, in their spare time, from things that have no further use. A return to traditional values. Waste not want not. I am not being wasted. Why do I want?

(Margaret Atwood, *The Handmaid's Tale*)

The speaker tells us factual details, then asks, "Why do I want?" Part of the answer lies in her voice—in the sound those details make as they slowly parade across the page in measured units of similar pitch, stress, and length. Her feelings are not listed but heard. And consequently, we feel the narrator's psychological numbness. Those details weigh us down; and we, like the narrator, carry them like heavy suitcases, setting them down at measured intervals, each thump making us more aware of psychic fatigue.

The interest, then, is not so much style as the effect of style. In particular, the interest is in discovering how certain combinations of stylistic features may create a voice each of us would want to claim as our own. Combinations, of course, are rich and varied, just as the possible voices resulting from them are.

VOICE AND THE RELATIONSHIP BETWEEN WRITER AND READER

Voice is, therefore, linguistically constructed to the extent that a writer can approximate in written symbols the particular speech patterns that reveal his or her intended relationship to subject, audience, and occasion at a given time. However, transferring voice from air to page also depends on a reader's ability to perform the opposite transference—from page to air. Consequently, voice is a conversation of sorts. Both reader and writer must be able to hear as well as see. Both must be sensitive not only to spoken voices but also to written ones.

The issue of authenticity (Is the voice on the page truly mine?) is problematic. The only one who can decide authenticity is the writer. And yet the writer may be unaware of the linguistic signals she is sending to readers that cause them to doubt authenticity. No writer can completely control how she will be heard. An authentic voice is one that the writer decides is her habitual way of responding to a given set of forces in the world impinging on her consciousness within a particular time frame. When those habits change in response to changing forces, so does her voice. Voice is constant yet always subject to change, as writers continue to react to social, cultural, political, and psychological forces.

Any reader, like any writer, is in a state of both constancy and flux—hence, the complexity of the authentic voice issue. Each writer strives to discover and communicate her private relationship to the world in which she lives, yet that same world pressures her to conform, to please. How do we know when we are responding to the pressure to please and when we are asserting our distinctive selves? This is a lifelong question. All we can do, I believe, is live with the tension. Its existence is part of what it means to be an individual and a member of a community. Every day, our voices are spoken and heard, written and read, within that tension. The sound of that struggle, however, is often what's missing in print.

Unless we are hearing and reproducing on the page the *sounds* of speech—those intonational contours that reveal our feelings as well as our knowledge—we are not conversing. We are only waving, at best, sophisticated signal flags.

THE STRUCTURE OF THE TEXT

To help you hear the variety of voices that can emerge from certain stylistic and rhetorical choices, the chapters of this book are organized by levels of discourse—colloquial, informal, and formal vocal registers. Voice is considered within the humanistic framework of social interaction. The value of stylistic forms and rhetorical choices is relative. Therefore, creating voices is a matter of understanding the interrelationships among writer, audience, subject, and occasion.

In each chapter that introduces a level of discourse, there are various exercises. These are intended as heuristic devices—that is, invention exercises to help you discover choices. They may strike you, at first, as extremely limiting. But what inhibits often frees. Many writers set up hurdles to force them in directions they may not otherwise have gone. Poets, for example, use rhyme and meter for this purpose. Given imposed restrictions, they often can't say what they intended to say or how they intended to say it; and consequently, they say something far more interesting. Poets, unlike other writers, have a stronger allegiance to manner than to message. (Yet if they want to say something badly enough, they do.) Your allegiance will be necessarily stronger to message, but your message can be made stronger with attention to manner, to the choices available to you for creating meaning.

The stylistic limitations imposed by the early exercises may lead you to some interesting discoveries, to voices you may not have realized you've heard or believed you could produce. As you practice and listen to each other, you will discover the characteristics of many types of voices. And as you experiment on your own, the hope is that you will develop a voice within and across the general categories of colloquial, informal, and professional speech.

To use an analogy, the first part of this book asks you to put on various costumes, find out where you can go in them, and discover who you become when so clothed. This analogy can be misleading, I think, if you feel that "putting on" means "pretending." But most writers develop a voice in much the same way that we learn to dress—by trying on whole ensembles, then borrowing items from various ensembles, mixing and matching, until they've found their own distinctive way of expressing their personalities. After that, they need only learn how to adapt to the occasion and company in which they place themselves.

You already know this experience as it applies to clothing. What you need to know is the experience as it applies to writing. The first part of this book attempts to give you that opportunity. The principle behind it is: Certain stylistic features evoke certain discourse occasions. Certain kinds of voices suggest certain occasions and audiences.

The last part of this book puts the principle in reverse: Certain discourse situations evoke certain stylistic features. Here you will be learning how to dress for the occasion and the company—adapting your writing to the audience, purpose, and occasion without losing your voice. What will be emphasized is compromise—the balance struck between private and public selves. The lesson is not just how to fit yourself to particular circumstances and company but how to assert your own private relationship to them. The early chapters focus on personal voice; the latter, personal and social voice.

In providing professional and student samples, I am not suggesting, "Write like this." It is always difficult, though, not to read examples as prescriptions. If I am prescribing anything, however, it's to let yourself experiment. The samples in this text are just such experiments. You may think some are successful and some not, just as in your own classroom. But developing a voice depends on risk taking, because to practice is to imitate other writers. And imitation is hard to manage at first. Your writing may seem to get worse. And it often does for awhile. You may even feel, as one student told me after working at imitation, as if you're "cheating." Yet writers steal from each other all the time. It's how they learn. "We talked about freedom," another student has said, "but then here we are following another writer's sentence patterns." Isn't that the paradox of freedom? You can't have any until you know what the choices are. And the more choices you're aware of and able to exercise on the page, the more freedom you have. But finally, the aim isn't even freedom: It's beauty. It's writing skill.

CHAPTER TWO

Colloquial Voices

Discovering Sounds
of Speech

Let's begin our ear training in vocal registers by listening to the sound of personal speech for a narrow, familiar audience, as in these excerpts from the professional samples appearing near the end of Chapter 3:

> She simmered in *The Witches of Eastwick*. Next she stole *Married to the Mob*. Then there were those close-ups in *Dangerous Liaisons*. Even crying she looked good. Her upper lip was puffier than ever. Puffier than Barbara Hershey's post collagen. Puffier than Kim Basinger's in the *Batman* lip close-ups. In the year of the puffy lip, Michelle Pfeiffer had the puffiest lip in Hollywood. Then came *The Fabulous Baker Boys* and that clinched it. Lips puffier than ever, Michelle Pfeiffer is now The Most Beautiful Woman in the World.
>
> (Patricia Volk—"Why I'm Glad
> I Don't Look Like Michelle Pfeiffer")

In the first place, thin people aren't fun. They don't know how to goof off, at least in the best, fat sense of the word. They've always got to be adoing. Give them a coffee break, and they'll jog around the block. Supply them with a quiet evening at home, and they'll fix the screen door and lick S&H green stamps. They say things like "there aren't enough hours in the day." Fat people never say that. Fat people think the day is too damn long already.

> (Suzanne Britt—"That Lean and Hungry Look")

It was 8:40 on a Friday night. The kind of night you get in Richmond when you know the full blast of summer is only days away, waiting for you like a mug with a sap in some dark alley, and you know you'd better enjoy the fact that the pavement is still cool beneath your feet. The cars on Broad Street were filled with working stiffs heading home late at the end of another day. A day like any other day, except that this one was different.

> (Michael Robinson—"Lights Are Low")

In this chapter, we'll note the differences between spoken and written colloquial voices, explore our assumptions about stylistic forms, and consider voice in relationship to audiences and our distance toward or away from them. Classroom samples will help you see some of the choices available for creating a personal voice for a familiar audience. You'll find opportunities to discover your own assumptions and practice your learning through various exercises in making voices, self-reflective analysis, and peer response. These tasks will lead you to Chapter 3, where you'll practice sustaining a personal voice for more than a few paragraphs.

SPOKEN AND WRITTEN COLLOQUIAL VOICES

Spoken

The colloquial voice is the sound of casual conversation. It is personal and direct, marked by simple word choice (often slang), contractions, use of first- and second-person pronouns, and loose sentence structure. Because casual conversation is spontaneous expression, audiences tolerate imprecision, ungrammatical structures, and the frequent stops and starts of speakers' working their way to a point.

The sound of spontaneous expression includes, usually, quick changes of pace, a sharp rise and fall of pitch, and heavy stresses. Speakers rely on the sound of their voices to organize loosely patterned ideas and to emphasize some points, minimize others.

Speech intonation—the patterns of pitch, quality (intensity or stress), and quantity (length or duration of sound)—often carries more message than the words themselves do. Although this point has been made in the introduction, it bears repeating. "Nice hat," for example, can be spoken to deliver opposite messages about the wearer's taste. Messages, therefore, can be clarified, reinforced, and even contradicted by intonation. Add gestures, and messages are further reinforced or altered.

Written

Although written conversation cannot be made to sound exactly like real talk, it can approximate some of the qualities of casual conversation. When we write personal letters, we try to capture some of our natural speech habits. We don't think about them much. We just produce them, imperfectly, perhaps, but there they are.

Some writers, though, do think about them. They work hard at producing writing that sounds like good speaking caught alive. They don't just go after easy game: simple words, loose sentence patterns, or the sound of general patter. They try to capture the energy of emphatic speech—the feelings driving the words. That feeling is in the manner, not in the direct statement. It's in the intonation of a sentence, across sentences, and across whole paragraphs. It's the sound of a distinct personality with a particular relationship to the subject, the language, the occasion, and the audience. That sound is not singular, but mixed. What we hear is a combination of personality features belonging to a particular individual. The writer is listening as she is writing, arranging patterns of speech on the page so that we hear the melody of feeling she intends.

The melody of real talk includes wide pitch intervals, loud stresses, and, most importantly, a variety of timbres (the subtle shades of feeling we identify as wry, ironic, mock serious, and so forth). It's the timbres of speech that are difficult to encode in printed symbols. For example, how can we capture in writing the particular blend of these speech qualities: serious, yet jokey; direct, yet discreet; accusatory, yet sensitive? What tools can we use for the job? These are problems writers try to solve in a number of ways, some of which will be discussed in this chapter, and some of which you may discover on your own through writing and listening.

Because people tend to associate lack of clarity and general imprecision with colloquial voices, some believe that this voice should be reserved for nonserious chat. That's not necessarily true. We often discuss serious matters in colloquial language. However, many people recognize that on the extreme side of colloquial speech, the exchange of ideas is less important than the gesture. So while the occasion and audience may allow for and, in some cases, demand colloquial language, we try to take special care in expressing ideas to avoid misunderstanding and to make clear a serious purpose.

Serious talk, though, does sometimes demand a leap to formality. Audience and occasion may demand it, just as in my earlier example, where Sidney Bechet's hypothetical music professor demanded a revision suitable to an academic audience. Formal speakers draw from a wider range of vocabulary choices (ideally, in the pursuit of the right word, not out of the belief that a less widely familiar vocabulary is in itself a mark of intellectual sophistication). They avoid slang, therefore, and (often) contractions. Because formality indicates distance between speaker and audience, they also avoid first- and second-person pronouns.

Formal speakers tend to use many qualifiers, again, for the sake of precision; and they elevate the style of sentence patterns to indicate a subject and occasion of high significance. One becomes cognizant of a serious speaker with an important message to deliver. Or, to put it less stiffly, we hear a serious voice talking about serious matters. Or, to put it casually, you know something big's at stake. Choice of formality level depends on three things: who you are, where you are, and who is listening.

Exercise I: Becoming Aware of Stylistic Features and How They Contribute to Voice

This exercise is designed to evoke some of the qualities that we associate with colloquial speech. But you may be surprised at the differences you hear as you read your paragraphs aloud to each other.

Write a fully developed paragraph (half a page) with the following constraints:

1. No punctuated sentence has more than 10 words; the shortest sentence, 1 word. A punctuated sentence is any

word or group of words that ends with a period, question mark, or exclamation point. You may therefore experiment with fragments, but try not to rely on them too heavily to satisfy the word limit.

2. No word has more than one syllable.

After you have written a preliminary draft of your paragraph, write an answer to the following questions:

1. What difficulties did this exercise pose for you, and why?
2. What do you believe is possible or impossible to accomplish, given the constraints?
3. Considering your answers to 1 and 2, what choices have you made in subject matter, audience, or occasion? What choices have you automatically excluded?

Classroom Activity: **Sharing Assumptions**

In groups of five, or as an entire class, read your preliminary paragraphs and answers to the previous questions to each other. What assumptions do you share?

The following common assumptions have been made in my classes:

1. Nothing sophisticated can be addressed. The subject must be simple.
2. No one would ever talk like this.
3. There is no way to make the paragraph interesting.

If you and your classmates agree with any of the assumptions I've listed, note them, adding any other commonly shared answers to the questions. These beliefs are the limitations you have set for yourself, apart from those imposed by the exercise. We will return to them later.

The "rules" of exercise I impose extreme limits on vocabulary and on sentence design and development. Although the specific limits are arbitrary, they are partly based on general principles of style, some of which may become evident as you try to solve problems. The following sections consider the limits of the exercise and how certain stylistic choices affect voice.

WRITING SHORT SENTENCES

Because there is little space within a 10-word (or less) sentence length, you have to say something fast. There is no time to gather speed, to paddle a few steps in the water. You have to take off. The first "rule" demands immediate flight to importance. As a consequence of the limit on sentence length, you will need to place key words of a sentence as close together as possible. The closer key elements come together, the more forceful the sound of the message is. Short sentences, consciously designed, emphasize information. Long sentences do not. The reasons are partly explained by the language code itself and partly by readers' attention patterns.

Language code: The most powerful positions in a sentence are the first and the last words. The closer these words come together, the more forceful the message is.

Reader attention: The shorter the sentence, the more likely it is that readers will remember it. If you want to make an idea memorable, compress it in a short space.

WRITING EFFECTIVE FRAGMENTS

An effective fragment follows logically from the sentence before it and forms a coherent, complete thought, even if, grammatically, the sentence is incomplete. One test for effectiveness is: Can the reader supply words or borrow sense from the sentence before it to make the fragment whole? (That is, is the fragment easily attachable to an adjacent independent clause?) And does the fragment serve to emphasize important information— that is, information important enough to warrant its own sentence space?

Although all experienced writers ask the first question in testing effectiveness, some pay less attention to the second question and more to this one: Does the use of a fragment or a short series

of fragments add rhythmical interest or help to establish an intonation pattern that will indicate the timbre (tonal shading) I
want heard in this piece? Consideration of rhythms and tonal
shading comes with practiced reading and writing. These writers have had several years of ear training. But they started just
as you are starting: trying to imitate on the page voices they've
heard in real conversations and those of writers they admire.
They began by experimenting.

Here are some examples of effective fragments.

> You reach a hallucinatory stage where everybody seems to
> be telling you that they are newly pregnant. Eva Gabor, the
> kid at your door taking a Thin Mints order, the trapped Arc-
> tic whales. All pregnant.
>
> (Colin McEnroe)

The sense of these two fragments can be easily derived from
the logic of sentence 1: "[Some examples are] Eva Gabor, the
kid at your door taking a Thin Mints order, the trapped Arctic
whales. [They're] all pregnant." The omission of the parenthetical words invites extra stress on the most important and interesting information. As listeners, we supply what isn't there by
stressing heavily what is. We also supply those fragmented sentences with the music and rhythmical interest of real talk—wide
pitch intervals, loud stresses, and a timbre reinforcing, in this
case, the speaker's comic exasperation.

The following sample is from my poem "Not for the Best."
It has been slightly altered to be understood out of context.

> Michael Buebles insisted Muffie Siegel change her name, then
> never spoke it twice in eight years. Nine.

To make the fragment "Nine" whole, readers borrow the
sense of the preceding sentence: "[Actually, come to think of it,
it was] nine [years]." The first sentence declares the appalling
fact. The fragment intensifies fact by correcting it, and the nature of correction demands a leap in pitch, heavy stress, and a
longer duration of sound than what would be heard if "nine"
had simply replaced "eight" in the preceding sentence. That
"nine" rings in Buebles's offense loud and long. The effect is
heightened information and emotional intensity.

This last example is William Gass's identification of a particular shade of blue.

Then there is the cold Canadian climate and the color of deep ice. The gill of a fish. Lush grass. The whale. Jay. Ribbon. Fin. (6)

In classifying items according to their special blueness, Gass reserves for each phenomenon its own sentence space. His possible reasons are that first, each phenomenon is to be savored for its blueness—no hurrying by the image. Second, Gass has arranged the list in a varying rhythmical pattern for added musical interest. The effect is weighted appreciation of color and sound. You might try rearranging his list to hear the differences in rhythm. What is musically lost in this version? "Fin. Jay. The whale. The gill of a fish. Ribbon. Lush grass."

VARYING SENTENCE LENGTH

If you are not in the habit of listening to sentence rhythms and varying length to add rhythmical interest to your writing (as well as to highlight important ideas), you may have created what those in the medical profession might call "flatliners"—a straight line of blips across the screen. No life there.

Richard Lanham, in *Revising Prose,* recommends making slash marks at every end punctuation mark on the page. If the marks occur at predictable, regular intervals (every three lines, say), you may be producing a flat, uninteresting speech pattern. Sometimes this method fails, however. A good second check is to make slash marks where you create an interruption in a sentence, such as the use of parentheses or other internal punctuation that produces a notable pause or notable break in the sentence pattern.

Slash marks at the end of sentences may also tell you how well you are helping your audience distinguish between important and less important information. In general, if you tend to write long sentences, one after the other, readers can't be sure which information to stress (short sentences emphasize ideas). And if you tend to write many short sentences, one after another, readers stress every one. If every idea is emphasized, nothing is. This principle was demonstrated in Chapter 1 where I played with Sidney Bechet's sentences, rewriting a short passage to show the impact punctuation can have on voice. Length variation affects, therefore, not only what you say but also how you sound when you say it.

USING MONOSYLLABIC WORDS

Monosyllabic words may help you recognize how many there really are and how often they can replace multisyllabic words, making ideas sound more forceful—often, surprisingly, without sacrificing clarity or precision of thought. The limit on syllables, of course, forces a generally simple, everyday vocabulary—the most used words. That is a feature of colloquial speech. But monosyllabic words don't have to add up to weak or loose expression.

When monosyllabic words end in a hard consonant, they form a power unit in English. When monosyllabic, consonant-ended words are placed at the end of a sentence (the most powerful position), their force is doubled. Listen to these lines from a poem called "Rattlesnake" by Brewster Ghiselin.

I crushed him deep in dust,
And heard the loud seethe of life
In the dead beads of the tail
Fade, as wind fades
From the wild grain of the hill.   (11.9–13)

In these final five lines of the poem, Richard Hugo tells us, "the poet kills the snake, faces himself and the moral implications of his act without a flinch or excuse, and we get no multisyllabic words in the entire passage." The act of killing had been prepared for earlier in these lines:

I saw the wedged bulge
of the head hard as a fist.   (11.5–6)

"With single-syllable words," Hugo explains, "we can show rigidity, relentlessness, the world of harm unvarnished." In the preceding lines, "the snake is seen as a threat, the lines slam home heavy as the fist the poet sees as simile for the head of the snake" (9). Hugo uses the language of the poem to talk about the effect of the words. But the general point is that monosyllabic words in succession, particularly if they end in hard consonants, tend to make the message sound emphatic and forceful.

In contrast, multisyllabic words "have a way of softening the impact of language. With multisyllabic words we can show compassion, tenderness, and tranquility" (Hugo 8). We can, but not exclusively so. In some rhetorical situations, we might show anything but compassion. Latinate legalese ("pursuant to the client's request") and other forms of professional jargon are notable exceptions to the compassion-and-tenderness claim. In these cases, multisyllabic words are often used to create wide distance between speaker and audience, sometimes for the sake of objectivity and high seriousness. But at other times, they are used to create intentional ambiguity, to establish superiority, and to exclude a general audience—those listeners who are not insiders, not members of the profession. This matter will be addressed more specifically in Chapters 4 and 5 on formal voices.

Revising Exercise I: **One More Time**

Try writing another version of your paragraph, having read the explanatory sections and having shared preliminary drafts and assumptions about possibilities.

After you have completed your paragraph, write in answer to these questions:
1. Who talks like this?
2. To whom?
3. For what reasons?
4. To what extent do you think your prewriting assumptions affected the subject matter as well as the intended audience and occasion?

Small-Group Exercise: **Reading Aloud**

In small groups of no more than five, read your new version aloud to each other. After each of you reads, allow time for the others to write their own answers to these questions: "Who talks like this? To whom? For what reasons?" Then listen to the answers of each group member. How do their answers compare with your own? Make note of each answer that differs.

After this exercise, read your paragraphs aloud again, one after the other, without interruption. How many different voices speaking about different subjects to different audiences for different reasons do you hear? Try to list those differences.

When your group has agreed upon a general set of categories, write in response to this question: "What hidden assumptions have I made that may have influenced the rhetorical context (subject, speaker, audience, occasion) of my paragraph, assumptions I did not notice before I listened to my peers read their paragraphs?"

Whole-Class Exercise: **The Memorable Moment**

Read paragraphs aloud, one after another, without interruption, until the fourth or fifth paragraph has been heard. (If you are not used to reading aloud and listening, you may need to stop after three paragraphs. That's ok. For the purpose of this exercise, it's necessary to hear a few at a time, though.) At the agreed stopping point, write what you remember most from what has been read. We usually remember what interests us: an unusual word for a familiar object or experience, an unusual analogy, a sentence, an attitude toward a subject, an interesting rhythm or sound pattern—whatever comes quickly to mind.

As a class, you might begin a list of memorable moments. If one of the shared assumptions of the class was that nothing very interesting or sophisticated could arise from adhering to the limits of exercise I, a helpful question might be: "If interest does not depend solely on big words and complex, lengthy sentences, what other things does it depend on?" Draw from your shared class list.

When students in my class read exercise I, they heard "simple and short." When they began to write, they unconsciously drew upon certain genres they remembered. Indeed, they had heard someone "talking like this." They had internalized particular forms, patterns, and rhythms, even if they could not produce perfect imitations or define the genre accurately in the abstract.

1. Some wrote primer prose, the Dick-and-Jane stories they remembered from early school years: "When you go to the store, take Spot." These writers assumed that nothing sophisticated could be said. They confined subjects to simple stories for young children, or in some cases, they produced refrigerator notes—casual reminders, directions, advice, or warnings.
2. Some heard the sound of religious passages: "The sun is God's light." These writers recalled biblical allegories, parables, or psalms.
3. Some heard a variation of the parable: fables, animal stories with a moral tag. Remember the one about the fox? "The grapes are out of reach."
4. Still others heard the voice of cryptic wisdom: "Ask the blind owl. He knows." This voice easily led writers to Oriental epigrams infused with mystery or simple philosophies for a virtuous life.

Contrary to what many writers initially believed, they did have sources to draw from, voice memories that suggested certain rhythms, subject matter, audiences, and speakers. These memories found their way into the exercise with only two small prompts: short sentences and simple words.

CLASSROOM SAMPLES

Here are some sample paragraphs that add to the list of possible voices emerging from the exercise you've been working on.

SAMPLE I: WINSTON GARLAND

My dad's mom is a pink old girl. Pink hats on hot days. Pink blush, pink lips. Her hair is curls of cream. To tell a tale is her art. Each move a part of the play. Last night she had guests. She wore a thin lace dress down to the floor. She sat in a large chair in the hall. To each guest—a smile or a kiss on the cheek. They held her hand. She spoke to the thirst in their eyes. Her tales pull fine mad men from the dust. She had a love of cake. And when a crumb dropped past her wrist, she rose. She'd sweep it from her dress. Her blue eyes pinch, then lift wide. They lock you in. Strong and deep. The guest's soft eyes do not see. See the death in her lungs: The black that preys on pink. But soon the guest is gone, the tale told. In her bed, there is no cheek to kiss. One night she will turn her breath to death's touch. Then I will sit in the chair in the hall. I'll drop a crumb. And tell the tale of a fine pink girl.

This example is Winston Garland's description of her grandmother. In planning a second version of this piece, Garland hoped to create "memorable sentences." She tried to write, she said, "a melody." Her audience is a younger person in her family, or anyone "whom you want to tell something about which you are an authority."

Describing her final version, Garland wrote, "I tried to alternate hard consonant and soft sounds at the end of words placed at the end of sentences. Most of my shortest sentences in exercise 1 ended in hard consonants. This adds emphasis." Garland also spoke of possible weaknesses: "The content of the short sentences was not always the material I planned to POWER." She was not always sure that a particular idea was worthy of its own punctuated sentence.

The limitations in exercise 1 help some writers, like Garland, discover a poetic voice. That sound is often made from sentences like those above: clusters of equally weighted clauses and phrases, or ideas that are unconnected by explicit transitions, that is, logical signals that subordinate some ideas to others. Although poets may omit overt patterns of direction that help readers get from idea to idea, they often imply connections by other means, such as alliteration, rhyme and other sound similarities, parallel structure and length, and repetition of words, phrases, and clauses. Such linguistic patterns can persuade readers of tight coherence even when, logically, connections are tenuous.

Winston Garland relies on the following patterns to hold her paragraph together (these patterns will be further described and illustrated in Chapter 4):

1. Repetition of an initial consonant sound in successive words (alliteration)

2. Repetition of the last word of a clause to begin the next (anadiplosis)
3. Repetition of the same word at the beginning of successive clauses or phrases, or a pattern of similar sentence openings (anaphora)
4. Rhyme
5. Repetition of key words
6. Phrases or clauses of equal structure and often of similar length (parallel structure)
7. Sentences or clauses that are not ranked by subordination (parataxis). Clause after clause is set down without signaling the relationship between or among them. Parataxis suggests that everything is equally related to everything else. No one idea is more important than the other. Parallel structure and repetition often accompany parataxis in the creation of equally weighted ideas.

Did Winston Garland consciously set out to create these patterns? Some, yes; others, no. Some she learned through class discussion. But others she discovered. The limitations of the exercise and her prewriting decisions about subject, audience, and occasion led her to make certain stylistic choices. The subject is of great significance to her, and so she weights her sentences in strong declarative statements. Parallelism is likely to follow, given the tendency toward direct statement and the limitation on sentence length. Short punctuated sentences and syllabic control leave little room for space-taking transitions and subordination; therefore, she relies on sound similarities and repetition for coherence.

Finally, there's Garland's own reading memory. She's heard a voice like this and she draws upon it consistently in the writing of her own paragraph, whether or not she consciously knows it.

Can you locate in Garland's paragraph examples of the rhetorical patterns I've listed? Do you notice any other means of connecting ideas? Do you notice any other features of her voice that make her sound "poetic"?

SAMPLE II: INDIA HENDERSON

In the following example, India Henderson captures her feelings during a practice session on the basketball court.

Here we go. One more day of this. It's the last day of the week. Oh no! It's not the last. We still have one more to go. I'm sick of it. All we do is run up and down the court. Sprint! That's the name of the game. Is that all coach can say? I think so! How 'bout you? Aren't you sick of it? How fast does she think we can run? We're not Carl. He's the one with all the gold. I think I'll ask her. Hey, coach! Why don't you give us a break? Uh, oh. Why did I do that? "On the line," she says. I knew that was next. Now the whole team is mad at me. "Ten sprints! Get on the line! Get set! Go!" One . . . two . . . I hope I don't die. I know I can make it. Three . . . four . . . five. Halfway there. "Five more to go, girls! Pick it up!" coach screams. We're up to six. Four more. These last three will be like hell! Nine. "Pick up the pace! You have one more left! run hard!" I made it. Now let's see if I can catch my breath. It'll take some time. Who knows? It could take weeks. Oh no! One more drill. I thought we were done. I have to catch my breath. Oh good, it's just free throws. We have to shoot six. If we don't make 'em all, we'll have to run sprints. Come on, girls! Sink those free throws and we're out of here. Good job! One more day. I'll keep my mouth shut next time.

Quite a different voice from Winston Garland's "My dad's mom is a pink old girl," isn't it? Yet India has conformed to the same limitations required by exercise 1. Within those limitations, she has created a strong speech personality, believably hers. Her voice pattern helps us share her external and internal experience that day at basketball practice. Unlike Winston's voice, which captures the sound of poetry (metaphor, leaps of logic, unusual information, balanced sentences of similar length), India's captures the vitality of everyday speech. When we read her description, we share her experience. We imitate her particular relationship to the world at a particular time and place. How does she manage it?

SAMPLE III: CATHY CURRAN

Not me. Oh God, don't call on me. I hate to speak in front of the class. Thank God. She called on him—the shy kid next to me. He's white with fear. His voice shakes while he reads. What will the class think? Will we laugh? Does he want us to laugh?

We'll do what he wants. Then he'll do what we want. It's the code. That way no one feels dumb. Oh no, he's done. She looks for the next one. I look at the floor. Then at the wall, the door. Is it too late to run out that door? I catch her eye. I feign a smile; I'm scared. Does she know I'm scared? Does she care? I should not have smiled. There's a glint in her eye. I look at the floor. Fast. It's too late. She calls on me. I clear my throat. I'm scared of what they will think. That's me on the page. Who I am. In print. I can't take back what I read. Can't change my mind. And if they laugh? Show scorn? What then? Is it me or the way I write? I won't know. That's the risk. That's why I'm scared. No choice now. I have to read. "Not me. . . ."

Same exercise, yet still different in voice from India's and Winston's. How does Cathy use the limitations to discover a voice? What emotion does she capture? How does she help us hear what she feels?

SAMPLE IV: CHRISTINE GOMOLA MULLIN

One last student sample, this one from Christine Gomola Mullin, produces yet another feeling, another voice to hear.

Those skis. They were the best I could buy at the time. And I still won't sell them. They may be three years old. They may be scratched. And they may not match my boots. But they're mine. Just the sight of them makes me laugh! Past trips, past pain, past fun—All race through my mind.

So where are my boots? In that box, I think. School bus gold. At one time they were in style. Not now. Now they're just boots. My friends all ski in pink and lime green. Those are the "in" shades this year. But I think I'll keep my school bus golds. They've kept me on the slopes and in one piece. You just don't trash what works well.

So I lift the skis to my back. The boot bar fits in the palm of my hand. It's time to take my skis out of the dark. I get the wax out first. Then I buff and shine 'til my hands hurt. The skis look great. And my boots still fit.

I could have new stuff now. I work full time and funds aren't tight. But this was the set I bought on my own. I worked months at that store. I saved. And I saved. My friends think I'm nuts.

But these are more than skis and boots. They're part of my youth. My heart's in them.

_____

Christine Mullin uses some of the same stylistic patterns as Winston Garland but her voice is nonpoetic. How would you describe it? What accounts for the difference in personality between Christine's piece and Winston's?

Taking My Own Advice

When I constructed this assignment, I wrote a paragraph myself.

> Here they are: small words in a small space. Strings of them, tied up in a box. What's the point, you might ask. It's this. When we write, we take care of our minds. We clean them up to see what we think. We take care of our guests too. We want to help them see what we do. So we pick crisp, clear, fresh words. Yet all must sound right and fit snug. That's hard. But it's not all. We want our guests to feel at home. To feel cared for by the way we speak our minds. With style, two things are at stake: your mind and your voice. Some reach for the phone. The risk is just too high. Some, though, reach for their pens. Their loops on the page catch the tunes of speech. And, in turn, those tunes rise from print to air. Back and forth. Loop de loop. It's how we train to hear, to speak, to write. We are not just what we say. But how we say it.

_____

How would you describe the voice in my paragraph? Who am I in that paragraph? Who am I talking to? What effects do you think my created persona and purpose might have on the audience you believe I'm addressing?

_____

Exercise: Following Through

After you have practiced listening to the voices that emerged from the exercise in your class and in this text, you might like to try a third version of your paragraph. After you have written the final version, make a record of your revising (or retuning) process based on what you've learned from reading, discussing, and listening to each other in class.

EXTENDING THE LIMITS AND CHOICES

This section builds from your learning so far. It begins with a new exercise and the rationale behind the stylistic limits. Following is a set of classroom examples with commentary and questions for discussion. The section ends with suggestions for revising.

Exercise II: Fewer Limits, More Choices

Write an extended paragraph or two (about a page) with the following constraints:

1. No punctuated sentence can have more than 18 words. Shortest, 1 word.
2. No words can have more than two syllables. At least half of the significant words must be one syllable.
3. Each sentence must be, at the very least, 4 words shorter or longer than the sentence before it.
4. At least half of the sentences must end in a consonant sound.

After you've written a preliminary draft, ask again the questions you addressed in exercise 1 of this chapter:

1. What difficulties did this exercise pose for you?
2. What do you believe is possible or impossible to accomplish within these limitations?
3. What choices have you already made about subject matter, audience, or occasion?

If possible, share these assumptions with your peers when you read your early drafts to each other. As a variation of this exercise, you might disregard the issue of subject matter in question 3 and, as a class, choose one particular subject to work with. If you can't decide on just one, try not to exceed three. A common subject may elicit interesting variations in rhetorical contexts, particularly if you can find one-word subjects that suggest more than one meaning. Some examples are "ties," "signals," "black" (or any other color with multiple associations), "fire," "rings." You get the idea.

Rationale Behind the Exercise

In general, the limitations of this exercise allow for greater possibilities of tonal blends and, thus, for the discovery of the blur between levels of formality. We might, for example, categorize a voice as colloquial or formal, but we know that rarely is a voice purely on one level or another. When we identify a level of formality, we are speaking of dominant features and locating those within a particular rhetorical context. Winston Garland's piece is made up of one-syllable words, yet the predominant sound isn't that of colloquial speech. Other features take center stage, features that we identify with literary language use; and so we disregard the monosyllabics in her paragraph as the primary test of low informality.

However, the limitations of exercise I are extreme. There's little room for mixing levels of diction to create a blended tone of voice. Exercise II frees diction to a much greater degree. But because words of more than two syllables are not permitted, the limits on diction level are still rather firm.

In relaxing the limits on sentence length, exercise II helps reduce the heavily emphatic sound that can easily be created in exercise I. For example, if you identify the audience in my own paragraph as college-age students, you might accuse me of being patronizing. The simple words plus short sentences help evoke that response, and my purpose—to explain—reinforces it. My very purpose puts me in a hierarchical relationship to my audience, so you might argue that I'm undermining your sophistication.

Attending to the variation of sentence length broadens tonal possibilities. A writer who ignored the principle about variation described earlier in this chapter could create a voice from exercise I that is completely flat (an effect that may or may not be desired). Exercise II attempts to make you more conscious of length patterns and their effect on tone as well as content.

The attention to monosyllabics in constraint 2 and to consonant word endings in constraint 4 reinforces the general principles behind exercise I. Opening the door to two-syllable words does not close the door on the use of monosyllabics to emphasize crucial information and to place that information in the most important spot of a sentence—the end. When writers consistently put the most important information at the end of sentences, they also help build coherence. The most important is often what's new. If the news is at the end, sentences are more likely to begin where the previous one left off, thus curbing the possibility not only of incoherence but also of wordiness and redundancy. Although it would be neither possible nor desirable to end every sentence on a monosyllabic word, much less a hard-consonant-ending monosyllabic word, any tendency in that direction is a good habit to develop.

All this attention to syllabics can make you more conscious of meaning too. Exercise II encourages you to ask why you choose particular words. For example, do you use a three-syllable-or-more word because it's the most precise expression for your idea? Or do you choose it because it sounds more impressive than a simpler word? Or have you not chosen at all but simply used the first word that popped into your mind, one that hazily approximates your idea?

Finally, an awareness of syllabic count can help you work at the rhythms within sentences as well as across them. By varying word length, you can build little rhythms within larger ones. Here is an example of such internal rhythmic interest:

If any of us were as well taken care of as the sentences of Henry James, we'd never long for another, never wander away: where else would we receive such attention, our thoughts anticipated, our feelings understood? Who else would robe us so richly, take us to the best places, or guard our virtue as his own and defend our character in every situation? If we were his sentences, we'd sing ourselves though we were dying and about to be extinguished, since the silence which would follow our passing would not be like the pause left behind by a noisy train. It would be a memorial, well-remarked, grave, just as the Master has assured us death itself is: the distinguished thing. (Gass 45)

To cite just one interesting series, listen to the rhythms of this short word list: "It would be a *memorial, well-remarked, grave. . . .*" In that piece of the sentence, words are chosen not only for their meaning but also for their palpability. The noun and postmodifiers are arranged as much for rhythmic effect as for sense. Notice too the monosyllabic "grave," ending as it does in a consonant sound—"grave," a significant idea at the clause end, followed by a significant break just before the dramatic resolution of the sentence, the paragraph.

Classroom Samples
I'll begin with my own writing sample.

Sample I: My Own

TIES

    I've never been tied up, but I've been tied to. Not to trees, to chairs, to beds, or railroad tracks, to nothing that suggests a crude restraint like rope. But I've been tied to lovers, to friends, to children, to books, to words that loop the air like jungle vines. From some, I've had a lifelong struggle to get free. It isn't always the bonds of greatest tension that make the struggle hardest, either. Sometimes it's the slackest ones. I don't believe even Houdini could have escaped the ties to my first husband. And they were the loosest of all. Yet I did it—a feat to rival the underwater trunk act. For this success, I neither expect nor want applause. I'd rather hear it for my magic in reverse, for those bonds I struggle to protect, to make tight. So much depends on the mystery of ties: the ones we keep, the ones we escape, the ones we trade for others. From here it's hard to say whether the master artist failed his greatest test of power. From there, no word comes.

Considering My Voice
To get a voice going, I relied heavily on contrasts and contradictions: "not this, but that" structures. And I relied on parallelism for balance. Parallel structure helped me maintain a level of seriousness, of weighted thought, in places.
    Three words in my paragraph break the "rules": Houdini,

underwater, and mystery. They seemed justifiable choices to me. However, in my earlier draft of this paragraph, I had nine multisyllabic words, all of which seemed necessary to sense and even sensibility. I found ways to eliminate six. Their absence changes little.

But you might want to test my judgment for yourself. Here are the original beginning sentences, complete with multisyllabic words: "I've never been tied up, but I've been tied to. Not to trees, to chairs, to beds, or railroad tracks, or to anything requiring physical restraint. No crudely visible ties like rope." What's lost or gained in sense or voice from one version to the other? Can the loss or gain be attributed in any way to multisyllabic words? Can you think of any defensible reasons for choosing the longer words in place of shorter ones?

The last two sentences in my original version contained the word *paradoxical*. I eliminated it in compliance with the rules for this exercise. They read: "From here it's hard to say whether the master artist failed his greatest, most paradoxical test of power. From there no word comes." Do you think *paradoxical* might be justified or not? On what grounds?

Let's look at some student samples of this exercise.

Sample II: Greta Mann

DRAGONS

All the people I know have dragons. These dragons lurk in dark places luring naive victims into their clutches. They have power. It's one we, their prey, can't always see, or feel, until we've slipped. Until we've lost control. Each dragon is different, but all hide in their caves, watching, waiting.

My biggest dragon is Sleep. His song is one of peace, comfort, warmth, dreams. He's dark, but not the frightening kind. His dark is simply the absence of things. It is the darkness of nothing. He offers a world of comfort—of beds, pillows, blankets. It's a comfort that extends to the mind. It surfaces in the world of dreams: a world without tests, work, pain, worries. Sleep argues: You can do that later.

"That" refers to all those chores on my list of things to be done. "Later" suggests a lesser dragon. His presence looms above me at all times of the day, telling me that "that" isn't crucial.

These two dragons haunt me most. I fight. I try to, anyway,

but their joint force is more than I can handle. I find myself slipping. I head towards my bed, ready to turn off the light and sink into that vast world of nothing. Later eggs me on. But I have one last defense against them. I stop myself and think. I do have power. If I can convince myself I create my own dragons, I win. They slip back to their cave, and I cross another job off my list.

Considering Greta Mann's Voice

Greta's piece was written after class members read their original drafts of exercise II. Several writers had picked subjects that didn't seem worthy of stylistic attention or fine tuning. Although I said nothing of the matter that day, they silently noticed how draft after draft reflected the safe routines of their lives. And since many students knew each other outside class, this observation was somewhat alarming to them, as you will see in the next sample. At our next meeting, I suggested this test question: Could anyone else have written your essay? If the answer is yes, then the essay isn't worth writing.

Greta's original version was about how tired she was. This had to be done, that had to be done, and so forth. So what? In her second version, she doesn't abandon the subject, but she abandons a tiresome way of talking about it. How does she make the subject interesting and more deservedly her own?

Sample III: Cathy Curran

Cathy Curran responds to her classmates' writing about the safe and predictable.

Last Tuesday in class I listened to the concerns of my classmates as they read their papers aloud. I was bored. We were supposed to write about something we cared about. Something that mattered. Surely it can't be grades and roommates and lack of sleep. Which is what most of us wrote about. Who were we kidding?

I know one student who just got engaged. What was his topic? He wrote about how messy his roommate is. Another student's grandma just died. She wrote a full page listing all the work she had. Who did we think we were kidding?

We left out our real interests, conflicts, and joys. Instead, we chose safe subjects. What were we afraid of? Exposing our feelings? Working? We stuck to polite, party topics that offend no one and interest no one. Not even ourselves. Why are we afraid to be human in our work? Do we only care about ourselves? Don't we connect to other people?

I left class puzzled. It had just started raining and people were running for cover. My hair's going to fall, I thought. I dodged in and out of students, heading for the Commons. So what mattered? What was so crucial to me that I could write about it? I'm getting a cold. I wish these people would hurry up so I could get inside.

People mattered. Why else did I join Amnesty International? When it came right down to it, people were all we cared about. I just needed a chance to prove I cared. I hustled up the hill to my dorm, thinking about what work I had left to do. I crossed through the archway and braced myself for three flights of stairs. But a shadow caught my eye. It was Sara, and she was crying. Should I stop to see what was wrong, to try to comfort her? I did not know her very well. The truth is, I really did not care. With a quick hello, I brushed past her and headed for my room. I should have stopped. This was a chance to show what mattered. But I let it go.

Considering Cathy Curran's Voice

Cathy talks about "we" in expressing her disappointment, but her voice suggests "them" until her concluding sentences. She speaks with some superiority, appearing to recognize what others do not. That's what her voice suggests both in message and tone. At the end, however, she reveals her own hesitance and failure to take her own advice. What does that suggest about her claim that she knows what matters because she joined Amnesty International (multisyllabics that are justified in her piece)? Does her admission of failure strengthen or weaken her voice? Do you think her essay stops abruptly or truly ends? To what extent does she succeed in creating a believable voice behind the page?

Sample IV: Brian Muldowney

In this final classroom sample, Brian Muldowney describes a long-awaited fishing expedition.

Break of dawn in early August—a day much looked forward to. The eastern sky, a subtle shade of pink. The only sign of life was the roar of the ocean and the bustling boat yard. The charter fleet was almost ready for daylong deep-sea angling in the Gulf Stream, thirty miles off the Jersey shore. I knuckled crust from my drowsy eyes. This was a dream come true. No worries here on the high seas, a place where time is not measured by a punch clock but by tides, shadows, and the spawning of speckled trout.

At forty knots, we'd reach Spensor Canyon in two hours. The strip of land faded in the distance with all my burdens on it. Fathoms of blue brine rose beneath the fifty-five-foot Viking Sport-Fisher as it cut through walls of water. By 8 a.m., six lines were being trolled. Each rig had a blue-and-green-skirted Sir Ace draped with cut mullet, but no results. If I were a fish, I'd bite. Midday, and not even a strike to liven our six-man crew aboard the *Dream Chaser.* Some of us slept. Others were awake but lulled by the mellow drone of diesel engines. I sat in the fighting chair on the transom. I was alone, but not lonely. Somewhere lurked a billfish that would make me famous from Mt. Sterling all the way to Charleston.

"Port rigger!" shouted the mate. The rod doubled over and line ripped off by the yard. A mighty yank of the rod firmly set the hook and the battle began. A blue marlin, of a quarter ton, in all its fury leaped with the grace of a ballet dancer. I had thought catching stripers in the surf of Martha's Vineyard was a thrill. Nothing could compare to this. We struggled to keep our poise, but the sight brought out the child in each of us.

"He's a beauty, look at him go!" stood out among the cheers. Vivid violet and bars of blue neon along the fish's side glistened in the sunlight. Hours had passed before the beast appeared to weaken. Then, in an instant, the line went slack. The rod returned to its normal upright position. No one spoke. Only the diesel engines now, humming their deep-throat song of sadness.

Considering Brian Muldowney's Voice

Lots of specific details are included in Brian's piece. He uses fishing terms and the names of specific places to give us the feeling of this trip. He uses parallel structure well. Here's one with alliteration and consonance: "a place where time is not measured by a punch clock but by tides, shadows, and the spawning of speckled trout." He even draws on repetition to weight the final sentence of the essay, calling back the image of the diesel engines that, at first mention, lulled some fishermen to complacency. At the end, the engines reflect loss. Brian's sentences are also built fairly tight. He doesn't waste space and he makes verbs count. Yet I wouldn't call the voice strong. It sounds rather flat to my ear. How would you account for the evenness of tone? How would you change it, if you could, to create a stronger sound of someone speaking to you behind the page? Or would you defend the even tone? How?

Brian's work with the exercise reflects what many students learned to do in the early weeks of the course. They may not have found strong speaking personalities yet, but they've honed their sentences and practiced stylistic patterns they've noticed and admired. They've made space for a voice to emerge.

Suggestions for Revision

After you've listened to each other's drafts and to the foregoing samples, try writing a second version of exercise II, "Fewer Limits, More Choices." Then answer the following questions: "Who talks like this? To whom? For what reasons?"

In small groups, read your new versions aloud to each other. After each person reads, write answers to the preceding questions. Share your responses with the writer. The similarities and the differences in reader response can help the writer hear how well he or she has produced not only the intended message but also the voice delivering it. As readers, your responses can also help you hear the voices you bring to a text, the tonal shadings you impose, given your own expectations and experience. As writers, you can begin to appreciate the degree to which you can control or not control how a text is heard and interpreted.

CHAPTER THREE

Toward a Developed Essay

Sustaining a Colloquial Voice

This chapter develops from your learning in Chapter 2. Here we will listen to both students and professionals writing in very personal and informal voices to narrowly defined audiences. The student samples include commentary and one self-reflective analysis. The professional samples include questions for discussion and exercises in imitation. At the end of the chapter, you'll find an essay assignment in developing and sustaining for a few pages a colloquial voice of your own. To create that sound on the page, you'll be drawing from all you've learned thus far.

Let's begin by listening to some very informal voices that are sustained for more than a few paragraphs. Our aim is to discover how these distinct voices are made and organized on the page.

CLASSROOM SAMPLES

The following pieces grew out of classwork for the exercises in Chapter 2.

Sample I: Winston Garland

Winston Garland is the author of the sample "my dad's mom is a pink old girl." She's not speaking as a poet this time.

> When I think of a feminist, I think of the women marching in Washington. You know, the older ones. The ones that always wear men's jeans that are too big for them, that are pulled up over

the waist with a big belt. They wear tennis shoes worn down on the outside from marching. And they have those T-shirts with bloody hangers on front. They have short hair, a little gray and fizzled. It's not that they don't wear makeup; it's that they have no color. And they're gruff, always snarling, never smiling. When they talk, it's a voice that grates on your nerves. I don't fit that image. My face, my hair—they're fiery. And though I love men's jeans and soleless shoes, I'm not going to wear a bloody hanger. I argue well for what I believe, but I'm also the warm voice on the phone. I know the value of a smile but just because I'm from a southern family doesn't mean I'm a southern belle. I know what a sexist is. The southern gentleman who puts his fair, virginal lady on a pedestal doesn't see her as equal. To him, she's fragile, a child who needs to be cared for. A feminist marches against such injustice. She makes change.

There's the feminist who screams so she won't be ignored. She doesn't care if she runs over other people's ideals. For her there's no compromise. One side must win; the other, lose.

I watch the mighty feminist like my father watched his father—a lawyer who fought to represent the rights of the individual. My grandfather moved just like a freight train. He made right and didn't give a damn who got in his way. The louder he was, the more offensive he was, the better he thought he did his job. My dad wanted to be like him. Fight the system. Stand up for freedom. My dad saw my grandfather hurt, but he also saw the best, the legend.

I know I can't always wear a white hat. Some people misunderstand me, though. They think I don't see the difference between men and women. A few even call me a "dike" or "feminist bitch." I have the courage to face them, but I want to be seen as feminine as well as feminist: To wear black lace when I choose. To be seductive. But also to stand up for what I believe. To demand respect for the person I am. To compromise as well as confront.

A personality emerges in this piece. We can hear Winston struggling with contradictions, trying to resolve them in her personal search for place within the feminist movement. We can hear her earnestness, too, in the quick shift from one view to another, from image to image. Where can she strike a balance between the "mighty" feminist and the feminine, or between her grandfather's single purpose and her father's awareness of others' pain? She asks herself a hard question, and we hear her struggle for an answer. Sometimes, I want her to slow down, to say more in places, perhaps to follow her "I am this but not that" lists with a paragraph of fleshed-out thinking, and to make bridges between her leaps of thought. But first things first. Winston has succeeded in getting the feeling into the facts. The rise and fall and stress of a speaking voice are entangled in those sentences. She can't do everything at once. No one can. If you could help her develop her thinking, without sacrificing her voice, what would you advise?

Sample II: Sarah Townsend

Sarah Townsend addresses her niece.

If you've ever eaten an orange, you'll know what I mean. You can be really hungry for one, and it can even be sitting right there in front of you, but the effort it requires changes your mind. Getting the skin started is the worst part; it hurts your fingers to peel so hard. Then the juice runs over your hands and you have to pick all those threads off. Of course, there are the endless seeds too. But when you've finished, and you've dried your hands, you eat the first section and nothing ever tasted so good. It's like that with much in life when you think about it. Everything worth something takes effort.

In Saint Exupery's *The Little Prince,* there's a scene where the prince meets a fox. "Please tame me!" said the fox, for he knew that one best understands the things one tames. But the Little Prince did not understand the word *tame.* The fox answered, "It is an act too often neglected. It means to establish ties." Establishing ties with someone or something means work: time, energy, effort. Today it seems we don't really have to put forth much effort to get by. When we want something, we go the store and get it. Or we pick up the phone and order it. Or we decide it's just not worth it and settle for something less, but easier.

It's easy to forget how the best things in life are usually the hardest to come by and the hardest to keep. Like your best friend, for example—the one with whom it would have been easier to remain casual acquaintances, but you really worked to get past the small talk, you took a chance and really invested time. What about the paragraph you wrote over and over and over again until it was perfect? You even hoped the teacher would call on you to read out loud. Or the time you spent months looking for the perfect Christmas present for Dad (who always gets books because he's impossible to shop for) and you found it and wrapped it and could hardly wait for him to open it just for the look on his face? Maybe it was how you ran on the track team for three years in high school, putting practice before almost everything else, even classes sometimes. How some days it would be pouring outside (or worse, snowing) and you think "this is crazy" but you run anyway until every muscle hurts. Then you make it to the state track meet, and you win, and the feeling when you cross the line is like nothing you can put in words. All the hard work was worth it.

Sometimes good things happen out of the blue, spontaneously. That's a great feeling. But most of the time what you worked hardest for feels even greater. My teammates and I always roll our eyes when our coach delivers this cliche: "The only time success comes before work is in the dictionary." We roll our eyes, but we know he's right. Not giving something worthwhile a chance because it may take too much effort is like never eating oranges because they're such a pain to peel.

Sarah Townsend's Self-Reflection

Students wrote analyses of their own essays, describing who they were as speakers, who their audience was, and what principles of voice they tried to apply based on our work in exercises I and II in Chapter 2. Sarah Townsend wrote the following analysis:

> The voice personality in my essay borders on being moralistic. I realized this from the very roughest draft and tried many revisions to avoid the sound, but it seemed to come through no matter what I changed. When I reviewed my prewriting questions, however, and considered who I was when I talked like this, my relationship to my subject and with my audience, I realized the tone was reasonable. I chose the subject because I was frustrated with the number of women who have come out for the track team, then quit after a week or less because it was too much work. I wanted to tell my niece about how I felt, I wanted to convey to her how I learned that things you work for mean the most to you. Thus, a moral. Because she is young, my diction needed to be simple. And because I feel so strongly about it, I tried to make words and sentences forceful.
>
> The principles that governed my voice were these:
>
> 1. Use shorter, more direct word choices to give the feeling

of efficiency and exactness (force, I mean). For example, I said in the last sentence, ". . . such a pain to peel" instead of "so extremely difficult."

2. Vary sentence lengths, using short ones to help avoid monotony. I tried dissecting my sentences, changing one long one to two, even three shorter ones.

3. Experiment with parallel lists. I tried to imitate what we saw in the sample from Saul Bellow. I made lists such as "time, energy, effort" for emphasis.

4. Make a conscious effort to end more words on stopped consonants for emphasis.

5. Use first- and second-person pronouns for familiarity. I tried to speak directly to my niece.

Considering Sarah Townsend's Voice

How well do you think Sarah Townsend succeeds in achieving her goals regarding purpose and audience? Are there places where she sounds too much like a morality teacher, or do you think she tempers that sound? Some might argue that she sounds like the "perfect student." Would you agree or disagree? Does she succeed in maintaining a diction level appropriate for a serious but informal conversation with a young girl? Where does she seem to strike just the right note? Where does she seem to miss the mark (if you think she does)?

PROFESSIONAL SAMPLES OF COLLOQUIAL VOICES

After each of the following three samples of professional writing, you'll find questions for discussion and exercises in imitation. Each writer creates a predominantly colloquial voice to speak personally to a narrowly defined, familiar audience.

Sample I: Michael Robinson

This first example is a restaurant review.

A CLASSY JOINT CALLED BENJAMIN'S:
LIGHTS ARE LOW, WAITERS KNOW

It was 8:40 on a Friday night. The kind of night you get in Richmond when you know the full blast of summer is only days away, waiting for you like a mug with a sap in some dark alley, and you know you'd better enjoy the fact that the pavement is still cool beneath your feet. The cars on Broad Street were filled with working stiffs heading home late at the end of another day. A day like any other day, except that this one was different.

The joint was called Benjamin's. I never did find out who Benjamin was, but it didn't matter. I wasn't there to make nice with the landlord. I had a job to do. A tough, dirty job. The kind of job where you come home to a seedy hotel room and a bottle of bourbon, instead of a white picket fence and a woman who knows your name.

Yeah, I'm a private reviewer. A few bucks a day and expenses—when I can get paid at all. Diners, clubs, hole-in-the-wall dives where no one asks your name—I do them all.

And I was getting ready to do Benjamin's.

It was the kind of place where the tables were far apart so you could keep your business to yourself. The light was low, and the waiters didn't ask too many questions. There were mirrors, but were all high up so the dame you were with had to look at you—that was the price she paid. At least, that was the down payment.

The waiters took their time and a little of yours, but they knew what they were doing, all right. Sure. They knew. I asked for a bottle, but they were out of rye so I settled for a Beaujolais-Villages. It cost 14 bucks, but after a few shots, a man could begin to forget. And maybe a dame could forget even quicker.

The doll with me was class all the way, so I asked for some of that pâté that the uptown money boys like and told them to throw in a seafood Norwegian while they were at it. I had nothing against Norwegians. The pâté ($4.95) was smooth as a silk stocking and surrounded by eggs and onions and coarse mustard like a ward heeler surrounded by relatives. It was as good as the feeling you get when the bullet meant for you misses.

The seafood was good, too. Oh, it was all there, all right: crab, shrimp, scallops. Just like they'd told me it would be, all the way down to the herb mayonnaise dressing. It was almost too good. Too neat. Why give me so much for a lousy $6.95? I felt like I was being set up for a sucker punch.

Then it came. The New Orleans Seafood Chowder ($2.25). I was waiting for it, but still, those peppers nearly caught me on the chin. Sure, they were hot, but I was a little too tough for them. What they didn't know was that I take to hot peppers the way some guys take to the sound of dice shaking in a sweaty fist. I laughed in their faces and was ready for more.

The doll had a Caesar salad for one. Nyeah, nyeah! It was a little Caesar salad. That's right, you mugs, a little Caesar. Got it? She'd already paid the $4.25 before I grabbed her and explained that we were doing film noir, not '30's gangster movies. I . . . I had to slap her around a bit, just to get her attention. She . . . she had to knee me in the groin. But it was worth it for the salad, and the taste of garlic and anchovies that filled your mouth like Esther Williams filled out a Catalina.

The waiter was back with more. Plenty more. He laid a plate of blackened salmon and crabmeat ($18.50) down on the table like a card shark laying down a fifth ace. Someone had painted a pattern of lemon butter and bordelaise sauces on the dish—someone who knew all about sauces. I began to get that funny feeling—the one that makes the little hairs on the back of your neck stand up. I couldn't see him, but somewhere back in that kitchen was a smart guy. A real saucier.

And then I didn't have to wonder any longer because my black and white tournedos ($17.95) were right in front of my face. Oh, there was a saucier, all right. The proof was right under my nose. Espagnole sauce on the first piece of meat, béarnaise on the other. And this saucier knew his business. I should have been keeping my eye on the doll, but all I could think of was how great it was to have perfect béarnaise joined to the charcoal of that fillet.

It was the music that jolted me back to reality. Cool jazz coming from the next room. The Anthony Dowd Trio and Big Jim Branch telling about that Devil Moon, while me and the doll spooned up chocolate pâté with raspberry sauce and pecan pie.

In the lounge we ordered our brandies and watched the band. I lit up a cigarette and gagged. Then I remembered: I don't smoke.

No, I'm no smoker. I'm just a private reviewer, doing a job. And on that warm Richmond night, in a joint named for a guy I never met, I knew it was an all-right job.

Questions for Discussion

1. Michael Robinson reviews Benjamin's in a familiar voice. What is it? Where have you heard it before?
2. Robinson lets us know that he's put on this voice. It's not his own. What are the clues?

3. What are the incongruities between the voice Robinson adopts and the real subject and purpose of this piece? How do those incongruities affect your response to the review?
4. Why would Robinson choose this particular voice? What's it good for?

Exercise in Imitation

Either alone or in pairs, go to a local restaurant, cafe, or fast-food chain. Take in not only the food but also the atmosphere. Later, write your own (or a collaborative) review in a voice that approximates the ambiance of the restaurant.

Sample II: Patricia Volk

WHY I'M GLAD I DON'T LOOK LIKE MICHELLE PFEIFFER

She simmered in *The Witches of Eastwick*. Next she stole *Married to the Mob*. Then there were those close-ups in *Dangerous Liaisons*. Even crying she looked good. Her upper lip was puffier than ever. Puffier than Barbara Hershey's post collagen. Puffier than Kim Basinger's in the *Batman* lip close-ups. In the year of the puffy lip, Michelle Pfeiffer had the puffiest lip in Hollywood. Then came *The Fabulous Baker Boys* and that clinched it. Lips puffier than ever, Michelle Pfeiffer is now The Most Beautiful Woman in the World.

This has never been my problem. I was born funny looking. Not like my friend Marjorie whose father took one look and said, "Give me a stick. I'll kill it." I simply didn't look like a baby. I was born looking like a twenty-three-year-old man. People laughed leaning over the carriage.

"She's the spitting image," they said to my father. "A little Cecil."

I was proud of looking like him. I thought it gave me an exalted position in the family. It wasn't till puberty that I found out I didn't look like other girls. The orthodontist said my mouth lacked "rhythm." My face was too generous. I had big hair.

Saturdays were spent in the photo booth anyway, checking out good angles, hoping to be discovered: "Oh miss?" the man stops you in the street. "My God. Could you . . . I was wondering— . . . would you mind posing for the cover of *Life?*"

Conventional ideas about beauty made me nervous. They precluded what you were born with. When all the girls in high school tried to look like Elizabeth Taylor in *Cleopatra,* I didn't. Of course, I couldn't. But I told myself even if I could, I wouldn't. Still, I was surprised when my college chose Bunny Gutfreund to represent us in the Miss America Pageant. Vapid, born-to-please Bunny Gutfreund, a professional contestant with a cocky little walk and an Ethel Merman hairdo, a girl devoted to practicing her dimples. Why would anyone admire that punctuated face? If this was what America wanted, I was happy to be out of step.

Basically, though, I liked my face. It was accessible. It was me people stopped to ask directions. "Where's Sixth Avenue?" or, "Which way to lingerie?" I never sat out a dance. People knew from my face I wouldn't hurt them. I never had good or bad days based upon how I looked, never suffered from the heartbreak of facial tyranny. Occasionally, someone would blurt, "You know . . . you're actually kind of beautiful . . . in a way," as if they'd discovered the tenth planet. I never woke up wondering if I looked better yesterday.

I used to think the Most Beautiful Woman in the World was my mother. "A Lana Turner look-alike," friends nodded in agreement. "You've got one gorgeous mother," relatives said. "You two sisters?" the butcher winked. My mother took this in her stride. If pressed, she would say Ingrid Bergman was the Most Beautiful Woman in the World. Despite a low hairline, my grandmother voted for Kay Francis. They laughed at Garbo. "She has big feet," Grandma would say. "I tank I go home," my mother would add, cracking them both up.

My father thought his mother was the Most Beautiful Woman in the World. Ethel Edythe Shure was the National Bank of Princeton's first calendar girl. She once received a letter addressed simply,

> Postman, postman
> Do your duty
> Deliver this letter
> To the Princeton beauty

But time, beauty's wrecker's ball, had its way. Six grandchildren used her arms as pillows. You could flick the upper part and it would swing. Always she laughed. Unlike Sean Connery who at fifty-nine became the Sexiest Man Alive, my grandmother accepted her evanescence. In our culture, once experience shows on a woman's face, she's through. Thanks to the miracle of plastic, you might get a decade. Look at Cher. She's spent megathousands on rhinoplasty, cheekplasty, riboplasty. Even so, you can tell Cher's no thirty. Maybe that's why she snarls through her video, "If I Could Turn Back Time."

"Do you think Michelle Pfeiffer's the Most Beautiful Woman in the World?" I ask my mother. "She looks like a skeleton," my mother says. And it comes to me that once you're the Most Beautiful Woman in the World, you can no longer be an outsider. Everyone has an opinion about you. Everyone has a claim. You no longer own yourself. People stare while you eat lobster in a restaurant. You're public domain.

So I count my blessings. No one's ever loved me for my looks. No one's ever hated me for my looks. No one will ever say, "Remember her? She used to be the Most Beautiful Woman in the World." The clock ticks. Poor Michelle Pfeiffer. Maybe next year will be the year of frizzy hair. Maybe Andie MacDowell will have her day. Andie MacDowell who ten years ago would have been too tall, too curly, too heavy-browed. I'd rather look like Mary McCarthy or Georgia O'Keeffe, face not an issue. Just my pal, my consort, my partner in crime. I'd rather be who I am not how I look. Like Margaret Atwood, Ann Beattie, Edna O'Brian, Mathilde Krim, Benasir Bhutto, Anjelica Huston, Toni Morrison or Virginia Woolf, too busy to notice I'm beautiful. (114)

Questions for Discussion

1. Patricia Volk reveals in her voice a blend of personal qualities that make us laugh yet take her seriously. Can you separate the humorous from the serious? Point out moments in her text where the voice suggests one attitude or another, or a blend of both. Try to say what in her language use makes you respond the way you do.

2. What specific language habits mark Volk's essay as colloquial speech directed to a familiar audience?

3. How might you define Volk's audience, based not only on what she says but also on how she speaks?

4. In what specific ways does Volk's voice seem to derive

from the principles we've been working with in this chapter?

Exercise in Imitation

Choose one of the following fill-in-the-blanks:

Why I'm glad I don't look like _____

act like _____

think like _____

talk like _____

Begin by making a list, freely adding names of people who are publically admired for qualities you'd rather not possess. After you have decided on one popular figure for your focus, write freely for awhile, listing reasons you don't want to have the particular quality for which he or she is generally praised. From your list, choose your best, most honest reasons. One or more of these will form the core of your essay. They should illustrate the contrast between the publicly admired figure and yourself. And they should explain the significance of that contrast—why you'd rather, finally, be you.

Decide on a familiar audience, one that might be most sympathetic to your argument. Write your essay directly to that audience. Your essay might be humorous too, like Volk's, but it doesn't need to be.

Sample III: Suzanne Britt

THAT LEAN AND HUNGRY LOOK

Caesar was right. Thin people need watching. I've been watching them for most of my adult life, and I don't like what I see. When these narrow fellows spring at me, I quiver to my toes. Thin people come in all personalities, most of them menacing. You've got your "together" thin person, your mechanical thin person, your condescending thin person, your tsk-tsk thin person, your efficiency-expert thin person. All of them are dangerous.

In the first place, thin people aren't fun. They don't know how to goof off, at least in the best, fat sense of the word. They've always got to be adoing. Give them a coffee break, and they'll jog around the block. Supply them with a quiet evening at home, and they'll fix the screen door and lick S&H green stamps. They say things like "there aren't enough hours in the day." Fat people never say that. Fat people think the day is too damn long already. Thin people make me tired. They've got speedy little metabolisms that cause them to bustle briskly. They're forever rubbing their bony little hands together and eying new problems to "tackle." I like to surround myself with sluggish, inert, easygoing fat people, the kind who believe that if you clean it up today, it'll just get dirty again tomorrow.

Some people say the business about the jolly fat person is a myth, that all of us chubbies are neurotic, sick, sad people. I disagree. Fat people may not be chortling all day long, but they're a hell of a lot nicer than the wizened and shriveled. Thin people turn surly, mean and hard at a young age because they never learn the value of a hot-fudge sundae for easing tension. Thin people don't like gooey soft things because they themselves are neither gooey nor soft. They are crunchy and dull, like carrots. They go straight to the heart of the matter while fat people let things stay all blurry and hazy and vague, the way things actually are. Thin people want to face the truth. One of my thin friends is always staring at complex, unsolvable problems and saying "the key thing is. . . ." Fat people never say that. They know there isn't any such thing as the key thing about anything. Thin people believe in logic. Fat people see all sides. The sides fat people see are rounded blobs, usually gray, always nebulous and truly not worth worrying about. But the thin person persists. "If you consume more calories than you burn," says one of my thin friends, "you'll gain weight. It's that simple." Fat people always grin when they hear statements like that. They know better.

Fat people realize that life is illogical and unfair. They know very well that God is not in his heaven and all is not right with the world. If God was up there, fat people could have two doughnuts and a big orange drink anytime they wanted it.

Thin people have a long list of logical things they are always spouting off to me. They hold up one finger at a time as they reel off these things, so I won't lose track. They speak slowly as if to a young child. The list is long and full of holes. It contains tidbits like "get a grip on yourself," "cigarettes kill," "cholesterol clogs," "fit as a fiddle," "ducks in a row," "organize," and "sound fiscal management." Phrases like that.

They think these 2,000-point plans lead to happiness. Fat people know happiness is elusive at best and even if they could get the kind thin people talk about, they wouldn't want it.

Wisely, fat people see that such programs are too dull, too hard, too off the mark. They are never better than a whole cheesecake. Fat people know all about the mystery of life. They are the ones acquainted with the night, with luck, with fate, with playing it by ear. One thin person I know once suggested that we arrange all the parts of a jigsaw puzzle into groups according to size, shape and color. He figured this would cut the time needed to complete the puzzle by at least 50 per cent. I said I wouldn't do it. One, I like to muddle through. Two, what good would it do to finish early? Three, the jigsaw puzzle isn't the important thing. The important thing is the fun of four people (one thin person included) sitting around a card table, working a jigsaw puzzle. My thin friend had no use for my list. Instead of joining us, he went outside and mulched the boxwoods. The three remaining fat people finished the puzzle and made chocolate, double-fudged brownies to celebrate.

The main problem with thin people is they oppress. Their good intentions, bony torsos, tight ships, neat corners, cerebral machinations and pat solutions look like dark clouds over the loose, comfortable, spread-out, soft world of the fat. Long after fat people have removed their coats and shoes and put their feet up on the coffee table, thin people are still sitting on the edge of the sofa, looking neat as a pin, discussing rutabagas. Fat people are heavily into fits of laughter, slapping their thighs and whooping it up, while thin people are still politely waiting for the punch line. Thin people are downers. They like math and morality and reasoned evaluation of the limitations of human beings. They have their skinny little acts together. They expound, prognose, probe and prick.

Fat people are convivial. They will like you even if you're irregular and have acne. They will come up with a good reason why you never wrote the great American novel. They will cry in your beer with you. They will put your name in the pot. They will let you off the hook. Fat people will gab, giggle, guffaw, gallumph, gyrate and gossip. They are generous, giving and gallant. They are gluttonous and goodly and great. What you want when you're down is soft and jiggly, not muscled and stable. Fat people know this. Fat people have plenty of room. Fat people will take you in.

Questions for Discussion

1. Suzanne Britt does not even try to appeal to logic. She appeals to our emotions instead: It's nicer to be around

fat people than thin people. To persuade you of that, she attributes sympathetic qualities to the fat, negative qualities to the thin. One could just as easily reverse the feeling by turning the qualities she attributes to fat people into vices instead of virtues. How does Britt make fat people seem socially superior? How does she manipulate meaning through images and word associations?
2. How does Britt use sound similarities to suggest similar meaning?
3. How does she use contrast to create an emphatic, truth-telling voice?
4. Britt's essay is largely list making. How does she build coherence from her pile of data? How does she hold things together, sentence to sentence, paragraph to paragraph?

Exercise in Imitation

Consider something people usually respond to negatively. Reverse the value by describing that same thing in positives. Try using images and associations the way Suzanne Britt does to enlist the sympathies of your audience. Talk about the positives in direct contrast to your topic's usual opposite, which is considered positive by most people. Reverse the value in the same way, making the positive negative. In other words, make fat seem good and its opposite, thin, seem bad. Appeal to sympathy, not reason.

Try organizing your essay the way Britt does—listing positive associations of one against negative associations of the other: Thin people are . . . but fat people are. . . . Divide paragraphs by category of qualities explored.

You might try suggesting coherence by using repetition of sentence openers and sound similarities (alliteration or rhyme, for example).

A Collaborative Exercise:
Writing the Music for Robinson, Volk, or Britt

After you have listened to the variety of personalities included in the professional samples, you may wish to try the following exercise: In a group of three to five students, describe the voice in one of the examples. Begin by listing the personality features of the speaker that you hear as you read. Then, try to support your list by identifying the language habits or combination of habits that seem to give rise to those features. Consider these elements, for example.

1. Level of vocabulary
2. Predominantly multisyllabic or monosyllabic words
3. Number of sentences ending on monosyllabic words, especially hard-consonant-ended words
4. Mainly simple sentences or complex sentences
5. Frequency of sentence fragments
6. Average sentence length (number of words). Does the speaker depend on mostly short or long sentences?
7. Length variation: varied a lot or a little. In a representative paragraph, mark the ends of sentences with a slash mark. Read the paragraph out loud. What does the rhythm of sentences tell you about the speaker?
8. Punctuation. Does the speaker rely much on punctuation within a sentence—interruptions, lists, clauses joined by semicolons? If so, read these sentences out loud. How does the intonation pattern created by internal punctuation contribute to the voice you hear?

If you were going to construct your own exercise to help writers imitate the voice your group described, what would you advise? What guidelines would you provide to produce the speaking personality heard in the example?

At the next class meeting, present your group report to the class.

ON YOUR OWN: WRITING A FULLY DEVELOPED ESSAY
Suggested General Class Topic

Try to explain something you know well to someone who knows little or nothing about the subject. You are speaking to one person, a peer or older adult with whom you have a relatively close relationship. Assume that you are somewhere quiet. There is no worry about interruption. And assume, too, that although your audience is ignorant about the subject, he or she would like to understand. You want to be patient, to take the time to explain carefully in terms familiar to your audience.

Let the subject be one that truly matters to you. Let's say that to explain your subject is to explain something important about who you are.

Getting Started

There is nothing like the tyranny of the blank page or computer screen. All writers face the defiance of the empty page. The only way to fight it is to write something, anything; but as Connor Freff Cochran, a music journalist, suggests in the following excerpt, "for God's sake . . . do something."

> Inaction is easy in the face of doubt and fear. That's why pressure is the creator's drug of choice, commoner than caffeine or cocaine. The longer you can avoid acting, the more the pressure builds, until finally it smashes the walls and carries you through work you believe yourself incapable of (forget that you've done it a thousand times before; fear doesn't answer to logic).
>
> But who respects a junkie? Certainly not the junkie. And while it seems easier not to act, to let the pressure do it for you, you realize that's a lie. Count all your emotional costs, both immediate and deferred, and you see that it's really much easier to simply begin, continue, and finish, than it is to gird yourself, hand the world a cat-o'-nine-tails, and beg it to whip you until you scream. Of course, it's not nearly as satisfying, not when you're addicted and your craving is no longer for the work, or for the satisfaction that follows, but for the stammer and steam and desperation of the rising pressure. . . .
>
> And yet, this thought: what a pleasure to toss an idea into the air, just for the fun of it. To tinker. To play again, free as when you were a child, but with your adult ability to treasure just how magical and important freedom is; and with your adult vision to guide you in a greater cause.
>
> You are standing on a bare stage. It may not look like it, of course. It might look like a bus or subway, or a recording studio. Maybe it's a waiting room or a street corner or a hospital bed or a coffee shop counter. It doesn't matter: They're

all the same bare stage, and you are a blank slate, your un-
realized possibilities infinite. Realize them. Wait no longer.
Fear no more. Put down your distractions. . . . As your
thoughts reach this end, unleash yourself and create something. Right now. Right where you are. With exactly what
you have at hand. It doesn't matter what—a riff, a song, a
dance, a rhyme, a bad pun, a circuit design—anything goes.
But for God's sake, for your sake, for your art's sake . . . for
the world's sake . . . do something. (20)

Working from Your First Draft

After you have written a preliminary draft, try to revise, using what you have found most useful in the past few weeks.
Draw from your textbook and from writing samples used in
class.

Attach to your draft a typed sheet on which you have described the "tools" you have used in creating a voice to speak
about your subject to a particular audience. Be sure to give examples from your draft that illustrate the use of each "tool" or
helpful guide. If you cannot identify it (that is, pin it down), just
try to explain, using an example from the textbook or a classroom sample to help you. For example, you may have tried to
imitate one of the writers you read for class because you wanted
to create a similar effect in your draft. In that case, describe the
effect you think the writer created and give an example from his
or her piece. Then give the example from your own draft to
show your attempt at imitation.

Sharing Drafts with Peers

In small groups of three or four, or in pairs, read your drafts
aloud to each other. Each writer may need to read twice. (It's
difficult to remember things if the essay is heard only once.) Let
the members of your group tell you how they understand the
following:

1. What they can tell about who you are from the way you
   explain your subject
2. Who your possible audience is
3. What might have occasioned this explanation

Next, let the members of your group tell you about the
following:

1. What seems most interesting to them
2. What they would like to hear more about
3. Whether the essay simply stopped or truly ended

Revising in Light of Peer Response

You are the author. That means you decide which advice to take and which to ignore. Sounds simple enough, but it's hard for writers to accept that responsibility. Two general tendencies are to begin arguing against reader response or to fall helplessly victim to it. Try not to argue at first. Just listen. Then wait awhile, maybe until the next day (I sometimes wait a week or longer if I have that much time to stew).

Read your essay aloud to yourself and reread your commentary following the essay. Consider to what extent your readers responded according to your professed goals. Then revise *in light of peer review, but not enslaved to it.* Prepare a second draft and revision notes—what you changed or did not change after listening to your peers read their essays and after hearing their response to yours.

Sharing a Second Draft

Bring to class a list of questions, such as "What do I still need to know from an audience to help me accomplish my goals?" Exchange your draft and your questions with one member of your group. (A group member will have heard your original essay as well as an entire set of commentaries on it.) Ask your reader to respond, this time in writing, to the questions you have posed. After your reader has answered your specific questions, ask him or her to respond to other things in the essay he or she finds interesting, puzzling, and so on. If there is time, you might exchange essays with another group member.

Finally, prepare your final draft and revision notes.

CHAPTER FOUR

Formal Voices, Part I
Pattern Play

In shifting from colloquial voices to formal voices, we will slide across the continuum—from low to high. It may seem more logical, at first, to move from low to middle, but the middle, when it comes to speech styles, can best be defined by the extremes. To move to the high end, you will need to make some big adjustments—socially, personally, and musically. We are leaving the piano bar and going to the opera. Here we will listen to the weighted sound of high seriousness directed toward unfamiliar, critical audiences, as in these operatic solos:

> Finally, to those nations who would make themselves our adversary, we offer not a pledge but a request: that both sides begin anew the quest for peace, before the dark powers of destruction unleashed by science engulf all humanity in planned or accidental self-destruction.
>
> (John F. Kennedy, inaugural address)

> And when the last Red Man shall have perished, and the memory of my tribe shall become a myth among the White Men, these shores will swarm with the invisible dead of my tribe, and when your children's children think themselves alone in the field, the store, the shop, upon the highway, or in the silence of the pathless woods, they will not be alone.
>
> (attributed to Seattle, Dwamish chief)

Because when we start deceiving ourselves into thinking not that we want something or need something, not that it is a pragmatic necessity for us to have it, but that it is a *moral imperative* that we have it, then is when we join the fashionable madmen, and then is when the thin whine of hysteria is heard in the land, and then is when we are in bad trouble. And I suspect we are already there.

(Joan Didion, "On Morality")

In this chapter, we'll examine the general features or language conventions of voices pitched high (in subject matter, importance of occasion, and distance of audience); yet any or all of these conventions may not produce an effective formal voice. Producing one depends on knowing what the choices are and exercising judgment. To discover our choices and decide among them, we need to practice various word and sentence patterns. These stylistic patterns, either alone or in combination, contribute to voice. We need to find out which are most effective for a given purpose, audience, and occasion, and which we are most attracted to. Different writers create different formal voices. And the same writer may create different kinds of formal voices, depending in part on the stylistic patterns he or she chooses.

Some examples in this chapter you'll like and want to imitate; others, you won't. Some you'll think are good for one occasion and audience but not for another. It's the same situation in life. Weddings and funerals are formal social occasions, yet you don't necessarily dress and act in the same way at both. Nor do you necessarily dress or act the same as other people gathered for the same event. To an outside observer, though, you all may be said to dress and act according to general expectations.

This chapter, then, focuses on general expectations, the conventions associated with, but not limited to, formal discourse. We will look specifically at choices in level of vocabulary, word and phrase patterns, individual sentence patterns, and patterns that run across several sentences. As you read examples and learn what certain patterns are good for—that is, what effects they can have on voice—you'll have opportunities to practice. There'll be short exercises along the way. These exercises invite you to imitate and test patterns, to combine and adapt them according to your own preferences, given the subject, occasion, and audience.

Chapter 5 extends our work with formal voices by offering practice at longer imitation, by providing several examples of professional prose and questions for discussion, and by showing the thinking and writing process of one student creating a formal essay. Our work with formal voices ends with an assignment for creating your own essay.

LATINATE OR MULTISYLLABIC VOCABULARY: THE TUXEDO OF WORD CHOICE

English words sprung from Latin roots have traditionally been associated with intellectual and social respectability because, historically, Latin was studied by the privileged social classes. Consequently, to sound classy and smart, many people choose Latinate words: They *demonstrate* instead of *show; initiate* instead of *start* or *begin; select* instead of *pick; increase,* not *add.* It's *mendacity,* not a *lie.* One is *inaccurate,* not *wrong.* One does not have a *bent* for art but a *propensity.*

Words we often label as "Latinate," however, are not exclusively of Latin origin. Because English has been influenced by so many languages and the influences are mixed, we tend to use the term loosely, indicating, generally, multisyllabic words. These have by nature a greater number of vowels, and so they are often softer in sound than short, simple words usually associated with Anglo-Saxon roots (see the previous word pairs for a few examples). As I explained in Chapter 2, multisyllabic words allow us to sound sympathetic, or, as George Bush would say, of "a kinder and gentler age." Part of the reason is explained by sound associations, and the other part, by social convention: We associate knowledge of Latin with civilized behavior. It sounds kinder, for example, to say "That's an inaccuracy" than "You are wrong."

No writer uses Latinate or multisyllabic diction exclusively, of course. But writers who aim toward a high style and who want to soften the impact of language will often make at least 20% of their vocabulary multisyllabic.

When we choose a multisyllabic word because it expresses the particular shade of meaning we intend, fine. But when we choose words only because they sound "nicer" or "smarter," we risk sacrificing our own ethical appeal, particularly if what we intend is deception. It's a mistake to think that sophistication and eloquence can be achieved simply by using a high-sounding vocabulary—"big" words. When the occasion, the audience, and the sense do not warrant such use, a predominantly multisyllabic vocabulary can make the speaker sound stuffy and can even hide the sense. What ought to govern our word choice are precision of meaning or feeling and the place and company in which we find ourselves. Here, for example, is an excerpt from an interdepartmental memo:

> The purpose of the council is to examine the multicultural identity of the College and make recommendations regarding such. To this end, we are informing you of our current status and solicit your input. The council will establish subcommittees as necessary to accomplish its responsibilities. These subcommittees may consist of persons from the X community and, when appropriate, outside resource persons. . . . We are soliciting your involvement via subcommittee participation and your assessment of the issues or concerns which should be given priority.

Given that the subject of the memo is people (the particular blend of cultures that comprise the community of students and faculty at the college), the use of "persons" only seems to emphasize, by contrast, the impersonal tone of the message. Recently, *persons* instead of *people* has become fashionable. It seems to connote, for the user, a sensitivity to people as individuals. However, the memo above is anything but a communication between and about "persons." It's relentlessly robotic.

The interesting thing about this example is that the language (the mix of jargon and level of abstraction) doesn't make the speaker sound sympathetic to any person or idea. Nor does it evoke any sympathy from the audience. Exactly the opposite effect of what the speaker intends, don't you think?

For instance, here is the final sentence in the memo: "We are soliciting your involvement via subcommittee participation and your assessment of the issues or concerns which should be given priority." The stylistic problems that affect my role as a sympathetic listener are these:

1. An invitation disguised as assertion. Why not just ask me directly?
2. Lots of nouns that could be verbs. Making nouns out of verbs is called "nominalization." It's a handy thing to be able to do at times, but it can make sentences overly passive and often clumsy and unclear, particularly when the nominalization occurs as the agent or subject of a sentence. *Participation* and *assessment* in the memo example describe what the writer wants me to do. Why not put the activity in the part of speech that normally carries it—the verb? That would also eliminate the sound of passivity (nouns plus weak verbs) and bridge the gap between speaker and audience. It would make the message easier to hear, too.
3. Two prepositional phrases plus the *which* clause. Important information is tucked into phrases that don't normally carry it. Why make *participation* the object of a prepositional phrase? It's the main thing the writer wants from me. Put the idea in a more prominent spot, the verb in this case. Many times, *which* clauses can be converted into adjectives, making information tighter, more direct. Aren't issues or concerns (do we need both?) "which should be given priority" simply the "most important" ones?

Here is a possible revision:

> Would you be willing to serve on one of the subcommittees to help us determine the most important issues?

Exercise: **On the Outside Looking In**

Find an example of jargon-laden prose, like the memo, that alienates you from the speaker and subject. Professional journals are a good place to look, but you might find examples in business correspondence and textbooks, too.

1. What role is the writer asking you to play? That is, what has the writer assumed about you as an audience—your background (cultural/social/educational), your interests, your values, your relationship to the writer?
2. How does the vocabulary make you feel like an outsider or at a great personal distance from the writer?
3. If the point of view seems to alienate you, can you say how?
4. How do the writer's sentence constructions affect your sense of exclusion from the discourse? Do they seem overwhelmingly long, complex in structure, hard to follow? Is it difficult to identify the important information in a sentence or in a series of sentences?

In small groups or as a class, choose one sample to work with. Discuss the questions above, and then try to revise the sample (or a short excerpt), making it more accessible to an audience like yourselves. As writer, you are changing the role for the reader.

Jargon itself is not intrinsically bad. It's a kind of shorthand for people who work within a particular field or share a particular body of knowledge. Using it establishes the speaker as an insider, as a member of the profession or special interest group. Consequently, it is often used for credibility. When the audience, however, is unfamiliar with the specialized language or when the occasion doesn't require it, jargon is alienating. In the memo you read earlier, the mix of jargon, the level of abstraction, and the point of view suggest a writer who has not fitted the discourse to the occasion and who has not, therefore, created the appropriate role for the audience. Instead of predisposing the audience to sympathy, the writer risks hostility.

CLASSICAL STYLISTIC PATTERNS

Formal speakers tend to favor figures of speech, particular kinds of word or phrase patterns, and elaborate sentence structure, such as a suspended syntax and periodic sentences. Some examples of these patterns occur in the sentences in the opening pages of this chapter. We will examine them (as well as other classic rhetorical patterns) more closely as we go along because they contribute to voice. What all of these patterns have in common is studied thought. Formal voices sound as if they have been mentally rehearsed before appearing on the page or ringing in the air. These voices rarely sound spontaneous, the way colloquial voices often do. When handled expertly, certain patterns in combination give weight and balance to ideas and thus help to produce the voice we hear on the page. It is the measure and pace of these patterns rather than a high-sounding vocabulary that leads us to identify a formal voice.

In contrast to colloquial voices, highly formal voices sound weighty; the rhythmic measures, longer; the pitch changes, less abrupt and not as wide; the stresses, farther apart. Compare one of the professional samples at the start of Chapter 2 with one at the start of this chapter to hear the difference in sound.

COLLOQUIAL

She simmered in *The Witches of Eastwick.* Next she stole *Married to the Mob.* Then there were those close-ups in *Dangerous Liaisons.* Even crying she looked good. Her upper lip was puffier than ever. Puffier than Barbara Hershey's post collagen. Puffier than Kim Basinger's in the *Batman* lip close-ups. In the year of the puffy lip, Michelle Pfeiffer had the puffiest lip in Hollywood.

(Patricia Volk, "Why I'm Glad
I Don't Look Like Michelle Pfeiffer")

FORMAL

Because when we start deceiving ourselves into thinking not that we want something or need something, not that it is a pragmatic necessity for us to have it, but that it is a *moral imperative* that we have it, then is when we join the fashionable madmen, and then is when the thin whine of hysteria is heard in the land, and then is when we are in bad trouble. And I suspect we are already there.

(Joan Didion, "On Morality")

The following discussion is a description and illustration of formal rhetorical patterns. The Greeks classified them and made them part of every student's training in rhetoric. Although many patterns are not confined to use only in formal discourse, experienced writers aiming at a high style, at the sound of solemnity, tend to make liberal use of them.

Before I begin listing and suggesting exercises for practice, let's consider what the wide variety is good for. The patterns give you many opportunities for mixing and matching as you seek your own brand of formality for those occasions and audiences that demand the sound of distinguished speech. Although few writers can (or even care to) remember the Greek names, most writers are familiar with the patterns themselves. They've assimilated them, they know from reading and writing experience what many are good for, and they draw on them almost unconsciously when they aim high—toward balance, emphasis, and the rhythms of solemn speech.

You can't be expected to begin writing with all the patterns in mind, but you can begin noticing patterns of language that create particular effects you admire. Experimenting will give you a larger repertoire for expression. You may write better music for your words. You may also discover ideas: If ideas and feelings give rise to particular forms, it can also be said that forms give rise to particular ways of thinking. You may find other pictures of the world when you use different frames of thought. For example, you may discover after experimenting with antithesis (opposing ideas placed in parallel structures) that you begin seeing an event in opposition to another—not this, but that.

John F. Kennedy relies heavily on antithesis in his inaugural address, implying his vision of the world (the entire inaugural address is in Chapter 5). To Kennedy, it is a system of polarities, the items in opposing pairs dependent on each other for what they signify. Kennedy's address also implies, however, that opposing realms can be reconciled. His worldview gives rise to juxtaposed, antithetical, parallel patterns. Placing opposites side by side in parallel structure tacitly argues the possibility of balance, because the grammatical framework on which the ideas are expressed is itself balanced. Thus Kennedy's extensive use of antithesis in equally ranked structures helps persuade his audience of reconcilable values. Here is an example of what I mean. It is excerpted from his inaugural address.

And if a beachhead of co-operation may push back the jungle of suspicion, let both sides join in creating a new endeavor, not a new balance of power, but a new world of law, where the strong are just and the weak secure and the peace preserved.

My more general point is this: The more frames you experiment with, the more likely it is that you will be able to see things from different angles, different points of focus, different sensibilities.

Let's examine the possibilities, then, of classic rhetorical patterns for what they may contribute to voice, beginning with figures of speech. Here is a chart of the figures described and illustrated in this chapter.

Figures of Speech: Tropes and Schemes

TROPES (uses of words)	SCHEMES (arrangements of words)	
Metaphor and simile	Of balance:	Parallelism
Synecdoche		Antithesis
Syllepsis		Isocolon
Anthimeria	Of unusual word order:	Anastrophe
Periphrasis		Parenthesis
Personification	Of omission:	Ellipsis
Litotes		Asyndeton
Oxymoron	Of repetition:	Alliteration
		Polyptoton
		Assonance
		Anaphora
		Epistrophe
		Epanalepsis
		Anadiplosis
		Tricolon/ tetracolon
		Chiasmus

The arrangement of rhetorical patterns on the following pages is borrowed from Edward P. J. Corbett's *Classical Rhetoric for the Modern Student*.

TROPES

A trope (from the Greek word *tropein,* "to turn") concerns a shift in meaning from the ordinary use of a word.

Metaphor and Simile

Metaphor and simile are basically the same. In both, two unlike things are said to be alike. The only difference is that in a metaphor the comparison is implied; in a simile, it's explicit. The words *like* or *as* signal a simile. Here are some examples of metaphors:

Alone in the livingroom at night, she often looked at the bowl sitting on the table, still and safe, unilluminated. In its way it was perfect: the world cut in half, deep and smoothly empty.

(Ann Beattie, "Janus," *Where You'll Find Me*)

In the following example, the metaphor is implied by a single verb.

Lyda was an exuberant, even a dramatic gardener. . . . When somebody walked past her in her work, she was always holding up a lettuce or a bunch of radishes, with an air of resolute courage, as though she had shot them herself.

(Renata Adler, *Speedboat*)

Here is another metaphor:

No matter how lovingly a person or doctor rapped at the door to Eddie's mind, Eddie refused to say "come in."
(Grace Paley, "In Time Which Made a Monkey of Us All,"
The Little Disturbances of Man)

Here are two examples of similes:

She is as tall blue lilacs are.
(Leonard Meyer, *Music the Arts and Ideas*)

Geography is life's limiting factor. . . . The rocks shape life like hands around swelling dough.
(Annie Dillard, *Teaching a Stone to Talk*)

Metaphorical language is used both as ornament and as a way of arriving at truth. We think not only with our reason but also with our intuition. Metaphors are an important means of making connections, connections that take into account the complexity and energy of human feeling. And yet the actual construction of metaphors, unlike similes, makes them look not like truth but lies. Because they are either categorically false (her head's in the clouds) or categorically true (no man is an island), we dismiss the literal truth and begin looking for implications. In that way, a metaphor invites us to do the comparing ourselves. It doesn't tell or explain; it intimates. Metaphors, like lies, concern not the meaning of words but their use.

You'll notice in the examples that not every use of metaphor is also an example of formal voice. Some voices are decidedly informal. A single stylistic pattern does not necessarily result in what we label "formal voice." Voice is the sum effect of several kinds of stylistic patterns. In the case of formality, the sum effect is the sound of weighted, balanced rhythms, of stresses that occur farther apart than in colloquial voices, and of pitch changes that are less abrupt and not as steep as in colloquial voices. That is why I am repeating throughout this text that stylistic patterns alone can contribute to voice, but no one style in itself is enough to create it. They must, in combination, be built into an intonation pattern that tells us, "This writer is speaking informally; this one, formally."

Synecdoche

A synecdoche is a figure of speech in which a part stands for the whole or vice versa. Substitutions can be made as follows:

Genus for species (or general for specific): "He's in trouble with the law." *Law* is substituted for *police*.
Species for genus (or specific for general): "They have no bread for their table." *Bread* is substituted for *food*.
Part for the whole: "If we can find some wheels, we can meet you Saturday night." *Wheels* is substituted for *car*. Or "We need a hand with this job." *Hand* is substituted for *another person*.
Material for what is made from it: "That's my own flesh and blood on the stage."

Syllepsis

Syllepsis is the use of one verb that is understood differently in relation to two or more objects. Here are some examples (the first two are my own).

Later that evening at Omar's, we tapped wine glasses and a variety of safe subjects.

He took the money and his time returning it.

Give me liberty or give me death. (Patrick Henry)

Anthimeria

Anthimeria is the use of a word in which one part of speech is exchanged for another—say a noun for a verb.

Let be be finale of seem. (Wallace Stevens)

"He slimed me," Bill Murray cried after his encounter with the protoplasmic ghost. (*Ghostbusters*)

Professional jargon is often created by anthimeria—*parent* and *impact,* for instance: "Edward and Elsa enrolled in parenting classes." Or "How does this loss impact on your daily life?" In these examples, words commonly used as nouns are used as an adjective and as a verb, respectively.

Periphrasis

Periphrasis is the substitution of one or more descriptive words for a proper name, or the substitution of a proper name for obvious associations with the name. The first three examples are my own invention.

I hope Blue-eyes croons another tune.

The Igniter ripped one up the middle for the Brewers' first base hit of the inning.

He had a Uriah Heep attitude toward his superiors.

She's got Bette Davis eyes. (rock tune)

Personification

Personification is the attribution of human qualities to inanimate objects or abstractions.

No one, not even the rain, has such small hands.

(e.e. cummings)

"When I asked why the Sun Dance ended at night, my friend said, 'So the sun will remember to make a complete circle . . .'" (Gretel Ehrlich, "To Live in Two Worlds: Crow Fair and a Sun Dance")

Litotes

Litotes is the use of understatement to intensify an idea. It usually involves denying the contrary.

[Grendel and his dam] guard the secret, somber land,
The wolf-denned hill, the windy bluff,
The savage fen-path where the mountain current
Descends beneath the darknesses under the bluff,
It is not far hence
The flood flows under the earth.
In measure of miles that the sea lies.
Over it hangs the encircling grove;
The firm-rooted wood hangs over the water.
There may [one] on any the evil-boding portent,
night see
The fire on the flood.

None lives of the sons of men
[Who is] ancient and wise to the point of knowing that bottom.
Though the stag, the heath- the strong-horned,
stepper,
Hard pressed by hounds, from afar put to flight,
Seeks the forest, sooner he gives up life, spirit,
Than he will [hide] his head It is not a heart-warmed
on that bank. place.

(*Beowulf*, ll. 1357–1372; translated by Elaine Penninger)

Oxymoron

An oxymoron is the juxtaposition of two contradictory words. An oxymoron is like a paradox in that both figures reveal surprising truths through contradiction. The difference is that a paradox involves an entire statement; an oxymoron involves only two words placed side by side.

Here are some examples of oxymorons: In "Easter 1916" William Butler Yeats describes the impact of the Irish Rebellion as "a terrible beauty is born." Walter Pater describes the artistic view of life as a "kind of passionate coldness." Also, some people might consider "military intelligence" an oxymoron.

Here are two examples of paradox. The first is my own:

Her professional success was her failure.

Cowards die many times before their deaths.
(William Shakespeare, Julius Caesar, act 2, scene 2)

Exercise: **What's My Line?**

Find an example of several tropes from your own reading. Then write a few examples of your own. Bring these to class and ask others to identify them. Can your peers tell which are yours and which are professional? In your journal, you might make a list of your favorite examples, both professional and peer. Try to say why you prefer the ones you do.

SCHEMES

Whereas tropes concern unusual uses of words, schemes concern unusual patterns of words. Tropes involve word meanings; schemes, word arrangements. Schemes fall into these categories: schemes of balance, schemes of unusual word order, schemes of omission, and schemes of repetition.

Schemes of Balance

Parallelism
Parallelism involves grammatical elements similar in structure.

There is a certain place where dumb-waiters boom, doors slam, dishes crash; every window is a mother's mouth bidding the street shut up, go skate somewhere else, come home. My voice is loudest.

(Grace Paley, "The Loudest Voice,"
The Little Disturbances of Man)

Parallel structure adds weight and force to ideas and thus affects the rhythm of the voice.

Ravenous fish and tasty plankton. Rain forests dripping with nameless reptiles, birds gliding under canopies of leaves, insects buzzing like electrons in an accelerator. Frost belts where voles and lemmings flourish and diminish with tidy four-year periodicity in the face of nature's bloody combat. The world makes a messy laboratory for ecologists, a cauldron of five million interacting species. Or is it fifty million? Ecologists do not actually know.

(James Gleick, *Chaos*)

The Gleick passage is also a good example of the parallel list, generally used to suggest breadth of knowledge and great numbers (possibly endless). Here the list of noun phrases is suspenseful—leading up to a climax in the last sentence. "The world makes" gains syntactical power because it resolves the tension created by the fragments, and gains persuasive power because of the preceding supporting details. These features help to create the sound of a knowledgeable, credible speaker, someone who suggests he knows more detail than he is listing here, and someone who, by the way he arranges information, feels that the information is highly significant. We hear his attitude in the voice of the sentence.

Antithesis

Antithesis is the use of parallel structure to emphasize contrasting ideas. More generally, antithesis can be defined as ideas or words in sharp opposition.

It is a sin to believe evil of others, but it is seldom a mistake.
(H.L. Mencken, *A Book of Burlesques*)

To every complicated problem, there's a simple solution—that is wrong.

(H.L. Mencken)

Marriage has many pains, but celibacy has no pleasures.
(Samuel Johnson, *Rasselas* XXVI)

I come to Hollins Pond not so much to learn how to live as, frankly, to forget about it. That is, I don't think I can learn from a wild animal how to live in particular—shall I suck warm blood, hold my tail high, walk with my footprints precisely over the prints of my hands?—but I might learn something of mindlessness, something of the purity of living in the physical senses and the dignity of living without bias or motive. The weasel lives in necessity and we live by choice. . . .
(Annie Dillard, *Teaching a Stone to Talk*)

Isocolon
Isocolon is the use of grammatical elements equal in structure and in length (the same number of words, and in its strictest use, the same number of syllables).

With *stars in her eyes and veils in her hair,* with cyclamen and wild violets—what nonsense was he thinking? She was fifty at least; she had eight children. Stepping through fields of flowers and taking to her breast *buds that had broken and lambs that had fallen; with the stars in her eyes and the wind in her hair*—He took her bag. . . . for the first time in his life Charles Tansley felt an extraordinary pride; felt the wind and the cyclamen and the violets for he was walking with a beautiful woman. He had hold of her bag. (emphasis added)
(Virginia Woolf, *To the Lighthouse*)

The studied use of balance and repetition, in structure and in rhythm, contributes to the sound of dignity in this passage.

Schemes of Unusual or Inverted Word Order

Anastrophe
Anastrophe is the use of inverted or unusual word order.

Insoluable questions they were, it seemed to her, standing there, holding James by the hand.
(Virginia Woolf, *To the Lighthouse*)

Something wicked this way comes.

(Ray Bradbury)

Yesterday morning, then, the first Park Keepers saw something afloat in the Serpentine— *What* it needed little looking to tell. Bodies in the Serpentine are not uncommon in the early morning.

(Virginia Woolf, from her unpublished journals)

Behind the crippled oak, beneath the rock big as ruin, lies the gold key.

(my own)

When words are wrenched from their usual positions in a sentence, they call extra attention to themselves through the intonation pattern because the *idea* order is indicated by *voice* rather than conventional syntax. The words are read with added stress and length, particularly when they occur at the beginning or end of a sentence—the two most powerful positions. Writers use anastrophe to emphasize ideas and thus make their importance heard in the voice of the sentence. Care must be taken, however, to avoid awkward expressions.

Parenthesis
Parenthesis is the insertion of a phrase or a clause that interrupts the main part of a sentence. It is an aside. The interruption is usually indicated by ( ) or by commas or dashes. The punctuation affects the way readers hear the parenthetical comment. Dashes generally signal a louder voice than commas; commas, a tone even with the sentence; and ( ), a whisper, often indicating intimacy.

And the very fact that he had had to choose respectability to hide behind was proof enough (if anyone needed further proof) that what he fled from must have been some opposite of respectability too dark to talk about.

(William Faulkner, *Absalom, Absalom!*)

Do we need blind men stumbling about, and little flamefaced children, to remind us what God can—and will—do?

(Annie Dillard, *Holy the Firm*)

Also, he was halfway through a new study of semantics, proving (as he so violently insisted) that sentence structure is innate, but that whining is acquired.

(Woody Allen)

When I am able to exercise my memory of the distant past, which is not often, I am able to do so with the precision of a stamp collector.

(John Hawkes, *Death, Sleep, and the Traveler*)

Can you hear how punctuation affects the parentheses in these examples?

Exercise: The Sense and Sound of Order and Balance

Write a sentence using a scheme of balance or a scheme of unusual or inverted word order. Then write another sentence using the same idea but eliminating the scheme, replacing it with another, or perhaps adding one. You may need to alter wording, but not necessarily. What changes occur in meaning and sound of meaning (voice)?

Here is an example of this exercise:

When I think about the accident, which is rare, I remember hearing your voice but not your words. (parenthesis, parallelism)

When rarely I think about the accident, your voice I remember hearing, but not your words. (remove parenthesis; add anastrophe—inverted word order)

Or if you like, choose one of the professional examples included in the sections on schemes of balance and unusual word order. (You might also find one in your own reading.) Rewrite that sentence, eliminating a scheme, substituting another, or adding one. Again, you may need to alter words. What changes occur in meaning and sound of meaning (voice) when you play with arrangement? Here is an example of what I mean:

Insoluble questions they were, it seemed to her, standing there, holding James by the hand. (anastrophe, parallelism)

It seemed to her they were insoluble questions as she stood holding James by the hand. (remove anastrophe and parallelism)

Exercise: **Psst!—The Sense and Sound of Interruptions**

Write a sentence that makes use of parenthesis. Punctuate the parenthesis three different ways: ( ), comma, and dash. Try to say how the punctuation affects the voice in your sentence. For example, here is a sentence by Alice Walker:

> Only recently did I fully realize this: that through years of listening to my mother's stories of her life, I have absorbed not only the stories themselves, but something of the manner in which she spoke, something of the urgency that involves the knowledge that her stories—like her life—must be recorded.
>
> ("In Search of Our Mothers' Gardens")

Take out the dashes before and after "like her life" and replace them first with commas, then parentheses. How does the change in punctuation affect the way you hear and understand the significance of the phrase? Now try working with a sentence of your own.

Schemes of Omission

Ellipsis

Ellipsis is the deliberate omission of a word or words that can be understood by the reader from the previous context and from the grammar of the sentence. The understood words must be compatible with the grammar. Strictly speaking, you can't omit what hasn't been supplied earlier. Writers use ellipsis for the sake of brevity, emphasis, and grace. Elliptical sentences gain emphasis and thus add force to the voice, because readers make up for what isn't there by stressing what is.

To some people that's the stuff of which legends are made, to others jokes.

> (Phyllis Rose, "Nora Astorga," *New York Times*)

With the missing words supplied:

To some people that's the stuff of which legends are made, to others [that's the stuff of which] jokes [are made].

Without the bracketed material, "legends" and "jokes" are syntactically brought close together to highlight the contrast, visually and aurally. When we read "jokes," we raise the pitch of our voices and add stress and duration of sound. We stress what's there to make up for what isn't. We hear as well as see the significance of ideas.

Here's another example:

When I read *King Lear* I realize that I'd be flattering myself to identify with Cordelia. I have the awful suspicion that I am much more like Regan or Goneril—from Lear's point of view monsters of ingratitude; from their own just two women taking their turn at the top, enjoying their middle-aged supremacy.

> (Phyllis Rose, "Mothers and Fathers," *New York Times*)

With the missing words supplied:

I have the awful suspicion that I am much more like Regan or Goneril—from Lear's point of view [Regan and Goneril are] monsters of ingratitude; from their own [point of view, they are] just two women taking their turn . . ."

Here's a simple example:

Vanessa had to leave her children and come running, nurses had to be hired, rest homes interviewed, transport accomplished.

> (Cynthia Ozick, "Mrs. Virginia Woolf:
> A Madwoman and Her Nurse")

With the missing words supplied:

. . . nurses had to be hired, rest homes [had to be] interviewed, transport [had to be] accomplished.

In the following examples, ellipsis occurs between sentences. It is a broader use of the device in which transitional logic is missing but implied. (See also the section on parataxis later in the chapter.) And unlike the omissions in the previous examples, these omissions do not depend on grammatical compatibility. Instead, the writer simply omits explicit links between sentences or clauses. Skillfully used, this kind of ellipsis forces stronger intonational patterns. Readers hear the voice behind the message.

> Conventional ideas about beauty made me nervous. They precluded what you were born with. When all the girls in high school tried to look like Elizabeth Taylor in *Cleopatra,* I didn't. Of course, I couldn't.
>
> (Patricia Volk, "Why I'm Glad
> I Don't Look Like Michelle Pfeiffer")

With the transitions supplied:

> Conventional ideas about beauty made me nervous. [The reason is that] they precluded what you were born with. [For example,] when all the girls in high school tried to look like Elizabeth Taylor in *Cleopatra,* I didn't. [I didn't try,] of course, [because] I couldn't.

In the Patricia Volk passage, the transitions are unnecessary. Readers easily infer the connections between sentences; the writer doesn't need make them explicit. By not doing so, the writer makes her voice stronger—the reader stresses the beginnings of sentences to close the gap between periods. The logic is implied and carried by the intonation.

Here is another example from the same essay:

> I'd rather look like Mary McCarthy or Georgia O'Keeffe, face not an issue. Just my pal, my consort, my partner in crime.

With the missing words supplied:

> I'd rather look like Mary McCarthy or Georgia O'Keeffe, [a woman for whom] face [is] not an issue. [Instead, it's] just my pal, my consort, my partner in crime.

In this final passage, Phyllis Rose uses ellipsis within and between sentences:

On the verge of assassinating Julius Caesar, Brutus—as imagined by Shakespeare—announces that he should be seen as a "sacrificer," not a "butcher." The ambiguity remains, however. You know the figure that from one angle looks like a vase and from another a witch? Same with Brutus: from one angle a noble idealist willing to assume the terrible guilt of murder to rid his country of a tyrant; from another a self-indulgent fool who deludes himself into thinking there is an excuse for murder. ("Nora Astorga")

Here is the missing logic supplied:

The ambiguity remains, however. [Here is a familiar example of such ambiguity. Do] you know the figure that from one angle looks like a vase and from another [angle the figure looks like] a witch? [If you do, you can see that it's the] same [kind of ambiguity] with Brutus: from one angle [he's] a noble idealist [who is] willing to assume the terrible guilt of murder to rid his country of a tyrant; from another [angle, he's] a self-indulgent fool who deludes himself into thinking there is an excuse for murder.

Reader expectations tell us that an example usually follows a major claim or assertion. So we assume that the question is an example of the ambiguity the writer describes. The writer doesn't have to tell us in advance that an example follows. We expect one to. The connection between sentences 1 and 2 in the example is readily inferred.

In compressing the sense between clauses by either omitting words or omitting logical connections between sentences, writers do need to be careful not to leap beyond what careful readers can supply. If words or connections are missing and the intonation can't carry the sense, coherence will suffer. For further discussion of ellipsis and cohesion, see Chapter 8, "The Voice of the Paragraph."

Exercise: X-cision—What's Gained
by Doing Without?

Find an example of ellipsis in your own reading. Rewrite the sentence or sentences, supplying the missing words (or transitional links). Can you say how the ellipsis strengthens the voice and message?

Asyndeton

Asyndeton is a deliberate lack of conjunctions between parallel or related clauses. One effect is to quicken the rhythm of a sentence or series of sentences. An asyndetic style often includes anaphora (repeated clause or phrase openers). And it tends to accompany parataxis (a series of sentences and clauses in which subordination is intentionally avoided). Here are a few examples:

> Now that science is looking, chaos seems to be everywhere. A rising column of cigarette smoke breaks into wild swirls. A flag snaps back and forth in the wind. A dripping faucet goes from a steady pattern to a random one. Chaos appears in the behavior of the weather, the behavior of an airplane in flight, the behavior of cars clustering on an expressway, the behavior of oil flowing in underground pipes.
>
> (James Gleick, *Chaos*)

Note how the use of anaphora in the last sentence brings the passage to a climactic close.

Polysyndeton

One way to notice the effect of asyndeton is to hear it in contrast with *polysyndeton*—the intentional use of many conjunctions. For example:

> Then the elephant had gone on into the thick forest and David had seen him ahead standing gray and huge against the trunk of a tree. David could see only his stern and then his father moved ahead of him and he followed and they came alongside the elephant as though he was a ship and David saw the blood coming from his flanks and running down his sides and then his father raised his rifle and fired and the elephant turned his head with the great tusks moving heavy and slow and looked at them and when his father fired the second barrel the elephant seemed to sway like a felled tree and came smashing down toward them. But he was not dead.
>
> (Ernest Hemingway, *The Garden of Eden*)

In the Ernest Hemingway passage, polysyndeton suggests a speaker whose consciousness is so immersed in the dramatic flow of events that he cannot pause or rank them but can only describe one after the other as they occur. The final sentence has climactic force because of the preceding rush of experience.

Here is another example of polysyndeton:

> It could be that the sort of sentence one wants right here is the kind that runs, and laughs, and slides, and stops right on a dime. (final sentence in Renata Adler, *Speedboat*)

Consider the difference between the Renata Adler excerpt and this sentence: "It could be that the sort of sentence one wants right here is the kind that runs, laughs, slides, stops on a dime." How does polysyndeton affect the voice and thus reinforce the sense of Adler's sentence?

Where conjunctions separate either grammatically complete or punctuated sentences, the effect can sometimes be one of solemnity: "And then, locked in her eyes, was remorse. And it was dark. And it was deep. And it was forever." How are the rhythms in my sentence here different from Hemingway's even though we both use polysyndeton?

Exercise: **Conjunction Junction**

Rewrite the Hemingway passage, removing the conjunctions and making his style asyndetic. Then rewrite the Gleick passage, adding conjunctions, making his style polysyndetic. What differences do you hear?

Schemes of Repetition

Alliteration

Alliteration is the repetition of initial consonants. Here are some examples.

The soul selects her own society.

(Emily Dickinson)

> I am firmly of the opinion that people who can't speak have
> nothing to say. It's one more thing we do to the poor, the
> deprived: cut out their tongues . . . allow them a language as
> lousy as their lives.
>
> (William Gass, *On Being Blue, A Philosophical Inquiry*)

Polyptoton
Polyptoton is the repetition of words with the same root but
different endings or in different forms. Here is an example:

> Poverty and isolation produce impoverished and isolated
> minds.
>
> (William Gass, *On Being Blue, A Philosophical Inquiry*)

The repetition reinforces the connection between quality of life
and quality of mind.

Assonance
Assonance is the repetition of similar vowel sounds. For
instance:

> The spider skins lie on their sides, translucent and ragged,
> their legs drying in knots.
>
> (Annie Dillard, *Holy the Firm*)

> The setting sun was licking the hard bright machine like some
> great invisible beast on its knees.
>
> (John Hawkes, *Death, Sleep, and The Traveler*)

Sound play is often used to connect important ideas and to
further emphasize already emphatic verbal patterns, such as parallelism, antithesis, or climax. Like sounds tend to suggest like
meaning, even when the logic doesn't support that connection.
Sound play, in other words, can help persuade readers what
logic would not.

Anaphora
Anaphora is the repetition of the same word or phrase at the
beginnings of clauses or sentences. Here are some examples.

> So the question is not whether we will be extremists, but
> what kind of extremists we will be. Will we be extremists for

hate or love? Will we be extremists for the preservation of injustice or for the extension of justice?

> (Martin Luther King, Jr., "Letter from a Birmingham Jail")

We forget all too soon the things we thought we could never forget. We forget the loves and the betrayals alike, forget what we whispered and what we screamed, forget who we were.

> (Joan Didion, "On Keeping a Notebook")

Note also Didion's use of antithesis in parallel structure. The combination of repeated words and repeated structures creates a balanced or even tone, one without steep rises and falls in pitch, a sound we associate with formal voices.

For more examples, see the Declaration of Independence. Or see the beatitudes in the Bible ("Blessed are the poor . . ."). The Bible is an excellent source for many formal rhetorical figures.

Here's an elaborate use of anaphora by Shakespeare in *King Richard II:* John of Gaunt's speech extolling the virtues of England.

> This royal throne of kings, this scepter'd isle
> This earth of majesty, this seat of Mars,
> This other Eden, demi-paradise,
> This fortress built by Nature for herself
> Against infection and the hand of war,
> This happy breed of men, this little world,
> This precious stone set in the silver sea . . .
> This blessed plot, this earth, this realm, this England. . . .
>
> (act 2, scene 1, lines 40–49)

Epistrophe

Epistrophe is the repetition of words or phrases at the end of subsequent clauses or sentences. For example:

What I do know is this. If you go so far out on a limb that it breaks, you have gone too far. If you lose your perspective, you have gone too far. If you don't see the joke anymore, you have gone too far. If you do anything you know you will regret (or know will be regretted by those who survive you) you have gone too far. And every time you go too far, in life or that subset of life which is art, you are giving a piece of yourself to death ahead of schedule.

> (Connor Freff Cochran, "Going Too Far")

Epanalepsis

Epanalepsis is the use of the same word or phrase at the beginning and end of a clause or sentence. Here are some examples.

Tribe follows tribe, and nation follows nation, like the waves of the sea.

(attributed to Seattle, Dwamish chief, in a speech to Isaac Stevens, Governor of Washington Territory, in 1854)

Blood hath bought blood, and blows have answer'd blows; Strength match'd with strength, and power confronted power.

(William Shakespeare, *King John,* Act II, Scene 1)

Anadiplosis

Anadiplosis is the repetition of the last word of a clause (or sentence) in the first word of the following one, therefore joining the two units. In a variation of anadiplosis, the repeated word occurs *near* the end of one clause or *near* the beginning of the next. Here are some examples.

How can people think that artists seek a name? A name, like a face, is something you have when you're not alone.

(Annie Dillard, *Holy the Firm*)

You want to be very careful about lying; otherwise you are nearly sure to get caught. Once caught, you can never again be, in the eyes of the good and the pure, what you were before.

(Mark Twain, "Advice to Youth")

And when he looked at you there wasn't anything in his eyes . . . it was like they were missing from his face, and his face, it had just come apart.

(Sidney Bechet, *Treat It Gentle*)

Tricolon

Tricolon is the use of three parallel phrases or clauses, usually climactically arranged. For instance:

But in a larger sense, we cannot dedicate—we cannot consecrate—we hannot hallow this ground.

(Abraham Lincoln, Gettysburg Address)

They had instilled in them, young, a certain discipline, the sense that one lives by doing things one does not particularly want to do, by putting fears and doubts to one side, by weighing immediate comforts against the possibility of larger, even intangible comforts.

(Joan Didion, "On Self-Respect")

Woody Allen plays against the tricolon scheme for comic effect in the following:

He [contemporary man] has seen the ravages of war, he has known natural catastrophes, he has been to singles bars.

("My Speech to the Graduates")

A series of four units in climactic order is called a tetracolon, as in Tennyson's phrase in "Ulysses": "to strive, to seek, to find and not to yield."

Chiasmus

Chiasmus is repetition in which the order of words in one clause is reversed in the second. (See also Chapter 1 for discussion and examples.) For instance:

Nature forms patterns. Some are orderly in space but disorderly in time, others orderly in time but disorderly in space.

(James Gleick, *Chaos*)

The press is so powerful in its image-making role, it can make a criminal look like he's the victim and make the victim look like he's the criminal.

(Malcolm X)

It's not the word made flesh we want in writing, in poetry and fiction, but the flesh made word.

(William Gass, *On Being Blue, A Philosophical Inquiry*)

Chiasmus is particularly effective when sentences are built tight, the language compressed. Chiasmus itself can be considered compressed antithesis. As such, it is a powerful construction, often persuading readers of an author's wit and insight.

Exercise: **When Once Isn't Enough**

Choose several examples from the listed schemes of repetition or find several examples from your own reading, each example illustrating a different scheme. Rewrite each one, eliminating the repetition. What differences do you hear in sense and sound?

Or make up a sentence of your own, employing one or more schemes of repetition. Then remove the scheme, or the two schemes, if you tried two or more in your sentence. What differences in effect do you hear?

Finally, you might try writing several sentences, each illustrating a different scheme of repetition. Which seemed easiest to write? Which hardest? Which schemes would you try to incorporate in your writing, and why? You might address these questions in your writer's journal.

PERIODIC STYLE: TWO TYPES

In a periodic sentence, the main event (the independent clause) comes at the end of the sentence. Periodic sentences are used for rhythm, balance, and emphasis. The key parts are suspension, parallelism, and climax. Mastery of periodic architecture depends on pacing—how well writers manage the building of phrases and clauses in their rise to an emphatic close.

Here are two examples.

Until justice is blind to color, until education is unaware of race, until opportunity is unconcerned with the color of men's skins, emancipation will be a proclamation but not a fact.

(Lyndon B. Johnson)

Because when we start deceiving ourselves into thinking not that we want something or need something, not that it is a pragmatic necessity for us to have it, but that it is a *moral*

imperative that we have it, then is when we join the fashionable madmen, and then is when the thin whine of hysteria is
heard in the land, and then is when we are in bad trouble.
And I suspect we are already there.

(Joan Didion, "On Morality")

In the Didion example, the dependent structure is inter-
rupted and thus sustained through antithesis to create greater
suspense. The resolution of the sentence is a series of three parallel clauses held together and emphasized through anaphora
(repeated phrase or sentence openers). The second short sentence is the coup de grace—the final blow that arrives after
readers have already believed it was delivered in "then is when
we are in bad trouble"—a clause that delivers its punch through
understatement.

Another kind of periodic style depends not on delaying the
independent clause by a series of dependent phrases or clauses,
but on interrupting the main parts of one independent clause. In
the following examples, the subject-verb-object of the main
clause are underlined:

The rest of the country—most of the rest of the planet, in
some very real sense, excluding a shred of British Columbia's
coastline and the Alaskan islands—is called, and profoundly
felt to be, simply "East of the Mountains."

(Annie Dillard, *Holy the Firm*)

So much depends then, thought Lily Briscoe, looking at the
sea which had scarcely a stain on it, which was so soft that
the sails and the clouds seemed set in its blue, so much depends, she thought, upon distance: whether people are near
us or far from us; for her feeling for Mr. Ramsey changed as
he sailed further and further across the bay.

(Virginia Woolf, *To the Lighthouse*)

Exercise: **Keeping Them in Suspense**

Find an example of a periodic sentence. If you notice any
other rhetorical patterns within the sentence, identify them

too. Then write an imitation of the sentence. Follow the sentence pattern but choose a different subject matter.

EXAMPLE

This sample gives a student example of imitation. It's based on the following passage from "On Being Sentenced to Death" by John Brown.

> Had I interfered in the manner which I admit, and which I admit has been fairly proved—for I admire the truthfulness and candor of the greater portion of the witnesses who have testified in this case—had I so interfered in behalf of the rich, the powerful, the intelligent, the so-called great, or in behalf of any of their friends, either father, mother, brother, sister, wife or children, or any of that class, and suffered and sacrificed what I have in this interference, it would have been all right.

PATTERNS IDENTIFIED

Anadiplosis (repetition of the last word in one clause in the beginning of the next); parenthesis; list; alliteration; parallelism—all in service of periodic structure for suspense and climax.

IMITATION

If I had planted in the spring as I should have, and as I was advised to have planted—because the time and temperature of the year during spring is ideal—if I had filled the pot with the correct level of dirt, fertilizer, water, and seeds, or filled the pot with mental messages like love, hope, encouragement, faith, strength, determination, or any other of that type, and prayed and promised that I would take care of these plants, the tomatoes might have grown. (Ben Polk)

Exercise: **Delivering the Goods—
Now, Later, or in Pieces?**

Find an example of a periodic sentence. Rewrite it, removing the periodic structure. That is, put the main clause in the front of the sentence and without interruptions between subject, verb, and object. Try to describe how the change in structure affects sound and sense.

Write a sentence of your own. First, write it in the usual order—independent clause followed by dependent structures. Second, write it in periodic structure—dependent structures first. Third, write it in periodic structure that does not delay the independent clause until the end of the sentence but, instead, interrupts it. How do the changes in structure affect the voice?

THE LIST

Listing is an alternative to periodic structure or suspension. Lists can imply endlessness or that writers have exhausted possibilities. Richard Lanham says, "List enough items and you'll have grasped the essence, generalized, grasped intuitively. It's not true, but it seems so" (135).

The following excerpt is a virtuoso display of listing by William Gass:

Blue pencils, blue noses, blue movies, law, blue legs and stockings, the language of birds, bees, and flowers as sung by longshoremen, that lead-like look the skin has when affected by cold, contusion, sickness, fear; the rotten rum or gin they call blue ruin and the blue devils of its delirium; Russian cats and oysters, a withheld or imprisoned breath, the blue they say that diamonds have, deep holes in the ocean and the blazers which English athletes earn that gentlemen may wear; afflictions of the spirit—dumps, mopes, Mondays—all that's dismal—low-down gloomy music, Nova Scotians, cyanosis, hair rinse, bluing, bleach; the rare blue dahlia like that blue moon shrewd things happen only once in, or the call for trumps in whist (but who remembers whist or what the death of unplayed games is like?), and correspondingly the flag, Blue Peter, which is our signal for getting under way; a swift pitch, Confederate money, the shaded slopes of clouds and mountains, and so the constantly increasing absentness of Heaven (*ins Blaue hinein,* the Germans say), consequently the color of everything that's empty: blue bottles, bank accounts, and compliments, for instance, or, when the sky's turned turtle, the blue-green bleat of ocean (both the same), and, when in Hell, its neatly landscaped rows of concrete huts and gas-blue flames; social registers, examination booklets, blue bloods, balls, and bonnets, beards, coats, collars, chips, and cheese . . . the pedantic, indecent and censorious . . . watered twilight, sour sea: through a scrambling of accidents, blue has become their color, just as it's stood for fidelity.   (3–4)

This passage is the beginning of Gass's *On Being Blue, A Philosophical Inquiry.* Through his formidable and wonderfully rhythmical list, Gass implies that blue is pervasive, the list infinite—and thus worthy of a book-length study. And, of course, the list further suggests that he has the breadth of knowledge to do it justice.

For other less overwhelming examples, see the samples by James Gleick in the sections on asyndeton (lack of conjunctions) and parallelism. Lists are always parallel and often without conjunctions between items.

PARATAXIS

In parataxis, clauses or whole sentences are not connected by explicit, logical transitional words. One idea is not subordinated to another. Instead, clauses are simply juxtaposed, their logical connections implied. The writer presents ideas equally (X and Y) or chronologically (X then Y). It is the reader who infers subordination.

A paratactic style is composed of simple and compound sentences. It often includes either asyndeton (lack of conjunctions) or polysyndeton (many conjunctions) and, generally, anaphora (repeated sentence openings). See Winston Garland's "pink old girl" in Chapter 2 for one example. Here are some other examples.

> Where I am, I don't know, I'll never know, in the silence you don't know, you must go on, I can't go on, I'll go on.
> (Samuel Beckett, *The Unnameable*)

> I come into the meadow with the abandoned apple orchard. The trees have leaves but have lost most of their blossoms. I feel as if I had caught strangers undressed.
> (Gretel Ehrlich, "Looking for a Lost Dog")

Turbulence was a problem with pedigree. The great physicists all thought about it, formally or informally. A smooth flow breaks up into whorls and eddies. Wild patterns disrupt the boundary between fluid and solid. Energy drains rapidly from large-scale motions to small.

(James Gleick, *Chaos*)

In the extreme, parataxis accompanied by asyndeton is indistinguishable from ellipsis—missing logical connections between sentences:

In the morning it was raining. A fog had come over the mountains from the sea. You could not see the tops of the mountains.

(Ernest Hemingway, *The Sun Also Rises*)

Sentences 2 and 3 are causally related, but that relationship is not explicit. Readers infer the connection—"consequently," "therefore."

A paratactic style can be considered formal when the sentences and clauses are heavily weighted by other rhetorical devices, such as parallelism and various kinds of repetition, and by similar or equal lengths (rhythmic units). The voice produced then is chantlike, a sound we associate with poetry and classical oratory—high style.

I sit on the downed tree and watch the black steers slip on the creek bottom. They are all bred beef: beef heart, beef hide, beef hocks. They're a human product like rayon. They're like a field of shoes. They have cast-iron shanks and tongues like foam insoles. You can't see through to their brains as you can with other animals; they have beef fat behind their eyes, beef stew.

(Annie Dillard, "Heaven and Earth in Jest," *Pilgrim at Tinker Creek*)

HYPOTAXIS

Hypotaxis is the opposite of parataxis. In a hypotactic style, the writer explicitly connects ideas, subordinating one to the other. Relationships are not equal, as they are in parataxis.

Hypotaxis is composed of complex sentences. For example, Hemingway's sentences given earlier could be made hypotactic:

> Because it was raining, a fog had come over the mountains from the sea. Consequently, you could not see the tops of the mountains.

Or Gleick's:

> Since turbulence was a problem with pedigree, the great physicists all thought about it, formally or informally.

Or Ehrlich's:

> When I come into the meadow with the abandoned apple orchard and see the trees have leaves but have lost most of their blossoms, I feel as if I had caught strangers undressed.

Or:

> When I come into the meadow with the abandoned apple orchard, I feel as if I had caught strangers undressed because, although the trees have leaves, they have lost most of their blossoms.

Exercise: **Equals or Subordinates:**
To Rank or Not To Rank

Find an example of either paratactic or hypotactic style from your own reading. Rewrite the example, making it the opposite style. Try to describe the difference in effect. Write a short paragraph of your own, first in hypotactic, then paratactic, style. Which do you prefer, and for what reasons?

The patterns you have been practicing in this chapter are not limited to formal levels of discourse. However, many of them are used in particular combinations to create the sound of high seriousness directed to an unfamiliar and, often, critical audience. Combinations change depending on the speaker, audience, and occasion.

No mechanical rules can be made for producing levels of discourse; yet experienced readers claim to recognize those levels when they hear them. They know the qualities associated with certain speech sounds and identify them as belonging to low, middle, high, or something in between (low-middle, middle-high, and the like). There's no shortcut to this knowledge. Readers learn to identify voices within levels of formality by reading, listening, speaking, and writing. They practice over and over. And the longer they practice, the more finely tuned their skills become. As they imitate and learn, writers become more aware of choices and effects. They can exercise more freedom and sounder rhetorical judgment.

The following exercises develop from your work at classical stylistic patterns. They are intended to help you not only see patterns (don't worry about memorizing the Greek terms) but also experiment with them, in isolation and in combination. Through imitation and practice, you will begin to notice how voice not only strengthens ideas but also helps to discover and develop them.

Whole-Class Exercise: Name That Tune

Here are some student examples of the various word, phrase, and sentence patterns described and illustrated in this chapter. As a class, you might begin by trying to describe or identify the most striking pattern in each example. In which examples are the patterns you notice most effective and why?

1. "The car turtled down the street, people staring at the creeping vehicle." (John Nichols)
2. "Returning from her blind date, she sighed, 'Well, he was surprisingly dull.'" (John Nichols)
3. "He stared at the window. The rain poured. The trees bent. Wind wound the branches round. The scene pressed against his pane, against his tired eyes, against his dulled, cold, stone mind." (John Nichols)
4. "She heard her name and approached the podium. As she passed through the crowd, smile followed smile, clap pursued clap, row succeeded row as the standing ovation began." (John Nichols)

5. "They marvel at the gifts and grace of God; they marvel at the destruction by their own hands." (Stephen Combs)

6. "Death pounds with impartial persistence upon the hovels of the poor and the palaces of princes alike." (Stephen Combs)

7. "When they went to see Grandma they were surprised. She wore a black miniskirt, black fishnet stockings, and a Madonna bustier. Grandma never wears black." (LaRanda Parker)

8. "Vague memories of the fading past: Kentucky, cattle to count and horses to ride, Big Red. These things were old and distant, but not out of reach. They were like cobwebs in the corner of the basement. To look beyond the cobwebs was harder. Like the spider dancing in and out of the shadows, these memories were hard to grasp. But they are there. Every now and then you can grab hold of that precious past—Florida, dolphins to swim with, boats to sail. Fofo." (Matt Witbeck)

9. "When we were performing I felt so much energy, I danced harder than I ever have and Marc sang even better than he did at rehearsal and when we sang together, we brought the house down. That was the best night of my life." (Delbert Rose)

10. "The new Nissan 300-ZX twin-turbo accelerates with a quiet storm of power." (Eric Poulsen)

11. "My behavior reflects my beliefs, and my beliefs, my behavior." (Anne Shepherd)

12. "The skies over Iran cried black tears—a direct result of the burning oil fields in Kuwait." (Clay Kannapell)

13. "The motive in any ministry is love. Love is the bond that holds people together when circumstances try to break them apart." (Rebekah Lassiter)

14. "She was Bangla Desh all wrapped up in the lithe body of a girl. Warm and spicy, she enticed me to follow her into the crowd." (Rick Smith)

15. "His body moved through the slalom course as smoothly as a river cuts a valley." (Kevin Redding)

16. "When people are faced with disaster, when their

world is disrupted by the unexpected and unwanted, when they have searched everywhere and find no answer, when they are brought to their knees in desperation—it is then they discover what is worthwhile in life." (Rebekah Lassiter)

Exercise: **Calling Your Own Tune**

To discover how several patterns together can generate, build, and strengthen ideas, try writing some sentences that combine two or more patterns. For example, you might generate a parallel list in a paratactic sentence style (no subordination) that makes use of asyndeton (lack of conjunctions) and anaphora (repeated sentence openers). Or you might write a periodic sentence that ends with a tricolon (three parallel structures in climactic order) in which three words alliterate. Building this way can present a tower of inspection: how certain patterns combine to create particular frames of thought, emphatic force, rhythmical interest, and so on.

It's best to begin with play. Make invention a game; truth will follow. After each attempt, try to describe how the pattern or combination of patterns affects meaning; or how meaning affects patterns. At the start, you most probably will be looking for ideas to fit a pattern; later, patterns to fit ideas. Eventually, patterns will present themselves according to your subject, purpose, audience, and occasion.

Exercise: **What a Difference the Frame Makes**

Write a sentence (or more if necessary) illustrating a particular combination of rhetorical patterns. Then, try to express the same idea(s) by using a different combination of patterns. Wallace Stevens said, "A change of style is a change of meaning." This variation can show you the truth of his words.

Formal Voices, Part II

From Pattern to Product

In Chapter 4, we examined stylistic patterns at the word, phrase, and sentence level to discover their effects on sense and sound of sense. In this chapter, we will examine combinations of patterns in a larger context. That is, we'll see how several different combinations operate together across an entire passage or essay to evoke the sound we associate with formal discourse. That sound on the page, just like speech, is not generic: We don't all sound the same when speaking formally, so naturally, we won't when writing, either. There's no formula, no mechanical set of rules to follow. At best, there are touchstones. Some stylistic choices are more likely than others, but no one choice is absolutely wrong. For example, simple sentences and everyday vocabulary are common to informal discourse, but as you've seen in one of the professional samples at the start of Chapter 4, a writer can produce a high formal voice using only simple sentences and simple vocabulary. It's a matter of balancing choices. In the case just described, the writer creates an intonation pattern across his sentences that makes them *sound* formal.

This chapter focuses on balancing choices across the space of a paragraph or more that results in a formal voice appropriate for a given audience and occasion. What's appropriate in a given rhetorical context is not fixed, not absolute. There's plenty of room for individual preferences and taste.

Our goal is to produce an extended piece of writing in formal voice. In working toward that goal, we'll concentrate on the following tasks:

1. We'll practice preliminary imitation of sentences within a passage of your own choosing.
2. We'll rewrite those sentences to discover how different structures produce different effects within the context of the whole.
3. We'll practice imitation, not of individual sentences but of whole passages, to discover how voice is created and sustained as well as how it can influence the discovery and development of ideas.
4. We'll read professional samples of formal voices to see the ways different writers make choices
5. We'll read one student's formal essay in various stages of planning and revising to see how she balances her choices against the needs of audience and occasion.

EXTENDED PRACTICE IN IMITATION: WRITERLY KLEPTOMANIA

In the following exercises, you will be focusing on a sustained piece of writing by an author whose voice you admire. Although kleptomania suggests an abnormal pyschology, writers who practice strict imitation, downright stealing, are in need of neither therapy nor criminal punishment. They are simply learning their trade the way writers have done for centuries. Their primary goal is not simply to parrot the voice of another writer, or to pass the imitation off as their original work (that would be criminal), but to see another way of thinking and to hear other ways of voicing ideas. Each imitation adds to a writer's repertoire of choices.

Exercise: **Preliminary Work with a Passage of Your Choice**

Bring to class a passage of formal writing that illustrates a strong voice. Bring both a reproduced copy and a handwritten copy. Copying the passage slowly in your most legible penmanship will not only help you to attend to individual words and sentence patterns but also help you to hear them.

After you have copied the passage by hand, extract several sentences in which you recognize particular stylistic patterns. Copy these on a separate sheet of paper. Beneath each sentence, identify the stylistic patterns; then write an imitation of the sentence. Your imitation does not need to be word by word, but it should follow the grammatical structure of the original sentence. In class, read both the original and your imitation.

This exercise will help you become familiar with the writer's general habits at the sentence level.

SAMPLES

1. Model Sentence
We face a challenge in Berlin, but there is also a challenge in Southeast Asia, where the borders are less guarded, the enemy harder to find, and the dangers of communism less apparent to those who have so little. We face a challenge in our own hemisphere.

(John F. Kennedy, July 25, 1961, *The Berlin Crisis*)

Patterns Identified
Parallelism, ellipsis, assonance (harmonized vowels), anaphora (repeated sentence openers)

Student's Imitation
I see the goodness in the good, but there is often goodness in the bad, where the positive is less obvious, the good so much harder to see, and the hope in life hidden from those who are pessimistic. I see goodness in all I encounter.

(Tracy Taylor)

2. Model Sentence
Suddenly—every movement, every sound was sudden in an atmosphere of such tension—a gong blared out.

(Virginia Woolf)

Patterns
Polyptoton (same root word, different endings or forms), parenthesis, anaphora

Student's Imitation
Instantly—each turn, each motion was instant in the attempt to avoid an accident—the cars collided. (Kevin Redding)

Exercise: How the Parts Affect the Whole

1. Using the same sample sentences extracted from your chosen passage, try reordering the words in each sentence. Do not change the words; just reorder them. Then after each, try to explain the effect of the change.

2. Next, write an entirely different version of each sentence. In other words, change the grammatical construction. This often means changing some words, but only change or add those words that the new construction demands. Again, try to explain the effect of those changes.

3. Finally, write a paragraph in which you describe what you have learned from this exercise about the relative strengths and weaknesses of the original sentences *as they occur in the context of the passage.* Be as specific as you can. (This exercise is adapted from Corbett's *Classical Rhetoric for the Modern Student.*)

In the following student example, Anne Shepherd completes parts 1 and 2 of this exercise.

MODEL SENTENCE

The world will little note, nor long remember, what we say here, but it can never forget what they did here.

(Abraham Lincoln, *Gettysburg Address*)

REORDERED CONSTRUCTION

What they did here, the world can never forget, but it will little note nor long remember what we say here.

ANNE SHEPHERD'S COMMENTARY

This reordering distorts Lincoln's message. This sentence seems to emphasize "what is said" rather than the important actions of the soldiers.

NEW CONSTRUCTION

The world will not remember what we say here but what they did here.

ANNE SHEPHERD'S COMMENTARY

This sentence emphasizes the right message, yet it doesn't have the same style—a blander version of Lincoln's intended high dignity.

Exercise: **Imitation of an Extended Paragraph**
and Analysis

PART I

1. Write an imitation of one full paragraph in the model passage. Your subject matter should be different, of course, but follow sentence patterns as closely as possible.
2. After you have written your imitation, try to describe what the process was like: What specific problems did you face? How did you solve them? What was easiest; what hardest? For example, how did you decide on subject matter? Did the original passage present some possibilities and rule out others? How did following the original sentence patterns affect what you wanted to say next; that is, how did form affect meaning?

PART II

1. What did you learn about the author's habits of mind and voice from your work at imitation?
2. What did you learn about your own habits of mind and voice in trying to imitate someone else's?
3. Finally, what will you take with you from this exercise that will be useful in your own writing? What tools will you add to your box?

Your answers to these questions will take the form of a two-part informal essay. The first part is imitation and process description; the second is critical, comparative analysis. In writing your analysis for part II, draw from your preliminary practice thus far.

Student Samples of Imitation and Analysis

The first student sample is the work of Rebekah Lassiter.

Model Paragraph 1

The band had been having a rest. Now they started again. And what they played was warm, sunny, yet there was just a faint chill—a something, what was it?—not sadness—no, not sadness—a something that made you want to sing. The tune lifted, lifted, the light shone; and it seemed to Miss Brill that in another moment all of them, all the whole company, would begin singing. The young ones, the laughing ones who were moving together, they would begin, and the men's voices, very resolute and brave, would join them. And then she too, she too, and the others on the benches—they would come in with a kind of accompaniment—something low, that scarcely rose or fell, something so beautiful—moving. . . . And Miss Brill's eyes filled with tears and she looked smiling at all the other members of the company. Yes, we understand, we understand, she thought—though what they understood she didn't know. (Katherine Mansfield, "Miss Brill")

Lassiter's Imitation

The troops were waging war. Now it stopped at last. And what the troops heard was empty, lonely, yet there was just a slight anticipation—a feeling, what was it?—not peace—no, not peace—a something that made you still want to fight. Their despair dwindled, dwindled, an elation rose; and it seemed to the commander that in another moment, all of his squadron would resume attacking. The younger ones, the frightened boys who were fighting for the first time, they would begin, and the older ones, experienced and courageous, would join them. And then citizens too, citizens too, and patriots all over the world—they would rally there with a kind of confirmation—something thunderous, that clamored and deafened, something so thrilling—inspiring. . . . And the commander's soul filled with pride and he looked smiling at all the members of his squadron. Yes, we must fight, we must fight, he thought—though why they must fight he didn't know.

Lassiter's Analysis

Selecting the subject matter is the hardest part of an assignment in which the subject matter is unbounded but everything else is defined. In my selection it was easy to think of something that related directly to my original passage, something about the drama of nature and the human soul. The challenge was to find something unrelated and to relate it to my original only by the literary forms they shared. I had several ideas from looking around my room, but when I looked at the literary forms in the original passage, the only ideas that seemed stylistically possible were either a mystery or something about war. Either of those could be used in a piece that needed something abstract, descriptive, and hesitant. I settled on the concept of war even though I knew many others would probably use it because it was on my mind and because I thought that through this piece I could view the war in a different light.

Following the patterns was also a challenge because it was limiting. Word choice was limited by rhythm and pattern to those words that would fit the context. Mansfield's style is different from how I would reflect on war because I rarely repeat or hesitate in my writing. The literary form of the original affected the mood of my piece because it required writing that moved from passive reflection to passionate climax. The beginning of Mansfield's paragraph is abrupt and moves through a struggle to a climax of emotion. To stay true to the format, I had to imitate a similar mood in my writing. Imitating the mood helped guide the direction and meaning of my imitation.

Through working at imitating this passage, I learned about Katherine Mansfield's style and how it communicated her thoughts. She did not see her subject as a black-and-white issue but, instead, saw how it related to the way people felt and thought. Her writing was reflective and did not focus on one aspect of the way Miss Brill thought, but it focused on everything she thought and felt during a restricted period of time. I enjoyed Mansfield's style of writing because I liked the poetic style, and I liked seeing the struggle she went through and resolved seemingly in the act of writing.

Katherine Mansfield did an excellent job of balancing repetition and hesitancy with other literary patterns such as parenthesis, polysyndeton, and parataxis. I would like to take back to my writing a developing patience. I would also like to learn how to balance the different patterns I've noticed in a way that makes the voice in my writing stronger.

The following student sample is the work of Matt Witbeck.

Model Paragraph 2
He lay flat on the brown, pine-needled floor of the forest, his chin on his folded arms, and high overhead the wind blew in the tops of the pine trees. The mountainside sloped gently where he lay; but below it was steep and he could see the dark of the oiled road winding through the pass. There was a stream alongside of the road and far down the pass he saw a mill beside the stream and the falling water of the dam, white in the summer sunlight. (Ernest Hemingway, *For Whom the Bell Tolls*)

Witbeck's Imitation

He sat back on the cold, concrete slabs of the porch, his tail on the frayed carpet, and just outside the birds flew to the shelter of the bird feeder. The yard ended suddenly where he looked; but beyond it were bushes and he could hear the movement of the rabbits jumping into their burrows. There was a time before the fence and long before the collar when he viewed the world alongside the road and the dirty alley of the city, free in his uncaged spirit.

Witbeck's Analysis

What specific problems did I face? I had a very hard time in the beginning matching what I wanted to do with what the author's work would allow me. I first took any random subject from my head: an airplane crashing, a boxer crashing, cooking breakfast, and tried to force it into the original paragraph. What happened was either I could not get past the first sentence or I came up with a paragraph that was so close to the original it bordered on plagiarism. I even tried finding a new model three times. (*U.S. News,* President Bush's national address at the start of the Persian Gulf War, and works of Stephen King. All flops.)

Finally, I decided to put some time into coming up with a subject that would or could parallel the Hemingway paragraph. I chose the subject of a stray cat I found, and how it always looked out the window like it wanted to be "free." (It got out one day and found its freedom.) This subject allowed me lots of room and also started out the same way as the original, with the cat sitting and viewing its surroundings. The first sentence came fairly easily since I could visualize it. After that, I would take each phrase of the original paragraph and say it over and over, trying to work in the story about the cat. This worked better than I had hoped, because while I was creating my sentences, I was fitting them to the form of the original paragraph.

I learned that Ernest Hemingway likes to put more than one main idea in a sentence. In the first sentence, he talks about the floor of the forest, the way the man is lying, and the wind blowing in the pine trees. Hemingway also seems to have a smooth, soft flow to his sentences. They're easy to follow and he does a good job of bridging them. It is almost as if he were there telling the story himself.

In the beginning it was very hard to imitate him. The first time I was trying to get an airplane crashing to fit into his paragraph. I just couldn't do it. It was hard for me to put so many different thoughts into one sentence, the way he does. I would rather write short sentences, each with its own idea. I am also fond of lists. Instead of incorporating the birds and rabbits as part of two different sentences, I most likely would have used them in a list.

In the end, I was very happy with my imitation. By imitating, I learned a new way of expressing myself. The smooth, flowing sentences explained what I wanted to say but in a different way than I normally would have chosen. I would have slowly led up to ideas. It would be hard for me to write like Hemingway, but at least I know there can be different ways for me to "sound" if I set myself to it.

What We Can Learn From Rebekah Lassiter and Matt Witbeck

As both students noted, writing a strict imitation of an entire paragraph limits not only choices in topic but also the exploration of topic. Because expression is not separate from ideas, but ideas themselves, it is best to begin with a topic that can take a number of directions. The more you restrict yourself in advance, the harder it will be to imitate the model. In a sense, you need to give yourself over to the model, to the writer's habits of mind.

Lassiter picks war as a topic and then lets the mood of Mansfield's paragraph limit and direct her ideas about war. Following the mood, the direction of emotion, makes it easier for her to employ repetition and hesitancy in the sentence patterns. And the mood, of course, influences her ideas.

Witbeck picks a stray cat for his topic. It allows him a vantage point, a beginning like Hemingway's, from which to generate concrete detail. As he describes the cat and its surroundings, he can integrate several points of information within a sentence the way Hemingway does. And he can hear Hemingway's voice— the sound of someone passively noting the flow of visual detail. That sound even enters Witbeck's last sentence, where unlike Hemingway, he reflects on his observations. Yet his reflection sounds weary, sadly wistful—the information there conforming to the passive voice in the paragraph. Repeating Hemingway's phrases, as Witbeck claims he did, helps him internalize rhythms. And those influence his "story."

In both samples, the writers learn experientially that "voice" is as much invention as ornamentation. It can discover as well as develop ideas. Paradoxically, imitation teaches discovery of choices through limitation of them. The more writers are aware of stylistic choices, and the more they exercise them, the more freedom of thought they have.

SUSTAINED PIECES OF PROFESSIONAL WRITING IN FORMAL VOICE

Let's look at some longer professional samples of formal prose. Here are four. Each style, I would argue, could be generally classified as formal—the voice aimed high. Yet each voice is decidedly different from the other. After each sample is a list of questions for discussion.

Chief Joseph's Surrender Speech

Tell General Howard I know his heart. What he told me before I have in my heart. I am tired of fighting. Our chiefs are killed. Looking Glass is dead. The old men are all killed. It is the young men who say yes or no. He who led the young men is dead. It is cold and we have no blankets. The little children are freezing to death. My people, some of them, have run away to the hills, and have no blankets, no food; no one knows where they are, perhaps freezing to death. I want time to look for my children and see how many of them I can find. Maybe I shall find them among the dead. Hear me, my chiefs. I am tired: my heart is sick and sad. From where the sun now stands, I will fight no more [forever]. (Turner 232)

Questions for Discussion
1. What rhetorical patterns do you notice in Chief Joseph's speech?
2. How would you describe the speaking personality? What qualities of mind and feeling do you hear as you repeat this speech in your reading?
3. How do the rhetorical patterns you have listed combine to create the voice you hear?
4. How might you argue that, despite the simplicity of diction and sentence patterns, Chief Joseph's speech is an

example of formality—speech aimed at high solemnity and eloquence?

An Excerpt from a Speech Attributed to Seattle, Dwamish Chief*

Every part of this soil is sacred in the estimation of my people. Every hillside, every valley, every plain and grove, has been hallowed by some sad or happy event in days long vanished. The very dust upon which you now stand responds more lovingly to their footsteps than to yours, because it is rich with the blood of our ancestors and our bare feet are conscious of the sympathetic touch. Even the little children who lived here and rejoiced here for a brief season will love these somber solitudes and at eventide they greet shadowy returning spirits. And when the last Red Man shall have perished, and the memory of my tribe shall have become a myth among the White Men, these shores will swarm with the invisible dead of my tribe, and when your children's children think themselves alone in the field, the store, the shop, upon the highway, or in the silence of the pathless woods, they will not be alone. At night when the streets of your cities and villages are silent and you think them deserted, they will throng with the returning hosts that once filled and still love this beautiful land. The White Man will never be alone.

Let him be just and deal kindly with my people, for the dead are not powerless. Dead, did I say? There is no death, only a change of worlds. (Turner 253)

Questions for Discussion
1. What particular rhetorical patterns do you notice in Chief Seattle's speech?
2. How do they compare with and contrast to those in Chief Joseph's?
3. How would you describe the speaking personality of Chief Seattle?
4. How does it compare with and contrast to that of Chief Joseph?

---

*This speech has been printed in several different translations, variations, and adaptations. The oldest recorded document is believed to be dated 1887, a translation written by H. A. Smith, derived from notes he made while listening to Seattle. The version quoted here is from Turner.

5. What rhetorical patterns seem to give rise to the particular voice you hear?

From *To The Lighthouse* by Virginia Woolf

There he stood in the parlour of the poky little house where she had taken him, waiting for her, while she went upstairs a moment to see a woman. He heard her quick step above; heard her voice cheerful, then low; looked at the mats, tea-caddies, glass shades; waited quite impatiently; looked forward eagerly to the walk home; determined to carry her bag; then heard her come out; shut a door; say they must keep the windows open and the doors shut, ask at the house for anything they wanted (she must be talking to a child) when, suddenly, in she came, stood for a moment silent (as if she had been pretending up there, and for a moment let herself be now), stood motionless for a moment against a picture of Queen Victoria wearing the blue ribbon of the Garter; when all at once he realised that it was this: it was this:—she was the most beautiful person he had ever seen.

With stars in her eyes and veils in her hair, with cyclamen and wild violets—what nonsense was he thinking? She was fifty at least; she had eight children. Stepping through the fields of flowers and taking to her breast buds that had broken and lambs that had fallen; with the stars in her eyes and the wind in her hair—He took her bag.

"Good-bye, Elsie," she said, and they walked up the street, she holding her parasol erect and walking as if she expected to meet some one round the corner, while for the first time in his life Charles Tansley felt an extraordinary pride; a man digging in a drain stopped digging and looked at her, let his arm fall down and looked at her; for the first time in his life Charles Tansley felt an extraordinary pride; felt the wind and the cyclamen and the violets for he was walking with a beautiful woman. He had hold of her bag. (24–25)

Questions for Discussion
1. Walking with Mrs. Ramsey, in particular, carrying her bag, is an exhilarating experience for Mr. Tansley. What rhetorical patterns help readers experience Mr. Tansley's anticipation, amazement, and pride?
2. How does Virginia Woolf turn this ordinary event into an extraordinary one? What lifts the voice from informal to formal description, from low to high?

John F. Kennedy's Inaugural Address

We observe today not a victory of party but a celebration of freedom, symbolizing an end as well as a beginning, signifying renewal as well as change. For I have sworn before you and Almighty God the same solemn oath our forbears prescribed nearly a century and three-quarters ago.

The world is very different now. For man holds in his mortal hands the power to abolish all forms of human poverty and all forms of human life. And yet the same revolutionary belief for which our forbears fought is still at issue around the globe, the belief that the rights of man come not from the generosity of the state but from the hand of God.

We dare not forget today that we are the heirs of that first revolution. Let the word go forth from this time and place, to friend and foe alike, that the torch has been passed to a new generation of Americans, born in this century, tempered by war, disciplined by hard and bitter peace, proud of our ancient heritage, and unwilling to witness or permit the slow undoing of those human rights to which this nation has always been committed, and to which we are committed today at home and around the world.

Let every nation know, whether it wishes us well or ill, that we shall pay any price, bear any burden, meet any hardship, support any friend, oppose any foe to assure the survival and the success of liberty.

This much we pledge—and more.

To those new states whom we welcome to the ranks of the free, we pledge our word that one form of colonial control shall not have passed away merely to be replaced by a far more iron tyranny. We shall not always expect to find them supporting our view. But we shall always hope to find them strongly supporting their own freedom, and to remember that, in the past, those who foolishly sought power by riding the back of the tiger ended up inside.

To those peoples in the huts and villages of half the globe struggling to break the bonds of mass misery, we pledge our best efforts to help them help themselves, for whatever period is required, not because the Communists may be doing it, not because we seek their votes, but because it is right. If a free society cannot help the many who are poor, it cannot save the few who are rich.

To our sister republics south of the border, we offer a special pledge: to convert our good words into good deeds, in a new alliance for progress, to assist free men and free governments in casting off the chains of poverty. But this peaceful revolution of hope cannot become the prey of hostile powers. Let all our neighbors know that we shall join with them to oppose aggression or subversion anywhere in the Americas. And let every other power know that this hemisphere intends to remain the master of its own house.

To that world assembly of sovereign states, the United Nations, our last best hope in an age where the instruments of war have outpaced the instruments of peace, we renew our pledge of support: to prevent it from becoming merely a forum for invective, to strengthen its shield of the new and the weak, and to enlarge the area in which its writ may run.

Finally, to those nations who would make themselves our adversary, we offer not a pledge but a request: that both sides begin anew the quest for peace, before the dark powers of destruction unleashed by science engulf all humanity in planned or accidental self-destruction.

We dare not tempt them with weakness. For only when our arms are sufficient beyond doubt can we be certain beyond doubt that they will never be employed.

But neither can two great and powerful groups of nations take comfort from our present course—both sides over-burdened by the cost of modern weapons, both rightly alarmed by the steady spread of the deadly atom, yet both racing to alter that uncertain balance of terror that stays the hand of mankind's final war.

So let us begin anew, remembering on both sides that civility is not a sign of weakness, and sincerity is always subject to proof. Let us never negotiate out of fear, but let us never fear to negotiate.

Let both sides explore what problems unite us instead of belaboring those problems which divide us.

Let both sides, for the first time, formulate serious and precise proposals for the inspection and the control of arms, and bring the absolute power to destroy other nations under the absolute control of all nations.

Let both sides seek to invoke the wonders of science instead of its terrors. Together let us explore the stars, conquer the deserts, eradicate disease, tap the ocean depths and encourage the arts and commerce.

Let both sides unite to heed in all corners of the earth the command of Isaiah to "undo the heavy burdens . . . [and] let the oppressed go free."

And if a beachhead of co-operation may push back the jungle

of suspicion, let both sides join in creating a new endeavor, not a new balance of power, but a new world of law, where the strong are just and the weak secure and the peace preserved.

All this will not be finished in the first one hundred days. Nor will it be finished in the first one thousand days, nor in the life of this Administration, nor perhaps in our lifetime on this planet. But let us begin.

In your hands, my fellow citizens, more than mine, will rest the final success or failure of our course. Since this country was founded, each generation of Americans has been summoned to give testimony to its national loyalty. The graves of young Americans who answered the call to service surround the globe.

Now the trumpet summons us again—not as a call to bear arms, though arms we need; not as a call to battle, though embattled we are; but a call to bear the burden of a long twilight struggle, year in and year out, "rejoicing in hope, patient in tribulation," a struggle against the common enemies of man: tyranny, poverty, disease and war itself.

Can we forge against these enemies a grand and global alliance, North and South, East and West, that can assure a more fruitful life for all mankind? Will you join in that historic effort?

In the long history of the world, only a few generations have been granted the role of defending freedom in its hour of maximum danger. I do not shrink from this responsibility; I welcome it. I do not believe that any of us would exchange places with any other people or any other generation. The energy, the faith, the devotion which we bring to this endeavor will light our country and all who serve it, and the glow from that fire can truly light the world.

And so, my fellow Americans, ask not what your country can do for you; ask what you can do for your country.

My fellow citizens of the world, ask not what America can do for you, but what together we can do for the freedom of man.

Finally, whether you are citizens of America or citizens of the world, ask of us here the same high standards of strength and sacrifice which we ask of you. With a good conscience our only sure reward, with history the final judge of our deeds, let us go forth to lead the land we love, asking His blessing and His help, but knowing that here on earth God's work must truly be our own.

Questions for Discussion

1. Kennedy's speech can be classified as ceremonial discourse—intended to please and inspire his audience (as well as to

inspire confidence in his leadership). Certain rhetorical patterns are used for that effect. Sentences are constructed to be "quotable," easily remembered because of their pithiness, sound play, and emphatic force. Note which sentences seem to you particularly "quotable" and try to identify their patterns.

2. Kennedy speaks not from across the table, the room, the pulpit in church, or even a high podium in a lecture hall, but from within a world theater. What in his voice suggests such space between himself and his audience?

3. How does Kennedy attempt to engage his audience, given the distance between them?

4. Kennedy attempts to persuade his audience not by appealing primarily to reason but to emotion. He does not develop the logic of his points through careful discussion, for example. Much of his speech could be described as a series of topic sentences. How, therefore, does Kennedy inspire our belief—in him, in the principles he lists, in the nation?

CREATING YOUR OWN FORMAL VOICE — A SUSTAINED PIECE OF WRITING

For this assignment, you will need to find a subject, an audience, and an occasion for which a formal voice is appropriate. You will also need to decide genre—a letter, a speech, an essay, a report.

In class, with your teacher and peers, explore possible subjects and rhetorical situations. After you've chosen what to write about, to whom, and why, begin your draft. As you write, do not try to force ideas into the rhetorical patterns you've been working with in this chapter. Just write. When you are first learning to play a Mozart concerto, you don't worry about phrasing. You just learn the notes and get a sense of where you are going and how things connect. In writing your first draft, see first what you have to say and how one idea leads to another.

Peer Review of a First Draft

In small groups in class, read your drafts to each other, making sure the group understands the rhetorical situation in which you have placed yourself. It's a good idea to type answers to the following questions on a separate page: Who am I in this piece of writing? Where am I? Who is my audience? What is my purpose? How do I want to sound in this piece? (List qualities.) This description of rhetorical considerations will help you as well as your classmates.

Questions for Group Discussion
1. Where are the moments of greatest interest in this piece?
2. Do I provide bridges to help an audience from idea to idea? Where might I expect too wide a jump?
3. How would you describe the speaking personality? What does my voice tell you about my relationship to my subject, my audience, and my occasion? Are there any places where I sound too stilted, too chatty, too cute/sweet, too tough?

Work on a Second Draft

Revise your draft in light of group discussion. Reread and rethink those moments in your text where others listened with interest and where they most strongly heard you behind the page. Are those places marked by any rhetorical patterns that you recognize as useful for creating balance, emphasis, or rhythmical interest? If so, try to revise other places in your piece, drawing on similar patterns for those effects. If people were responding mainly to a notion here and there that caught their attention, try strengthening those ideas by drawing on patterns you have studied and admired: schemes of balance (parallelism, antithesis, tricolon, chiasmus); ellipsis (for emphasis); tropes or periodic structure (suspense, balance, emphasis).

Other Rereadings and Retunings

Listen for how ideas are connected. Where might you need more explicit transitions—patterns of logical connection—hypotaxis, or patterns of repetition (anaphora, anadiplosis, epistrophe), for example?

Listen for the sound of weighted seriousness that we associate with formal speech. Remember that producing formal discourse is not a matter of following mechanical rules. There aren't any. Formality is not a matter of high vocabulary and complex sentence structure. Reread Chief Joseph's speech, for example. The difference between formal and informal is more a matter of rhythm than anything else. In contrast to informal speech rhythms, as I described in Chapter 3, formal rhythms are weightier; the pitch changes, less abrupt and not as wide; and stresses, farther apart.

Avoiding the Pitfalls

As you aim toward high seriousness, you don't want to sound stilted, awkward, or rhythmically flat. Here are some habits to avoid:

1. Overuse of Latinate vocabulary. Try not to make more than 25% of your vocabulary multisyllabic; less is better.
2. One long sentence after another without rhythmical breaks or without space for readers to assimilate the important ideas. See Chapter 2 for a discussion of the value of varying sentence lengths.
3. Many long subordinate or dependent clauses. Keep them under 15 words, for the most part, and don't let them dominate the general sentence design of the whole piece. This habit, like that in item 2, affects readability.
4. Too many similar sentence styles in succession without defensible purpose.
5. Too many weak or passive verbs. This habit may signal that you are shunting verb power into nouns or relying overmuch on adjectives. For example, do you say "reach a conclusion" or "conclude"; "make a proposal" or "propose"; "is in need of" or "needs"?
6. Several prepositional phrases in a row. Three or more prepositional phrases usually means that you are stringing together nouns and weak verbs. See item 5. Both affect readability.
7. Too many abstract nouns as subjects. Is the subject of your sentence the true agent in the sentence, or have you buried the agent or omitted it? This habit often reveals itself in "there is/are" sentences in which *there* is not the true subject: "There are several trees in this forest that were destroyed in the fire." *There* can then lead to an unnecessary *that* clause. Revised: "Several trees in this forest were destroyed in the fire." Too many abstract nouns or *there* sub-

jects can also lead to wordiness and lack of clarity. Make some of your subjects *people* instead of abstract nouns. In general, make the real subject the grammatical subject of your sentence.
8. Habitual interruptions of main sentence parts. Use interruptions between subject and verb sparingly.

Lastly, listen for where might you sound too chatty, too colloquial in word choice and rhythm, or too loose and rambling in sentence structure.

The Relative Value of Stylistic Taste

The list of habits to avoid comes from several sources on modern style, most notably, Richard Lanham, *Revising Prose;* Joseph Williams, *Style, Ten Lessons in Clarity and Grace;* and Walker Gibson, *Tough, Sweet, and Stuffy.* The same general advice can be found in many style texts. The reason? Stylistic preference, or taste, is the product of an age. What we often consider "stuffy" or "artificial" was not considered so in the seventeenth, eighteenth, or early nineteenth centuries. In the seventeenth century, a decorative, often convoluted sentence style enjoyed high praise. John Lyly's prose, for example, was marked by extremes in style. It was loaded with schemes and tropes, particularly schemes of balance, alliteration, and strained figures of speech.

But changes in taste were developing as early as the Restoration period. John Dryden was already advocating a shift toward a middle style, a more "natural," less Latinate style in both vocabulary and syntax. In the eighteenth century, this trend continued, with less and less emphasis on stylistic precepts inherited from formal classical rhetoric and more emphasis on individual stylistic freedom.

Now, even in formal, expository prose, praise generally goes to expository writers who avoid a highly mannered, ornate style and the features that often accompany it: heavy reliance on multisyllabic vocabulary; a parade of long, complex sentences with embedded clauses; an elaborate display of figures; passive and indirect expression—the longest distance to a point. But no one set of aesthetic values ever reigns supreme. Even today, not all the roses go to short, plain, direct sentences, despite the influence of George Orwell and E. B. White. So if individual taste leads writers against the current preference for a plain, unmannered style in expository prose, the previous guidelines can, nevertheless, help writers avoid clumsy, unnecessarily cloudy, or rhythmically flat sentences.

Peer Review of a Later Draft

After you have revised according to the suggestions above and to those of your teacher and peers, prepare a page of notes (what you changed, added, deleted, and why) and questions for your reviewers. See where you have succeeded and where you need to make further changes to accomplish your goals for meaning and voice.

In small groups, exchange drafts, revision notes, and questions for reviewers. Read each other's drafts and then write in response to the author's revision notes and questions. If there is time, pose other questions the author could consider in his or her final draft.

There is no magic number of drafts to tell you that a piece of writing is finished. "Finished" is a matter of time (your boss wants the report by 5 p.m. today), a writer's ability to make several kinds of revisions in a single draft, level of audience satisfaction, and, finally, the level of writer satisfaction. An experienced writer may compose one or several drafts over a short or long period, depending on the nature of the task, its complexity, the intended audience, and self-expectations. Most writers agree that at some point in the drafting process, the writing should be tested on an appropriate audience. The success of writing tasks often depends on helpful response from several readers, and occasionally, it depends on direct collaboration.

After it has been decided by the deadline, your peers, your teacher, and yourself that the piece is "finished," write a page of final revision notes. You might address some of the following questions in your writer's journal:

1. What significant changes have you made regarding your subject—purpose, progression and connection between ideas, conclusion?
2. How do you define your specific audience for this piece?
3. How would you describe yourself in relationship to your subject, your audience, and your occasion?

4. What stylistic choices did you make to create not only a formal piece but also the persona you've described in answering question 3?
5. What specific revision(s) would you like your reader to pay close attention to when he or she reads this draft? Your answer to this question should be addressed directly to the person reviewing your draft.

A SAMPLE STUDENT ESSAY FROM START TO FINISH

The work used in this section is that of Anne Shepherd.

Planning Stage: Rhetorical Situation

I am a member of the charter volunteer program—the Class of 2000. Founders of the program intend to supply third graders of an inner-city public school with mentors and role models to help them cope with troubles in their lives and to develop values necessary to survive. Part of this survival includes gaining an appreciation for education and eventual graduation from high school. If they graduate, they will receive a scholarship to a Richmond college.

I have been chosen to speak to the 25 charter volunteers because I have overcome some of the obstacles in establishing relationships with those involved in the program. My purpose is to boost morale during this support-discussion meeting. I want to convey to my audience my struggles as well as the rewards. Most of all I want to clarify the importance of the children and our dedication to them.

Anne Shepherd's Second Draft

Five months ago, 75 strangers gathered in Room 308 of the Commons. There Tom Panther and David Dorsey described an abstract plan of a charter volunteer program. Expectations were high, curiosity great, but details scarce. Those who sat in that room were moved by the words of these men. They told us that this program required serious commitment. They told us competition would be stiff. Blind and brave, we took the risk. Those of us sitting here today are the finest 25 for the challenge. If once we were blind, we now see the mountain before us. We are beginning to face not what we imagined but what exists.

I speak to you today in many voices. One is enthusiastic, one is concerned, one is frustrated. All are in response to the same terrain. The climb has been rocky, at times treacherous. My efforts have been blocked by prejudiced teachers, unwilling children, resentful parents, skeptical administrators. These scratches, bruises, I have endured; once healed, I am satisfied. I am satisfied because I have succeeded in this day's climb. I am higher on this mountain than the previous one. I have earned the respect of a classroom teacher, the faith of the principal, and most importantly, the trust of the students.

I am not alone. I now carry three young boys who cannot endure this climb alone. I'm dedicated to these children. I persevere in giving them support. I encourage their respect for their key to survival—education. I am patient while they grow. And they have grown. They have grown in that they have learned to hold on—to trust the grip of my hand. I will help them fulfill their curiosity. In return, they will fulfill mine. There may be many more valleys, but we will persevere. I may survive alone, but alone these children will perish.

Don't you lose patience either. Try to cross the valleys. By doing so, you will escape despair, provide hope, and with the children you help, feel the victory of the climb, together.

Endurance. That is why you are the select 25. You possess endurance. It is not physical endurance to maintain your posture, or mental endurance to calm your mind, but spiritual endurance to help others who need you to guide them. Feel this strength—let it be the love to overcome your disappointments. Feel this strength—let it be the joy to celebrate your victories. Feel this strength—let it be the force that gives these children hope.

Anne Shepherd's Analysis

I used many schemes of balance (parallelism, tricolon, and antithesis) in this piece because they emphasize my feelings about my work in the program, and all are equally powerful. The tricolon offers me a way of listing feelings and progressions so that all receive equal attention. I use repetition in the piece to emphasize that "I am not alone" but am responsible for the growth of three youths. "And they have grown." I also use a lot of repetition. I think it's appropriate, considering that we must keep repeating words of encouragement to ourselves to keep our spirits high.

In my first draft, I made an awkward shift from a vague introduction to a very abstract poetic analysis. I had many problems battling with my first product because I was pleased with many of the poetic comparisons. Yet my language was distant and not clearly relevant to my audience.

In my second draft, this element is still present. I've tried to add some examples, making the more abstract statements tangible to my audience. The topic is typical of discussions that arise at our support meetings—I have reflected on our beginnings; shared my personal feelings, intentions, ideals, frustrations, and goals; and encouraged perseverance. It is most important that we remember the children and our commitment to them.

Our Class Discussion of Anne Shepherd's Draft: A Summary

We put ourselves in the audience. We're frustrated volunteers who believed our efforts would be met with applause but discovered the contrary. We, like Anne, heard the initial pep talk by Tom Panther and David Dorsey. Now we have heard another one.

What's missing? I asked. Everyone so strongly heard the rhythms of the rhetorical patterns Anne used, they substituted sound for substance. If you're a disgruntled volunteer, what can Anne tell you to get you back into that school? "I want to know what happened to her—if it was as bad as what I experienced, what she did to turn things around, and how much can I really expect?" That was the class consensus. A few felt there was still too much distance. Martin Luther King, Jr., and Abraham Lincoln had enthralled several members of the class—rich sources of rhetorical patterns, but some wanted the reality behind the metaphors, too.

Anne Shepherd's Final Draft

Five months ago, 75 strangers gathered in Room 308 in the Commons. There Tom Panther and David Dorsey described an abstract plan of a charter volunteer program. Expectations were high, curiosity great, but details scarce. Those who sat in that room were moved by the words of these men. They told us this program required commitment. They told us competition would be stiff. Blind and brave, we took the risk. Those of us sitting here today are the 25 finest for the challenge. If once we were blind, we now see the mountain before us. We face not what we imagined but what exists.

I speak to you today in many voices. One is enthusiastic, one is concerned, one is frustrated. All are in response to the same terrain. The climb has been rocky, at times treacherous. I believed teachers would welcome help from an enthusiastic volunteer. Children would be flattered by my individual attention. Parents would be pleased by the tutoring and moral support their children would be offered. And administrators would be exhilarated by the promise of this rising program. With these expectations, I faced my first day.

Yet these expectations were paradoxical to what I experienced. I was greeted by the cold eyes and suspicious voice of the third grade teacher who questioned my purpose and presence. She had never heard of the Class of 2000. She randomly called three boys; they were not necessarily the ones who needed my attention most, but the boys she could first recall. They were unwilling, reluctant to even share their names. They wanted little to do with me. Still I returned week after week, trying to inch my way to their approval.

Today the third grade teacher called me by name with a smile on her face. Today, three boys were happy to see me. Principal Crockett even flattered me by inquiring about my progress. Jamal remembered $1/3$ of what I had taught him about Ella Fitzgerald and other famous jazz musicians last week. Marcell trusted me with his sorrow: His brother was murdered last weekend. And Michael, well, Michael has a very small attention span, but he demonstrated his welcome by jumping up and down and clapping his hands. So now I am not alone.

I've learned to be patient while they grow. And they have grown. They have learned to hold on—to trust the grip of my hand. Don't you lose patience either. There may be many more valleys, but we can persevere. We may survive alone, but alone these children perish. Try to cross the valleys. By doing so, you will provide hope and with the children you help, feel the victory of the climb, together.

Endurance. That is why you are the select 25. It is not so much physical endurance, or mental endurance, but spiritual endurance to help others. Feel this strength—it will ease your disappointments. It will allow you to celebrate your victories. It will be the force that gives these children hope.

Excerpt from Anne Shepherd's Final Revision Notes

In this draft, I provided concrete examples with which my audience could identify. I described the obstacles that they may have faced or can expect to face as well as the rewards. I am able to talk more directly, yet I did not sacrifice the formality or my purpose—inspiration. The use of specifics also allowed more focus on the children. I would most like my readers to respond to the examples I provided.

My Commentary

The sample essay grew out of one student's admiration for the voice she had been imitating. For Anne Shepherd, discovering sentence patterns was like discovering chocolate. Suddenly, there was all this available richness. She stuffed her prose with the chocolates she liked best—schemes of repetition and balance, lofty metaphor.

Her final draft may seem extravagant—too "heavenly" sweet for some palates. But what I admire most is her willingness to experiment. To *do something* with what she has heard and enjoyed. I'm inclined to say, "Go ahead—be extravagant. Put it all in there." Then see what disappears from the menu when you discover the next voice and the next. Eventually, after much experimentation, writers create their own menu of stylistic options and variations—one that suits their own temperaments, their own linguistic preferences, given the subject, occasion, and audience.

CHAPTER SIX

Informal Voices
The Middle Ground

Informal voices are neither colloquial nor formal but somewhere in between. In general, the speaker avoids either extreme. The speaker sounds intelligent and educated but is not at pains to display it. He or she seems relaxed, though not loosely casual. In other words, informal voices tell us that the speaker is personal, yet maintains a respectful distance. These qualities describe the midpoint on a continuum of middle-range levels of discourse. Informal voice, then, is the sound of personal speech for a broad, familiar, and moderately critical audience.

There is no pure level of informality. Depending on the subject, occasion, and audience, informal speech may move closer toward colloquial or formal levels of discourse. Labeling it low-middle, middle, or high-middle is a matter of how much is borrowed from one or the other end of the continuum. The key to maintaining a level squarely in the middle is to borrow evenly across the range from informal to formal. Neither low nor high governs the tone, and thus the level of discourse belongs to neither end of the range.

The discussion of Sidney Bechet's piece in Chapter 1 illustrates the differences among very colloquial (Bechet's original passage), a middle range of informality (my first revision), and high-middle (the second revision). The analysis after each describes what has been borrowed from where and the effects on level of discourse. A rereading of that section may help you hear the possibilities across the range of informality, from low to high-middle.

In this chapter, we will examine many samples of informal voices, beginning with three that illustrate different levels within the middle range. Each sample is followed by an analysis of how the writer holds the middle ground. Next, you will have an opportunity to investigate possibilities by reading and analyzing several other voices. Throughout these pages are exercises to help you practice what you read and perhaps discover more than you can from reading alone. The chapter ends with an essay assignment in creating an informal voice and offers a student example of that assignment.

LEVELS OF INFORMALITY
High-Middle

Let's begin, then, by looking at some examples to use as touchstones, since, as in all levels of discourse, fast rules for creating them can't be made. I'll begin with a voice that aims at high-middle informality, on the verge of high, a level common to essays found in journals written for well-educated, though not necessarily specialized, audiences. The following is excerpted from "Rock and Sexuality" by Simon Frith. Frith is both a sociologist and a rock journalist.

Excerpt from Simon Frith
   Nineteen-fifties rock'n'roll is usually described as a particularly sexual form of expression, a source of physical "liberation," but teenage culture was already sexualized by the time it appeared. The question we really have to examine concerns the use of music not in the general expression of sexuality but in its ordering. Sexuality is not a single phenomenon that is either expressed or repressed; the term refers, rather, to a range of pleasures and experiences, a range of ways in which people make sense of themselves as sexed subjects. Sexual discourses determine prohibitions as well as possibilities, what can't be expressed as well as what can. But the most important function of 1950s teenage culture wasn't to "repress" sexuality but to articulate it in a setting of love and marriage such that male and female sexuality were organized in quite different ways. And rock'n'roll didn't change that sexual order. Elvis Presley's sexuality, for example, meant different things to his male and female fans. There was an

obvious tension between his male appropriation as a cock-rocker and his female appropriation as a teeny-bop idol. Rock'n'roll was, say its historians significantly, "emasculated," but its "decline" (from crude, wild dance music to crafted romantic ballads and spruce idols) marked not a defused rebellion but a shift of sexual discourse as the music moved from the street to the bedroom. In neither place did it challenge the conventions of peer-group sex.

Exercise: **High-Middle versus Out of Range**

The Frith passage is considered academic discourse, but it's not as elitist and distant as it often can be in specialized journals. As a short exercise similar to the one you did in Chapter 4, read an academic journal within a field of your own interest (sociology, English, or psychology, for example) to see the extreme of academic discourse. Bring to class a short excerpt from a piece that you feel excludes you from the discourse community. Discuss the writer's use of language: What role has he or she created for the audience? In what way has the writer defined the rhetorical context— occasion, audience, speaker—that does not address your own needs as a reader?

How Frith Controls the High-Middle

What keeps the Frith passage from soaring to the heights of formal academic prose are some speech habits attributed to lower levels of informality (the middle range) and an intonation pattern that is not flat but is occasionally marked by the pitch changes and stresses we associate with strong personal speech.

You can easily pick out the multisyllabic vocabulary associated with formal speech. But notice that these words are not out of the range of generally educated readers. They wouldn't need a glossary.

Here are some of the features of informality found in Frith's excerpt:

1. Writers who aim at an unspecialized, but well-educated, audience often express the same idea in both high and low levels of discourse. The habit is an attempt not only to

clarify but also to personalize the information, to bridge the distance between speaker and audience. Frith does this.

Here is an example of what I mean: "Sexual discourses determine prohibitions as well as possibilities, what can't be expressed as well as what can." The second clause tells you the same thing, but at a lower point on a continuum from low to high. The same point is made more forceful in the second instance because of the *sound* of compressed antithesis (not fewer words, but shorter, simpler ones) and the *sound* of emphatic personal speech. That is, the big stresses fall on "can't" and "can" in "what can't be expressed as well as what can."

2. Frith follows long sentences with shorter, emphatic ones not only to highlight key points but also to vary his rhythms. Notice that the short sentence, "And rock'n'roll didn't change that sexual order," after the long one just before it, adds the force of personal speech by its break in rhythm and its use of simple vocabulary and contracted verb.

3. Frith makes frequent use of antithesis in parallel-structure, "not this, but that" constructions to create pitch changes and stresses on particular ideas, and to therefore infuse those ideas with the *sound* of importance—the importance to Frith, and through Frith's voice, the importance to us. There's a personal stake in the information. His voice tells us he's not removed. We hear his feeling about the message in the intonation pattern. Even though Frith does not use *I*, his sentences imply the *I*, because of the strong speech rhythms entangled in the syntax.

4. He uses contractions. A small thing, I know, but it tugs and holds back the aspiring climber from the high peaks.

5. He occasionally interrupts the main parts of a sentence or clause with parentheses, creating abrupt pitch changes and stresses that we associate with strong speech. Such interruption needs to be made cautiously, however. If the interruption occurs too often or is too long, the opposite effect can be created: not strength, but stuffiness or flatness. Effective examples from Frith:

. . . the term refers, rather, to a range of pleasures. . . .

Elvis Presley's sexuality, for example, meant different things. . . .

Rock'n'roll was, say its historians significantly, "emasculated." . . .

Middle

The next example is from William Styron's *Darkness Visible.* Styron is talking about his depression. It is a serious subject, discussed in a serious manner, yet the voice is personal. The level of discourse is middle, not as high as Frith's piece, but not as low as my first revision of Bechet's piece. It's a middle informality that includes much from the diction and rhythms of literary voices (lots of parallelism, images, alliteration, assonance, and finely tuned phrases, rising and falling in measured pace). It includes some language from science that raises the level of discourse, but it also has some vocabulary and speech patterns that belong to low-middle informality.

Styron's voice is, I would say, poised on a middle note—personal and markedly so, yet maintaining a respectful distance from the audience. This is neither journal writing—self-expression intended only for the writer's ears—nor one side of a private conversation about what it feels like to be depressed. In other words, Styron talks informally about a personal subject, but he maintains some distance from it as well as from his audience.

Excerpt from William Styron
But I felt an immense and aching solitude. I could no longer concentrate during those afternoon hours, which for years had been my working time, and the act of writing itself, becoming more and more difficult and exhausting, stalled, then finally ceased.

There were also dreadful, pouncing seizures of anxiety. One bright day on a walk through the woods with my dog I heard a flock of Canada geese honking high above trees ablaze with foliage; ordinarily a sight and sound that would have exhilarated me, the flight of birds caused me to stop, riveted with fear, and I stood stranded there, helpless, shivering, aware for the first time that I had been stricken by no mere pangs of withdrawal but by a serious illness whose name and actuality I was able finally to acknowledge. Going home, I couldn't rid my mind of the line of Baudelaire's, dredged up from the distant past, that for several days has been skittering around at the edge of my consciousness: "I have felt the wind of the wing of madness."

Our perhaps understandable modern need to dull the sawtooth edges of so many of the afflictions we are heir to has led us to banish the harsh old-fashioned words: madhouse, asylum, insanity, melancholia, lunatic, madness. But never let it be doubted that depression, in its extreme form, is madness. The madness results from an aberrant biochemical process. It has been established with reasonable certainty (after strong resistance from many psychiatrists, and not all that long ago) that such madness is chemically induced amid the neurotransmitters of the brain, probably as the result of systemic stress, which for unknown reasons, causes a depletion of the chemicals norepinephrine and serotonin, and the increase of a hormone, cortisol. With all this upheaval in the brain tissues, the alternate drenching and deprivation, it is no wonder that the mind begins to feel aggrieved, stricken, and the muddied thought processes register the distress of an organ in convulsion. Sometimes, though not very often, such a disturbed mind will turn to violent thoughts regarding others. But with their minds turned inward, people with depression are usually dangerous only to themselves. The madness of depression is, generally speaking, the antithesis of violence. It is a storm indeed, but a storm of murk. Soon evident are the slowed-down responses, near paralysis, psychic energy throttled back close to zero. Ultimately, the body is affected and feels sapped, drained. (46–47)

* * * *

What I had begun to discover is that, mysteriously and in ways that are totally remote from normal experience, the gray drizzle of horror induced by depression takes on the quality of physical pain. But it is not an immediately identifiable pain, like that of a broken limb. It may be more accurate to say that despair, owing to some evil trick played upon the sick brain by the inhabiting psyche, comes to resemble the diabolical discomfort of being imprisoned in a fiercely over-heated room. And because no breeze stirs this cauldron, because there is no escape from this smothering confinement, it is entirely natural that the victim begins to think ceaselessly of oblivion. (50)

How Styron Holds the Middle Note

In the first paragraph, you can see how Styron integrates occasional high-sounding words into the neighborhood. In sentence 2, paragraph 2, for example, beginning "One bright day on a walk," 21 words are monosyllabic in the clause ending at the semicolon. The only words not in anyone's 500-most-used list are *ablaze* and *foliage*. Similarly, in the rest of the sentence, high-sounding words are sparse: *stricken by, actuality, acknowledge.* The sentence is long but loose; and though there are parallel lists, they are patterned to provide breaks within the sentence and even within the list. The rhythm keeps the parallelisms from becoming too evenly toned, too much like chant—the high, solemn, formal chant of Chief Joseph, for example.

In the third paragraph, words like *affliction* and *banish,* for example, continue the pattern of high-sounding, literary words among common words. Parentheses do their part to vary the intonation pattern, causing changes in pitch and stress and thus avoiding the sound of flat, unrhythmical prose. The two long sentences are broken by parentheses, for example, and they are followed by this series of shorter and more emphatic, hard-hitting sentences:

> The madness of depression is, generally speaking, the antithesis of violence. It is a storm indeed, but a storm of murk. Soon evident are the slowed-down responses, near paralysis, psychic energy throttled back close to zero. Ultimately, the body is affected and feels sapped, drained.

Notice how many significant ideas are expressed in short, consonant-ended words. And notice too how those words belong to common speech. These techniques help balance the level of discourse and contribute to the voice we hear on the page.

Exercise: Discovering Voice
by Working Against It

In class, rewrite the last paragraph of the Styron excerpt in the following way: Remove the interruptions (the parentheses) in sentences 1 and 3 in paragraph 4. Remove the periodic structure of the last sentence in that paragraph by placing the subordinate clauses (*because*) at the end instead of at the beginning. What happens to the coherence, the connections in sense from one sentence to another? And what happens to the voice?

Lower-Middle

In this third excerpt, from "Mum's the Word" by Austen A. Ettinger, we can hear another middle-range voice. It is, like Styron's, an educated, personal voice, one with an important truth to tell, yet it does not sound as literary as Styron's. It's not as noticeably full of parallelisms and harmonized word pairs— the rhythmical balance of literary prose. It's directed to the audience of the *New York Times,* a middle-class, fairly well-educated audience, but a general one. The rhythms in Ettinger's piece are closer to that of colloquial speech, but the vocabulary level and frequency of image making raise the level of discourse to the middle range.

Excerpt from Austen A. Ettinger
Do you want to close that big sale? Firm up a friendship? Get your spouse to regard you with the unqualified adoration you haven't known since Mom? Place your bet on communication. Over cocktails or back fences, and of course on analyst's couches, we earnestly extol the rewards of communicating effectively— redemption through understanding.

I grant you, communication is sometimes a good and useful thing, undoubtedly one crucial component of an orderly, humane society. For healing the lesions that are likely to afflict every relationship from time to time, it can be just the soothing poultice that is needed. But always a panacea? Not in my marriage. And not in many others I have observed. Far from always providing a hoped-for balm of bond, the very act of communicating may set off or exacerbate painful conflicts rather than quiet them.

Is that because many of us are inept at this subtle social art? On the contrary, we are too perilously good at it.

Our talents for unfettered expression, after all, have been honed by talk-radio jocks exhorting us to give full vent to our pet notions about everything from the Middle East to abortion rights and wrongs to baseball's latest trades. All the while, television hosts on newlywed and dating shows tempt us with offers of one-week vacations in Ottumwa, Iowa, matched luggage thrown in, if we will reveal the delights or deprivation of our sex lives. And all Americans automatically assume that it is their cherished, democratic prerogative to utter whatever crosses their minds, whenever they wish, telling it like it is. Or like they want you to think it is.

Indeed, some among us have cunningly developed an arsenal of conversational gambits that masquerade as true communication and are especially handy whenever clouds darken our marital landscape. Each presents a Potemkin-like facade of civility from behind which we can safely lob grenades—of evasion, denial, put-down—at our spouse on the other side of the argument. It is communication, all right, communication at its most insidious.

Let me be honest with you. Disarmingly, the words seem to solicit permission to speak out; artfully, they claim the moral high ground, and above all, they promise truth-telling. Yet why does the truth invariably turn out to be uncomplimentary? Why is the "honest" message never good news? Because, as any black-belt marital combatant knows, this particular overture is less calculated to open a forthright exchange than it is to open a wound.

Please don't take this the wrong way. "As you probably will" is the unvoiced coda. What's also unsaid is, "Besides the blunder you have already committed, don't make matters worse by taking my shot across your bow mean-spiritedly."

I know I have faults, too, but. . . . "Nothing close to the enormity of yours" is never spoken but clearly understood. And the critic's prudent strategy of up-front self-depreciation neatly preempts any chance for retaliation.

In the face of such vocal game-playing, is it any wonder that I concluded long ago that too much talk can be like social cholesterol, clogging the channels of genuine communication, blocking real contact, dangerous to the health of relationships?

I realize that the very idea of substituting silence for communication may seem somehow un-American: repressive, hostile to the expansive image we have of ourselves, just plain wrong for a people who grew up in the bleachers of a thousand stadiums and now have their say on public access television.

Yet silence gives space for perspectives to be altered, affords an opportunity to separate what is vital (and worth dwelling on) from what is not (and thus better ignored)—all before words burst forth like missiles from their silos, on their lethal way and impossible to call back.

There are many times, my wife and I have learned, when the best way to clear the air is quite simply to clear the air of verbal weapons camouflaged as reasonable discussion and oh-so-calm analysis.

That's when we can be truly open and ready to share the loving, laughing, warmly satisfying kind of communication that makes everything else—including the rough spots—worthwhile.

How Ettinger Holds His Ground

Ettinger borrows many expressions from colloquial speech—"telling it like it is," "rough spots," "clear the air," "taking my shot," "firm up," "up-front," "handy," and so forth. These are blended into sentences that include formal expressions and higher-sounding vocabulary. The mix is fairly even and in context makes Ettinger sound smart but hip, a man who's been educated and who knows that making a show of his intelligence will alienate or "turn off" his broader audience.

But he's also trying to show he knows the language of the pop psychology that supports open talk about one's feelings. He adopts some of that trendy language to place one world view against the other. He peppers his speech with colloquialisms to let us know that he's not just a regular guy but also a guy who knows the score, the truth, about these matters. Popular speech habits are neatly tucked into the surrounding tissue so that he sounds neither high nor low.

He's careful not to make any gaffes—big incongruities in diction that will make him sound unintentionally comical. (He comes close, though, at times.) Ettinger's middle range is lower than Styron's. He draws from the lower ends of both extremes. Styron draws from the higher ends. Imagine if Styron, for example, used some of the colloquial expressions of Ettinger in his piece: if, instead of saying "It may be more accurate to say that despair, owing to some evil trick," he said this: "To tell it like it is, despair, owing to some evil trick" Given the word *despair,* a formal literary choice, *to tell it like it is* is incongruous in this context. Styron would now sound oddly folksy and literary at the same time.

Although Styron uses some colloquial expressions such as "around the corner," they are not modern slang, and so he avoids mixing very low diction with high. Ettinger borrows far more freely from the low end of the continuum and distributes those choices evenly across his entire piece.

Often, he uses both styles in the same sentence, as in "And all Americans automatically assume that it is their cherished, democratic prerogative to utter whatever crosses their minds, whenever they wish, telling it like it is." In that sentence, *telling it like it is,* a modern slang expression, brings home his higher point. It punctuates the intellectual with plain truth. This isn't just some political science or sociology talk, he seems to say. This is an idea whose truth is in everyday experience. And for the other types, he suggests the opposite: This isn't just homey observation; this notion is embedded in our culture, and you can see by my language that I'm fairly sophisticated about it. In aiming at the middle, speakers need to borrow evenly and at the same points on both sides of the low-high continuum. Wild incongruity occurs if they don't. It would be like Minnie Pearl singing country, with the Boston Symphony Orchestra playing Mozart behind her.

Lastly, Ettinger makes his speech sound conversational, despite the overall sophistication of his language, by using sentences that sound like the emphatic speech of conversation. He uses lots of questions, pithy remarks, and contrasts that make our voices rise and drop often, and sharply in places. For example, note the quick changes in pitch, stress, and rhythm in this sequence: "But always a panacea? Not in my marriage. And not in many others I've observed. Far from always providing a hoped-for balm of bond, the very act of communicating. . . ." Parentheses also do their part to move our voices up and down as we repeat Ettinger's vocal behavior on the page. From our reading performance, we make judgments about his personality, his attitudes, and his message.

Exercise: **Separating High from Low**

Rewrite one paragraph of Ettinger's essay, removing all the features belonging to the low end of informality, making the language sound uniformly high—that is, no longer a blend of two levels of discourse. Then rewrite the original paragraph a second time, removing all the features that belong to the higher end of informality, making the language sound uniformly colloquial. In both rewritings, you will need to change more than vocabulary. As you've been discovering, sentence style affects the level of discourse too.

How does each of your revisions affect the way you perceive the writer's role—his persona, his attitudes, and his message? How does each affect your role as audience?

THREE VOICES POISED ON
A MIDDLE NOTE: EAR-TRAINING
AND READING PRACTICE

Sample I: Ann Beattie

The first voice is heard in an excerpt from Ann Beattie's *Picturing Will*.

Does it seem impossible that the child will grow up? That the bashful smile will become a bold expression? The sparkling eyes in need of corrective lenses? That fevers will subside, that there will be no more bloody knees, that a briefcase will replace the blue security blanket? You must resist the tendency to think ahead; wishing for peace is *not* the same as wanting things to change forever, and when all is said and done (a state only songwriters believe in), the child will never really be gone, even though he grows up. You will find that although the child may be remembered in association with one or two prized toys, more likely the child will be remembered alone, standing with his legs parted, his arms dangling at his sides, pants fallen down a bit so that only the toes of the sneakers are visible. He will be standing the way he stood in the snapshot, with an expanse of field—or maybe the beach—around him. A little thing but you will remember that distinctly without having a photograph in front of you. That will be the way, in fact, the child will stay: a visual image—one that, even at the time, you squinted to look harder at, whether or not a camera was raised to your eye.

When you are thirty, the child is two. At forty, you realize that the child in the house, the child you live with, is still, when you close your eyes, or the moment he has walked from the room, two years old. When you are sixty, and the child is gone, the child will also be two, but then you will be more certain. Seeing pictures of your child at different ages, you will not hesitate for a moment. You will point to the two-year-old, not the ten-year-old or the twenty-year-old. He will always be that high. With a nick above the eyebrow. Those eyes, at that point a bit too large for his face, so that, in remembering the eyes, you are sure that your child possessed startling intensity. He might be wearing some article of clothing purchased for a special occasion, but unless the picture of the shirt with the anchor and the sheepshank knot is right in front of you, you will not think much about that. He will be in typical little-boy clothes, smiling or looking straight at the camera with a tolerant expression that may show a hint of fatigue: Another picture? Why do you want it? What can it mean to you? He will be there with you without special costumes or toys as the years go by: the child alone, more and more a fact. Your life before the child seems too long ago to think of. What happened with the child, something of a blur. There were late-night walks in the summer heat, weren't there? Didn't the child once assume that you could give him pointers about how to fly? Didn't he think he was recreating the rumbling of Vesuvius with the plastic straw in the glass of chocolate milk? You go on—and the child goes on—but you change, as the child sees you. You do, but he does not. He stays the same, no matter how many marriages, mortgages, dogs, and children he may surround himself with—he does not change, so he is not vulnerable. It becomes difficult to remember that he ever was. That the dog snapped at him, and he was afraid. That the cut got infected. That night after night, the same blue-bodied demon flicked its tail in his dreams. Sticky fingers. Wet sheets. Wet kisses. A flood of tears. As you remember him, the child is always two. (53–54)

Questions for Discussion
1. Who is the narrator talking to? For what reasons? What seems to be at stake for her in this subject?
2. How would you describe the voice you hear? What are its special qualities? How do they affect your response to the subject matter and to the speaker?
2. Where would you place the level of discourse on a continuum from low to high-middle? Is it closer to Frith, Styron, or Ettinger, or nowhere near any of them?
3. What blend of stylistic and rhetorical choices account for your placing the discourse at the level you do?
4. Does subject matter influence your judgment or not?

Collaborative Exercise: **Writing Against the Narrator's Voice in** *Picturing Will*
In groups, work collaboratively, each group directing itself to one of the following suggestions.
1. Repunctuate a few long sentences in either paragraph. Make them short, or relatively so. Then, aloud, read your revised sentences in context with the sentences before and after them. What happens to the voice?

2. Eliminate a series of fragments in either paragraph, making Beattie's punctuated sentences grammatically complete ones. Read your revised sentences, again in context with the sentences just before and after them. What happens to the voice?

3. Choose a short section in a paragraph—a few sentences. Rewrite them, making all the vocabulary colloquial. What happens to the voice then? (For example, a colloquial revision of the sentence "You must resist the tendency to think ahead" is "try not to think ahead.")

As a class, try to describe what you've learned about the level of discourse in Beattie's piece, the quality of voice, and the role created for the reader. How would you compare or contrast her voice to other voices you've heard so far in this chapter?

Sample II: Zora Neale Hurston

The following excerpt is from Zora Neale Hurston's "How It Feels to Be the Colored Me."

At certain times I have no race, I am *me*. When I set my hat at a certain angle and saunter down Seventh Avenue, Harlem City, feeling as snooty as the lions in front of the Forty-Second Street Library, for instance. So far as my feelings are concerned, Peggy Hopkins Joyce on the Boule Mich with her gorgeous raiment, stately carriage, knees knocking together in a most aristocratic manner, has nothing on me. The cosmic Zora emerges. I belong to no race nor time. I am the eternal feminine with its string of beads.

I have no separate feeling about being an American citizen and colored. I am merely a fragment of the Great Soul that surges within the boundaries. My country, right or wrong.

Sometimes, I feel discriminated against, but it doesn't make me angry. It merely astonishes me. How *can* any deny themselves the pleasure of my company? It is beyond me.

But in the main, I feel like a brown bag of miscellany propped against a wall. Against a wall in company with other bags, white, red and yellow. Pour out the contents, and there is discovered a jumble of small things priceless and worthless. A first-water diamond, an empty spool, bits of broken glass, lengths of string, a key to a door long since crumbled away, a rusty-knife blade, old shoes saved for a road that never was and never will be, a nail bent under the weight of things too heavy for any nail, a dried flower or two still a little fragrant. In your hand is the brown bag. On the ground before you is the jumble it held—so much like the jumble in the bags, could they be emptied, that all might be dumped in a single heap and the bags refilled without altering the content of any greatly. A bit of colored glass more or less would not matter. Perhaps that is how the Great Stuffer of Bags filled them in the first place—who knows?

Questions for Discussion

1. How would you describe the speaker in this piece? What are her special qualities?
2. How would you describe her attitude toward herself and to her subject?
3. What role has the speaker created for her audience? How do you respond to that role in your reading?
4. Where do you place the level of informality—low, middle, or high-middle? To what degree does that affect your response as a sympathetic audience?
5. What rhetorical and stylistic choices does Hurston make to create the level of discourse and the voice you hear? Consider the blend of vocabulary choices, sentence structure and rhythms, use of figures of speech, point of view, and tone.

Sample III: Annie Dillard

This final, short example is Annie Dillard's introductory paragraph to "Living with Weasels."

A weasel is wild. Who knows what he thinks? He sleeps in his underground den, his tail draped over his nose. Sometimes he lives in his den for two days without leaving. Outside, he stalks rabbits, mice, muskrats, and birds, killing more bodies than he can eat warm, and often dragging the carcasses home. Obedient to instinct, he bites his prey at the neck, either splitting the jugular vein at the throat or crunching the brain at the base of the skull, and he does not let go. One naturalist refused to kill a weasel who was socketed into his hand deeply as a rattlesnake. The man could in no way pry the tiny weasel off, and he had to walk half a mile to water, the weasel dangling from his palm, and soak him off like a stubborn label. (11)

Questions for Discussion

1. How would you describe the speaker in this passage? What are her special qualities?
2. How would you describe her attitude toward her subject and her audience?
3. What role has Dillard created for her readers? How sympathetically can you respond in that role?
4. Where would you place the level of discourse? How does it compare with other examples of informality in this chapter? Would you say it's lower or higher than, say, the Hurston passage?
5. Styron, Ettinger, Hurston, and Dillard use metaphor and simile. How might you compare their uses of metaphorical language? What effect do they have on level of informality? If you hear a difference, is it the nature of the metaphor or the manner in which it is expressed?
6. What stylistic and rhetorical choices does Dillard make to create the level of discourse and voice you hear on the page?

ESSAY ASSIGNMENT FOR INFORMAL VOICES

Choose one of the pieces in the previous sections as a model. (Or choose your own model of informal discourse, using those in this chapter for guidance.) Write an essay in loose imitation of it—not a formal imitation like those you wrote in Chapter 5, but a few pages *in the manner of.*

Your objective is twofold: to attain a middle level of informal discourse, neither too low nor too high, neither casual nor formal; and to create a strong speaking personality within that level of informality.

Planning Your Essay

How to Begin

Let's say, for example, that you have chosen Austen Ettinger as a model. Here are some points to consider for analysis:

1. Say what his topic and purpose are.
2. Describe the audience he is aiming at, the audience most likely to respond with interest.

3. Describe his attitude toward his subject and his audience.
4. List the stylistic and rhetorical choices that might have generated the level of informality, and describe the voice you hear speaking to you on the page.

After you have analyzed the model, choose your subject. It might be close to Ettinger's; for example, you might discuss a societal value that you're skeptical about.

Considering Your Audience
Think about who are you writing to and for what reasons.

Writing Your Guidelines
From your analytical description of the model, decide what stylistic and rhetorical guidelines you will use to produce the level of informality required and to create the voice you want your audience to hear.

Your First Draft

After you have written your draft, listen to the voice you have produced. To what extent do you believe you have succeeded in achieving your prewriting aims? Write your response in connection to purpose, audience, and voice.

Peer Review

Exchange drafts with members of your group. Ask them to respond to the following questions:

1. What do you understand to be the purpose and intended audience for this piece?
2. Who do you hear speaking to you from behind the page? Describe both the level of discourse and the personal qualities of the speaker.
3. What stylistic principles or guidelines might have given rise to the voice you hear?

Revision

In preparing a second draft, compare your prewriting analysis with the analysis offered by your peers. How does your desired effect measure up against what your audience heard? Revise your draft by trying to reconcile your intentions with what your audience heard.

SAMPLE STUDENT ESSAY: EXCERPT FROM PLANNING AND SECOND DRAFT

Mindy Rettew chose to write about the effects of her parents' divorce. The voice she tries to imitate loosely is William Styron's.

Planning

I am writing to young adults whose parents have been divorced. Particularly, I am addressing high school students. I would like to share my experiences and my point of view.

I plan to loosely imitate Styron's work. These are the techniques I plan to use:

1. Blend high and low levels of discourse as he has done.
2. Incorporate listing, because I think it is very powerful.
3. End some important words in hard consonants. Styron reveals strong feelings with that technique.
4. Aim toward general informality, because I want to use a personal anecdote and bring the audience close to me.
5. Use longer sentences in the anecdote but incorporate rhythmical breaks, as Styron has done.
6. Vary sentence lengths. At times, I will use short, emphatic sentences to express an important idea or opinion.
7. Try to use some figures of speech like metaphor and simile.

Second Draft

I never truly understood the situation. Years of loving and living with two parents, and two sisters, in the same house as a close family, had, without warning, come to an abrupt end.

The custody battle began a year and a half after the divorce. Each probably fought just as hard as the other, one parent fighting for one reason and the other parent for another, both knowing the entire time that the decision really lay in our hands. But when the judge, sitting in that great leather chair that almost swallowed him, but not quite, since he was a very large man, asked us individually and privately who we wanted to live with, our mother or our father, how were my sisters and I, being only five, seven and ten years old, supposed to answer? It was an unfair, but necessary, question.

We had made our decision. We chose my father. I am not quite sure why all three of us made that decision. Maybe it was because she had moved to an apartment in another town, and my father chose to remain in our home. We also wanted to stay in the same area as our friends. With so many changes falling on us like snow, we didn't want to be buried. I needed something stable: our house, my room, my bed, my Winnie the Pooh comforter. I don't know if she resented us for choosing my father, but I resented her for leaving me. However, the resentment did not surface until I was much older. When she discovered the judge's verdict, she was very upset. I remember sitting on her lap, hugging her and crying with her, not really understanding why. I did not comprehend the consequences of our decision; I only knew that my mommy was deeply hurt because of it.

A few years after the custody battle, my father remarried. There were some new additions to the family. Now it was not only my father and the three of us but a stepmother and three stepsisters. The living arrangements did not work well after this drastic change. My sisters and I needed a new atmosphere. My father understood our reasons and did not resent us for our decision. Living with my mother worked well for all of us for awhile. Then some time after my half-sister was born, my resentment towards my mother began to surface.

Resentment has built, since then, some consciously, some unconsciously. Now that I am mature enough, my mother and I have spoken on the subject. Some feelings are resolved, but not all. . . .

In writing loose imitations (instead of the strict type you practiced in Chapter 5), you are working the way many professional writers do—learning how to develop your own voice by selectively imitating other writers' rhetorical and stylistic choices. By experimenting in this way, you discover how to create new roles for yourself as writer and new roles for your readers. Different roles suggest different perspectives and attitudes. How you see yourself and your audience influences what you say about your subject. So the more you imitate and practice, the more ways of thinking you discover. And the more freedom and judgment you can exercise within a given rhetorical situation.

CHAPTER SEVEN

Informal Voices

Special Effects of the Wild Mix

In Chapter 6, we listened to different personalities speaking seriously about subjects in which they have a personal stake. Each chose a particular level of informality appropriate to the intended audience. In each speaker's attempt to establish a middle range of discourse, that writer made stylistic choices that derived from the same points on either end of the continuum from low to high. None of the professional writers created wild incongruities in vocabulary choices—slang right next to high formal choices, for example. The vocabulary or diction level was kept in balance. Nor were there wild incongruities between vocabulary level and sentence structure—loose colloquial talk trapped in long periodic or formal sentence patterns. Nor were there incongruities between subject matter and the voice describing it. The melody created, the voice, was in harmony with the lyrics, and vice versa.

Some voices, however, are neither loose colloquial speech nor formal speech; they speak in the middle range, and yet they depend on the incongruities described above to create particular tonal blends. These we identify as wry, ironic, spoofy, mock-serious, tongue-in-cheek, affectionately teasing—all those in a class that mix serious with comic to give voice to a particular complex of emotions. We don't have a precise vocabulary for describing the mix of attitudes we feel toward certain subjects and even audiences, but we recognize particular blends, even quite subtle ones, when we listen to people talk. Capturing those sounds in writing is difficult, as I've partly described in Chapter 2 on colloquial voices. Here I'm inviting you to listen to writers who have deliberately created incongruities for special effects in voice. We have heard a variety of speech melodies across three levels of formality. We have been to the casual piano bar, the pops concert, and the opera. Now we will listen to jazz—where the mix is jagged, where the sounds are both disjunctive and connected. The effect is a coherent speech melody that arises from disparate yet compatible feelings and attitudes. It's jazz—like Dorothy Donegan mixing "Tea for Two" with the "Second Hungarian Rhapsody," modulating the feelings into one complex set of sounds. We perform similarly when we catch in our speech a surprising blend of contrary feelings heard and understood by our listeners.

In this chapter, we'll listen to three distinctive voices, each one an example of the effects created by intentionally juxtaposing high and low—formal syntax and colloquial diction, formal and colloquial diction, and so forth. The first example is followed by critical commentary, and each model is followed by questions for discussion. The chapter ends with an essay assignment based on the models and offers two student essays in response to the assignment.

THREE PROFESSIONAL MODELS
Model I: Colin McEnroe

Let's begin with an excerpt from Colin McEnroe's "How to Get a Baby." We used examples from this article in Chapter 2 to illustrate effective use of fragments.

> Once upon a time my wife and I decided to have a baby. Weeks, months, and years drifted by. No baby. We entered the world of fertility medicine, which is somehow both perched on the leading edge of scientific technology and trapped back in the age when a hunched-over person with a lot of split ends would shake gourds and throw pulverized lizard entrails at you.
> For a period of time—our Von Bulow period—I would inject my wife with this stuff we had to keep in our refrigerator. It was

made from the refined urine of menopausal women. The primary source in the early days of its manufacture was (I swear this is true) Italian nuns. Someone told me the Vatican got wind of it and told the nuns to knock it off. I'm not sure I believe this. We never achieved a pregnancy, but my wife kept buying more and more black and white clothes and issuing calls for spiritual renewal.

Although the burdens of fertility treatment fall most heavily on the woman, the man has some interesting moments. I was required to produce specimens of something I am not accustomed to handing over to anyone I haven't had at least a few dinner dates with. The circumstances under which I was required to coax out these substances became less and less cozy with each new lab study until—in Self-Abusers Anonymous, this would have been my "bottom"—I was ushered one day into a standard, clinical gynecological examination room, stirrups and all, handed a cup and shown the location of the light switch. No Mantovani, no shellfish, no Rita Moreno telling me what a man I was. An additional millstone was the knowledge that this particular sample would be combined with the eggs of a hamster (ach, the ignominy) to see whether my little guys really knew how to secure a beachhead.

Unless you have a swab and tongue depressor fetish, you really have to pull out all the stops on your fantasy machine if you want to break the tape in this situation. I'm talking Mary Lou Retton *and* Ladysmith Black Mambazo *and* Wonder Woman— wielding steam irons and hunks of ginseng. That's not even good enough. You think I'm going to tell you what I really thought about? Hell, I may be a magazine writer, but I have a scintilla of dignity. OK, a demi-scintilla.

You come out of that room with a saffron container's worth of vital fluids, and you feel as though there should be one of those boxes you step up on when you win the Olympics, and martial music of several nations playing. And forgive me for swaggering, but I passed. There are a few left-handed hamsters with thick glasses and halfway decent turnaround jump shots walking around today. A few cedar chips off the old block. I reckon they may show up at my door some day and hit me up for a couple of new water bottles or even a little treadmill wheel, but what the hey. You reap what you sow.

Time drifted on. Hamsters, si. Ninos, no. The fertility doctors began to remind me of me trying to hook up a VCR. Plug this into that, turn on the driveway lights and hum the Mr. Ed theme song. Trying new combinations of stuff just to be doing something. You reach a hallucinatory stage where everybody seems to be telling you that they are newly pregnant. Eva Gabor, the kid at your door taking a Thin Mints order, the trapped Arctic whales. All pregnant.

We decided to adopt. In order to adopt, you have to go through a home study, usually with a good-hearted social worker who is only trying to ascertain that you are not a member of a paleo-Christian corporal discipline cult or a Medellin drug-cartel franchisee or an officer in the Elks. But you, the prospective parent, may have become a little thin-skinned. After all, shotgun maintenance technicians for the Baader-Meinhof gang or cyberpunk computer hackers with bad skin, even people who host home satellite shopping network programs, can get pregnant and have children and never have to answer questions about their characters. However, you, a person who has given money to save otters and who subscribes to the *Utne Reader,* are going to be obliged to prove you are Penelope Leach and Jane Brody and Jiminy Cricket all rolled into one. This is not true, but try telling yourself that.

Social worker: "And where do you work, Mr. Pimento?"

You: "Oh, sure I know what you're getting at. Yeah, I took a couple of packages of Post-its out of the office supply cabinet and brought them home for my own use. What does that make me, a criminal? A mutant unfit parent? Yeah, I filled the supervisor's briefcase with cannoli. It was a *joke.* DON'T YOU PEOPLE HAVE ANY SENSE OF HUMOR?"

Social worker: "Let's try that one again."

What I'm trying to say here is that, sure, if you own eight vacuum cleaners and they all have different names and personalities, maybe the agency is going to suggest gently that you'd be better off starting a stamp collection. If you are just a garden-variety neurotic American couple, one of whom may even occasionally dream of being forced to walk across a field of bird feet growing up backwards out of the ground, you can probably get yourself a baby. We did.

One day last fall, my wife and I found ourselves on a plane to Texas to pick up our baby son, Joseph. . . . (153)

Critical Commentary

Although the speech rhythms in this piece can be identified as colloquial—the intonation patterns we associate with casual speech—the diction level is not consistent with those patterns.

McEnroe draws from across the board, low to high, and often mixes the extremes within a single sentence.

In paragraph 3, for example, notice these disparate vocabulary choices:

FORMAL	COLLOQUIAL	POPULAR MODERN TECHNOLOGY
burdens (literary word)		*fertility treatment*
interesting moments (tongue-in-cheek cliché)		
fall most heavily (literary cliché)		*produce specimens*
required		
I am not accustomed	*handing over*	
circumstances under which	*dinner dates with (slang)*	
	coax out	*these substances*
ushered in	*cozy (tongue-in-cheek)*	*lab study*
		clinical gynecological examination
	and all	
	handed a cup	
shown the location of	*what a man I was (colloquial cliché)*	
additional millstone		
the knowledge that		
ach, the ignominy (jokey use here because of the ach*)*	*my little guys*	
secure a beachhead		

The mix, as you can see from the chart, is rough. But it's that very mix that creates the special brand of humor in this piece, particularly the sound of "tongue-in-cheek" we hear when formal bumps hard against informal. Notice what happens if I collapse the vocabulary into consistently colloquial expressions and remove the tongue-in-cheek cliche of "interesting moments" (jokingly coy evasiveness) in the first sentence:

Even though it's mostly women who have to put up with fertility treatments, men put up with their share too. I had to give specimens of something I'm not used to handing over to anyone I haven't had a few dinner dates with. And I got less and less comfy with each new lab study until I was taken into a standard, gynecological examining room one day, stirrups and all, handed a cup, and shown where the light switch was.

Can you hear what's missing when this particular passage is plainly colloquial? What personality quality is lost? How does it affect the way you judge the speaker—in particular, his attitude toward this experience, his sense of himself?

Questions for Discussion
1. Try to identify the personality you hear speaking to you. How would you describe his relationship to his subject, his audience, and to the language he uses?
2. How does the speaker mix seriousness with unseriousness? What effect do those techniques have upon the voice you hear, the emotions behind the information?

Model II: Donald Barthelme

Our second model is a fictional letter by Donald Barthelme, entitled "The Sandman." The writer addresses his girlfriend's psychiatrist, arguing that Dr. Hodder should accept her decision to discontinue therapy and buy a piano. The voice is comic, but not as broadly comic as McEnroe's. The voice is also very educated, the sophistication itself part of the joke.

Dear Dr. Hodder, I realize that it is probably wrong to write a letter to one's girl friend's shrink but there are several things going on here that I think ought to be pointed out to you. I thought of making a personal visit but the situation then, as I'm sure you understand, would be completely untenable—I would be *visiting a psychiatrist*. I also understand that in writing to you I am in some sense interfering with the process but you don't have to discuss with Susan what I have said. Please consider this an "eyes only" letter. Please think of it as personal and confidential.

You must be aware, first, that because Susan is my girl friend pretty much everything she discusses with you she also discusses with me. She tells me what she said and what you said. We have been seeing each other for about six months now and I am pretty familiar with her story, or stories. Similarly, with your responses, or at least the general pattern. I know, for example, that my habit of referring to you as "the sandman" annoys you but let me assure you that I mean nothing unpleasant by it. It is simply a nickname. The reference is to the old rhyme: "Sea-sand does the sandman bring/sleep to end the day/He dusts the children's eyes with sand/And steals their dreams away." (This is a variant; there are other versions, but this is the one I prefer.) I also understand that you are a little bit shaky because the prestige of analysis is now, as I'm sure you know better than I, at a nadir. This must tend to make you nervous and who can blame you? One always tends to get a little bit shook when one's methodology is in question. Of course! (By the bye, let me say that I am very pleased that you are one of the ones that talk, instead of just sitting there. I think that's a good thing, an excellent thing, I congratulate you.)

To the point. I fully understand that Susan's wish to terminate with you and buy a piano instead has disturbed you. You have every right to be disturbed and to say that she is not electing the proper course, that what she says conceals something else, that she is evading reality, etc., etc. Go ahead. But there is one possibility here that you might be, just might be, missing. Which is that she means it.

Susan says: "I want to buy a piano."

You think: She wishes to terminate the analysis and escape into the piano.

Or: Yes, it is true that her father wanted her to be a concert pianist and that she studied for twelve years with Goetzmann, but she does not really want to reopen that can of maggots. She wants me to disapprove.

Or: Having failed to achieve a career as a concert pianist, she wishes to fail again. She is now too old to achieve the original objective. The spontaneous organization of defeat!

Or: She is flirting again.

Or:

Or:

Or:

Or:

The one thing you cannot consider, by the nature of your training and of the discipline itself, is that she really might want to terminate the analysis and buy a piano. That the piano might be more necessary and valuable to her than the analysis.[1]

What we really have to consider here is the locus of hope.

1. For an admirable discussion of this sort of communication failure and many other matters of interest see Percy, "Toward a Triadic Theory of Meaning," *Psychiatry*, Vol. 35 (February 1972), pp. 6–14 et seq. [*Editor's note:* This and all subsequent footnotes to this story are part of the text.]

Does hope reside in the analysis or rather in the piano? As a shrink rather than a piano salesman you would naturally tend to opt for the analysis. But there are differences. The piano salesman can stand behind his product; you, unfortunately, cannot. A Steinway is a known quantity, whereas an analysis can succeed or fail. I don't reproach you for this, I simply note it. (An interesting question: Why do laymen feel such a desire to, in plain language, fuck over shrinks? As I am doing here, in a sense? I don't mean hostility in the psychoanalytic encounter, I mean in general. This is an interesting phenomenon and should be investigated by somebody.)

It might be useful if I gave you a little taste of my own experience of analysis. I only went five or six times. Dr. Behring was a tall thin man who never said anything much. If you could get a "What comes to mind?" out of him you were doing splendidly. There was a little incident that is, perhaps, illustrative. I went for my hour one day and told him about something I was worried about. (I was then working for a newspaper down in Texas.) There was a story that four black teenagers had come across a little white boy, about ten, in a vacant lot, sodomized him repeatedly and then put him inside a refrigerator and closed the door (this was before they had that requirement that abandoned refrigerators had to have their doors removed) and he suffocated. I don't know to this day what actually happened, but the cops had picked up *some* black kids and were reportedly beating the shit out of them in an effort to make them confess. I was not on the police run at that time but one of the police reporters told me about it and I told Dr. Behring. A good liberal, he grew white with anger and said what was I doing about it? It was the first time he had talked. So I was shaken—it hadn't occurred to me that I was required to do something about it, he was right—and after I left I called my then sister-in-law, who was at that time secretary to a City Councilman. As you can imagine, such a position is a very powerful one—the councilmen are mostly off making business deals and the executive secretaries run the office—and she got on to the chief of police with an inquiry as to what was going on and if there was any police brutality involved and if so, how much. The case was a very sensational one, you see; *Ebony* had a writer down there trying to cover it but he couldn't get in to see the boys and the cops had roughed him up some, they couldn't understand at that time that there could be such a thing as a black reporter. They understood that they had to be a little careful with the white reporters, but a black reporter was beyond them. But my sister-in-law threw her weight (her Councilman's weight) around a bit and suggested to the chief that if there was a serious amount of brutality going on the cops had better stop it, because there was too much outside interest in the case and it would be extremely bad PR if the brutality stuff got out. I also called a guy I know pretty high up in the sheriff's department and suggested that *he* suggest to his colleagues that they cool it. I hinted at unspeakable political urgencies and he picked it up. The sheriff's department was separate from the police department but they both operated out of the Courthouse Building and they interacted quite a bit, in the normal course. So the long and short of it was that the cops decided to show the four black kids at a press conference to demonstrate that they weren't really beat all to rags, and that took place at four in the afternoon. I went and the kids looked O.K., except for one whose teeth were out and who the cops said had fallen down the stairs. Well, we all know the falling-down-the-stairs story but the point was the *degree* of mishandling and it was clear that the kids had not been half-killed by the cops, as the rumor stated. They were walking and talking naturally, although scared to death, as who would not be? There weren't any TV pictures because the newspaper people always pulled out the plugs of the TV people, at important moments, in those days—it was a standard thing. Now while I admit it sounds callous to be talking about the degree of brutality being minimal, let me tell you that it was no small matter, in that time and place, to force the cops to show the kids to the press at all. It was an achievement, of sorts. So about eight o'clock I called Dr. Behring at home, I hope interrupting his supper, and told him that the kids were O.K., relatively, and he said that was fine, he was glad to hear it. They were later no-billed and I stopped seeing him. That was my experience of analysis and that it may have left me a little sour, I freely grant. Allow for this bias.

To continue. I take exception to your remark that Susan's "openness" is a form of voyeurism. This remark interested me for a while, until I thought about it. Voyeurism I take to be an eroticized expression of curiosity whose chief phenomenological characteristic is the distance maintained between the voyeur and the object. The tension between the desire to draw near the object and the necessity to maintain the distance becomes a libidinous energy nondischarge, which is what the voyeur seeks.[2]

2. See, for example, Straus, "Shame As a Historiological Problem," in *Phenomenological Psychology* (New York: Basic Books, 1966), p. 219.

The tension. But your remark indicates, in my opinion, a radical misreading of the problem. Susan's "openness"—a willingness of the heart, if you will allow such a term—is not at all comparable to the activities of the voyeur. Susan draws near. Distance is not her thing—not by a long chalk. Frequently, as you know, she gets burned, but she always tries again. What is operating here, I suggest, is an attempt on your part to "stabilize" Susan's behavior in reference to a state-of-affairs that you feel should obtain. Susan gets married and lives happily ever after. Or: There is within Susan a certain amount of creativity which should be liberated and actualized. Susan becomes an artist and lives happily after.

But your norms are, I suggest, skewing your view of the problem, and very badly.

Let us take the first case. You reason: If Susan is happy or at least functioning in the present state of affairs (that is, moving from man to man as a silver dollar moves from hand to hand), then why is she seeing a shrink? Something is wrong. New behavior is indicated. Susan is to get married and live happily ever after. May I offer another view? That is, that "seeing a shrink" might be precisely a maneuver in a situation in which Susan *does not want* to get married and live happily ever after? That getting married and living happily ever after might be, for Susan, the worst of fates, and that in order to validate her nonacceptance of this norm she defines herself to herself as shrink-needing? That you are actually certifying the behavior which you seek to change? (When she says to you that she's not shrinkable, you should listen.)

Perhaps, Dr. Hodder, my logic is feeble, perhaps my intuitions are frail. It is, God knows, a complex and difficult question. Your perception that Susan is an artist of some kind *in potentia* is, I think, an acute one. But the proposition "Susan becomes an artist and lives happily ever after" is ridiculous. (I realize that I am couching the proposition in such terms—"happily ever after"—that it is ridiculous on the face of it, but there is ridiculousness piled upon ridiculousness.) Let me point out, if it has escaped your notice, that what an artist does, is fail. Any reading of the literature[3] (I mean the theory of artistic creation), however summary, will persuade you instantly that the paradigmatic artistic experience is that of failure. The actualization fails to meet, equal, the intuition. There is something "out there" which cannot be

---

3. Especially, perhaps, Ehrenzweig, *The Hidden Order of Art* (University of California Press, 1966), pp. 234–9.

brought "here." This is standard. *I* don't mean bad artists, I mean good artists. There is no such thing as a "successful artist" (except, of course, in worldly terms). The proposition should read, "Susan becomes an artist and lives unhappily ever after." This is the case. Don't be deceived. What I am saying is, that the therapy of choice is not clear. I sympathize. You have a dilemma.

I ask you to note, by the way, that Susan's is not a seeking after instant gratification as dealt out by so-called encounter or sensitivity groups, nude marathons, or dope. None of this is what is going down. "Joy" is not Susan's bag. I praise her for seeking out you rather than getting involved with any of this other idiocy. Her forte, I would suggest, is mind, and if there are games being played they are being conducted with taste, decorum, and some amount of intellectual rigor. Not-bad games. When I take Susan out to dinner she does not order chocolate-covered ants, even if they are on the menu. (Have you, by the way, tried Alfredo's, at the corner of Bank and Hudson streets? It's wonderful.) (Parenthetically, the problem of analysts sleeping with their patients is well known and I understand that Susan has been routinely seducing you—a reflex, she can't help it—throughout the analysis. I understand that there is a new splinter group of therapists, behaviorists of some kind, who take this to be some kind of ethic? Is this true? Does this mean that they do it only when they want to, or whether they want to or not? At a dinner party the other evening a lady analyst was saying that three cases of this kind had recently come to her attention and she seemed to think that this was rather a lot. The problem of maintaining mentorship is, as we know, not easy. I think you have done very well in this regard, and god knows it must have been difficult, given those skirts Susan wears that unbutton up to the crotch and which she routinely leaves unbuttoned to the third button.)

Am I wandering too much for you? Bear with me. The world is waiting for the sunrise.

We are left, I submit, with the problem of her depressions. They are, I agree, terrible. Your idea that I am not "supportive" enough is, I think, wrong. I have found, as a practical matter, that the best thing to do is to just do ordinary things, read the newspaper for example, or watch basketball, or wash the dishes. That seems to allow her to come out of it better than any amount of so-called "support." (About the *chasmus hystericus* or hysterical yawning I don't worry any more. It is masking behavior, of course, but after all, you must allow us our tics. The world is waiting for the sunrise.) What do you do with a patient who finds the world unsatisfactory? The world *is* unsatisfactory; only a fool would deny it. I know that your own ongoing psychic structuralization is still going on—you are thirty-seven and I am forty-one—but you must be old enough by now to realize that shit is shit. Susan's perception that America has somehow got hold of the greed ethic and that the greed ethic has turned America into a tidy little hell is not, I think, wrong. What do you do with such a perception? Apply Band-Aids, I suppose. About her depressions, I wouldn't do anything. I'd leave them alone. Put on a record.[4]

Let me tell you a story.

One night we were at her place, about three a.m., and this man called, another lover, quite a well-known musician who is very good, very fast—a good man. He asked Susan, "Is he there?," meaning me, and she said "Yes," and he said, "What are you doing?," and she said, "What do you think?," and he said, "When will you be finished?," and she said, "Never." Are you, Doctor dear, in a position to appreciate the beauty of this reply, in this context?

What I am saying is that Susan is wonderful. *As is.* There are not so many things around to which that word can be accurately applied. Therefore I must view your efforts to improve her with, let us say, a certain amount of ambivalence. If this makes me a negative factor in the analysis, so be it. I will be a negative factor until the cows come home, and cheerfully. I can't help it, Doctor, I am voting for the piano.

With best wishes,

Questions for Discussion

1. The letter writer's audience is Dr. Hodder. How might Dr. Hodder respond to this letter? What would he make of the concerned boyfriend? The content of his letter? The voice?
2. What appears to be the letter writer's view of himself in relationship to Dr. Hodder? What does his voice tell you about his self-image and his image of Dr. Hodder?
3. The author's real audience is us. How do we respond to

4. For example, Harrison, "Wah Wah," Apple Records, STCH 639, Side One, Track 3.

this letter? How is our response dependent upon our knowledge of the fictional Dr. Hodder's response?

4. Certain sentence structures in this letter tell us a lot about the boyfriend's attitude toward Dr. Hodder. Trace the instances of parentheses and suspended syntax in the letter. How do these affect the letter writer's voice as he presents his case to the psychiatrist?

5. Although the letter writer uses a sophisticated vocabulary, the formality is not consistent nor infused with the dignity and solemnity we associate with serious formal discourse. Yet there is seriousness in this letter as well as sincerity. Where do you take the letter writer seriously? Where do you respect his intentions and concern?

6. How would you compare the voice in the anecdote with the voice in the rest of the letter?

Model III: Stanley Elkin

This final sample is an excerpt from Stanley Elkin's "The Future of the Novel: A View from the Eight-Seated Spaceship."

From time to time, when I was 7 or 8 years old, I had a chance to stay home from school and live the high life, this on the evidence of a slightly elevated temperature, the merit of a marginally swollen gland. It was a sort of willed, maybe even willful hypochondria that did no real harm and drew no real blood but just sufficiently rasped my throat or, in certain acrobatic positions, ached my head to keep me if not exactly honest then at least within the fudged and fuzzy range of a judgment-call credibility, my mom's hung jury, that would not, back in those old polio-fraught days, take on either the risk or responsibility of sending an only child out into the first- or second-grade world when a day or two in quarters might provide if not the cure then perhaps the prevention (a limited, voluntary quarantine back then being a kind of quasi, self-imposed exile, part stylite, part masque of the red death). In any event, there I would be, still in my pj's and all cozed out in the apartment, by the grace of having pleaded my iffy fifthy. All dressed down and nowhere to go and, all comic books read and all radio serials heard, nothing to do.

Except, of course, there were always the dining room chairs. Because there would come a time, often in the late forenoon or the early postprandial, during that part of the day at any rate when my fraction of a degree of fever had broken—"the crisis,"

I believe, was the official medical term we used in those days—and the idea of school, while still not attractive, had, on the scale of things to which I refer, abated upward—at least recess-wise, at least assembly-wise. (I've always been a sucker for a good assembly, or even not such a good one, and enjoyed them even on those occasions when they were called by the principal—there was no public address then, no Big Sister whose voice boomed out at you, like a pilot's on an airplane, from the very walls—for the purpose of reaming out at one time in one place an entire grammar school for the infraction of some rule—certain hooligans didn't obey the patrol boys; those among us raised in barns had chewed gum in class; there was talking in the halls.) This was a time of day conducive to the development of bedsores, to ennui, to, I mean, getting the hell out of bed to begin one's recuperation, to start the blood up again, to play, I mean, with all the toys of one's stuffed and blunted imagination, to have kick in, I mean, without ever having to leave home, some out-of-doors, out-of-body experience. To seek, I mean, after all the hard work of filling the minutes, quarter-hours and hours of that wasted, drowsy day, some crisper, more brisk sense of life.

So I'm at my dining room table, under it, examining the latchwork there, the minimal, limited machinery whose pulled levers permitted the insertion of additional leaves to accommodate company and special occasion, or heighten those lazy Wednesday and Tuesday afternoons of which I speak. This dining room table, this reddish runway, this wooden playground, this long, manipulative mahogany toy. And I'm under it, lost in its carved, ball-and-claw stump forest, supine on the queer, colored grasses of the dark Oriental like a mechanic beneath a car, all the juices of possibility running now, loose, amok even, alerted by some programmed tropism for snug adventure. When I come out it's to arrange, rearrange, the dining room chairs, not just, in our small and, at least in Chicago, practically relationless family, the three for ordinary meals, but pulling away from the walls, too, and from beside our breakfront, the additional unused (at least except for dinner parties or anything more specially occasioned than a poker game) five.

Lining them up into an eight-seated spaceship or, alternating the configuation, into a comet like a comma, riding my frozen, bunched celestials, yippee-yiyo-kaiyay, like The Cowboy From the Furthest North. Did I say there were broom handles poking through the fret of the back of the lead chair? These were the spaceship's controls, the comet's accelerator lever, the joy stick for its brakes. Or did I tell you that blankets hung along the positioned chair-backs like a sort of space laundry, or lined the seats like flying carpet? Did I mention the neatly folded blanket in the commander's cabin at the front of the comet? The bars of soap I dropped on enemy planets? My flashlight and extra batteries? The toolbox for emergency repairs? The purred, back-of-the-throat noises of warp speed, the whishes and whooshes of intergalactic steering? The folded Illinois map by which I negotiated the universe? My just cause? The cookies and milk, raisins and oranges stashed away in the sky furniture?

Because if ever there was an essential trope or basic dynamic of fiction, this is surely it. And if the rest of the novel is like the rest of the novel, its truly essential trope and basic dynamic is *certainly* this—action and respite, tension and release. All rat-a-tat-tat, take-this-you-guys one minute, all cookies and milk the next. *Story,* I mean, life and death followed by remission, by all contented suck-thumb abeyance, gravity defied, the dining room chairs made up into high contingency machines that don't skimp on the cookies and milk. (*Or why are there candy counters in movie theaters? Or why do we watch TV and plays in the dark?*) Story finally—consider the exhalated endings of novels, their sense, happy or otherwise, of frozen ever-afterness—something to go to sleep by—death's mood music. (11–13)

Questions for Discussion

1. Elkin's subject is literary—the nature of fiction. He talks about it in a very sophisticated way and a highly mannered one. Despite the level of vocabulary in places and the long, winding sentences, Elkin's voice is not formal. And despite the looseness of sentence structure and the often hip, inventive vocabulary, his voice isn't easily defined as informal either. It's a wild mix.

   Take a small section of his prose and try making a chart of the vocabulary, categorizing his choices the way I did in discussing the McEnroe essay. What do you find? How does Elkin's mix compare with McEnroe's?

2. Try to describe how his sentences work. Take a few really long ones. How does he make them sound elaborately complex and studied, yet loose and breathless, like someone so bursting with ideas that they just spill into the air, onto the page, like the contents of Hurston's bag?

3. How does Elkin keep his sentences from sheer collapse? By what means does he connect parts of sentences?
4. How does Elkin build emphasis and create rhythm across long sentences so that we hear someone speaking earnestly, someone who has a stake in the subject matter? Try working with two long sentences: Put slash marks where you hear pauses. Underline the words that you hear loudest. And indicate, with arrows pointing up, where you hear the pitch rise; arrows pointing down, where you hear it fall.
5. In the last section, Elkin uses an extended analogy to illustrate his ideas about the nature of fiction. How does he connect the concrete experience with the abstract ideas? That is, how does he link the images of building a spaceship to notions about fiction? How might you argue that the analogy becomes more than a useful illustration, that the story is written as much for its own sake as for the point it serves?
6. Who is Elkin's intended audience? How would you describe his audience's background, interests, and the like? To what degree do you feel included or excluded from this audience? How does that affect your ability to respond with interest and pleasure to his essay?

EXPERIMENTING WITH THE MIX

Your aim in this assignment is to create a mix of tone and level of discourse similar to that in one of the models. As in Chapter 6, you are not writing a formal imitation but a few pages *in the manner of.*

Planning

Begin by choosing a speaker whose voice you admired and would like to experiment with. Although it may be helpful to choose a topic that's in the general subject arena of the model, you don't have to. It's the voice you want to imitate. But to do that, you still need to view the whole writing first: What's the subject? Who's talking? To whom? For what reasons?

Next, try to describe the governing tone, the mix of attitudes in the essay toward the subject, the occasion, the audience. Then find a paragraph that illustrates your description. Read it aloud several times. That will help you internalize the melody and rhythm of the voice. After you've practiced performing the piece, try to determine these things:

1. How the writer mixes vocabulary from different levels of formality
2. How the writer makes sentences—the general pattern of style, length, variation
3. How the writer uses speech rhythms—How far apart are the big stresses, how wide and abrupt are the pitch changes? Where are the pauses? How long do they tend to be? Try marking a few sentences within the paragraph as directed earlier: Put slash marks at significant pauses. Underline the words that get the most stress. Use arrows pointing up for a rise in pitch, pointing down for a fall.
4. What the connection is between the speech rhythms you hear and the style, length, and variation of sentence pattern

Let your work at this representative paragraph serve as a minimodel for the kind of stylistic options available to you in creating a similar voice, a similar set of relationships among speaker, audience, and occasion.

General Subjects Suggested by the Models

Here are the general subject models, if you choose to follow one of them.

Colin McEnroe

Make your topic a personal experience that was frustrating or exasperating. Let it be something that happened far enough in the past or something that has since been resolved pleasantly so that you can reveal in your voice both the exasperation of the experience and some comic distance from it. It's that mix of tone that's entangled in McEnroe's sentences and creates some of the incongruity in vocabulary and the strong rhythms of personal speech.

Donald Barthelme

Try writing a letter of concern to someone in another's behalf. You are trying to assert your own expertise or your knowledge of the person you're concerned about. To create a similar persona, you'll need to mix the tone: genuine concern and presumption, concern and self-indulgence, and self-assertion and arrogance.

If you want to mirror Barthelme more closely, you'll need a tonal mix obvious to a second audience—an eavesdropper who sees the comedy of your errors (in audience awareness) but also sees, behind the comedy, a serious point to be made.

Stanley Elkin
Write an anecdote, a personal experience, that will later serve to illustrate an abstract idea. Give in to the anecdote; that is, write the story as much for its own sake as for the point it serves. Fill the story with concrete details. Then tie the story to an abstract idea, a general point, by using some of the images and words from your story as you make your point.

What to Keep in Mind

After you have chosen a topic and model, write in answer to the following questions:

1. Who are you writing to and for what reasons?
2. From your analytical description of the model, what rhetorical and stylistic guidelines will you use to produce the voice you want heard?

Your Draft

Read your draft out loud and listen to the voice you have produced. To what extent do you believe you have succeeded in achieving your prewriting aims?

Peer Review

Exchange drafts with members of your group. Ask them to respond to the following questions:

1. Who do you hear speaking to you? What role has the writer created for himself or herself?
2. What role has the writer created for the audience?
3. What is the purpose, the occasion?
4. How would you describe the level of discourse?
5. What specific stylistic choices might have given rise to the voice you hear?

6. To what extent do you think the writer succeeded in creating the voice described in his or her prewriting aims?

Revision

In preparing a second draft, compare your own analysis and draft with the analysis offered by your peers: How does your desired effect measure up against what your audience heard? Revise your draft by trying to reconcile your intentions with what your audience heard. After you've completed your final draft, write a short self-evaluation of your successes.

SAMPLE STUDENT ESSAYS
Model I: Tracy Taylor

The first student sample is written by Tracy Taylor. Like Mindy Rettew, whose voice we heard in Chapter 6, Taylor writes about divorce. The model she uses, however, is not William Styron but Colin McEnroe. Side by side, Taylor's and Rettew's essays make an interesting contrast in voice. Included here are also excerpts from Taylor's prewriting aims and her postwriting commentary.

Planning
After working with Colin McEnroe's essay, Taylor wrote the following plan.

Deciding on a topic for my own writing based on Colin McEnroe's essay took some thought. I wanted an experience that had frustrated me, but was far enough in my past that I could joke about it. My parents have been divorced since I was in second grade. Since that time, I've experienced many frustrating and annoying situations. I was the oldest child and really the only one my parents could hope to explain the divorce to. Now that I can look back on those years, I see humor in many of the predicaments I found myself in. Any older (by this I mean, mature) child who has been through his or her parents' divorce could relate to my topic.

More importantly, I would like parents to read my piece and realize what travels through a child's mind. Children might sympathize; parents might, I hope, understand.

As Colin McEnroe did, I will need to portray myself as a close friend—one able to talk frankly to my audience. Since the subject is personal, I will also distance myself when I begin to feel embarrassed. It will be challenging for me to write so personally and, occasionally, loosely. But to appeal to children, I need to sound close. To appeal to parents I need, at times, to sound mature, more formal.

Taylor's Stylistic Guidelines
McEnroe techniques to use:
1. Abrupt changes in diction—formal to informal (works to make the voice personal, yet distant)
2. Shift in pronoun from first person to second person (also works to make voice shift from personal to distant)
3. Exaggerated examples and description
4. Asides, fragments, short sentences—conversational sound

The Essay
It was February 1, 1969. It was a day of joy. Two people were to be joined in holy matrimony and live happily ever after. Law school, two children, and nine years later—forever came. It was the end of a marriage and the beginning of a new life.

The couple was Noreen and Bob Taylor. (Notice the similarity in their name and mine.) They were my parents and as their life together ended, a new life for me began. No more happy Beaver Cleaver life, no Cosbys. I was part of a dysfunctional family. Simply stated, we weren't normal. It's an odd feeling, visiting a parent. But that's what my sister Jen and I had to do. Dad moved out and every other weekend we went to stay with him. Of course, my parents went to court over and over again. Settlement, child support, the proverbial works. Custody included.

The previous arrangement was changed and the court order stated that my parents had joint custody. No big deal for them, but now every two weeks, Jen and I packed our clothes and our books and moved to a new house with a new room, new parent, and new rules. As step-parents entered the picture, things remained the same. Pack and move. Pack and move.

I never saw or heard my parents fight at the end. In fact, in none of my childhood memories, can I catalog arguments. It seemed as if all of a sudden things changed. Just like that.

Kablooey. Questions enter your mind. Why me? Why them? Why us? Why can't things be the way they were? All those stories you hear about kids thinking it's their fault—what did I do?— that wasn't me. I was smarter that that—even at seven. I knew I wasn't the reason for what was happening. I knew it was them. I knew things were different. I knew I hated it. What did I know?

They thought Jen and I should begin sessions with a psychologist. We needed to sort through our emotions and get in touch with our feelings. Never! There was no way I was going to a shrink—and I let them know. I could handle my own feelings and make sense of my life. After all, I was seven.

Then it happened. Mr. Hyde. My parents became monsters. They began to inquire about each other. Not nice questions that when someone asks them, you know the person is genuinely concerned. No, not those. These questions were mean. "Why does he/she do that?" "What is he/she thinking?!" And the comments. The little asides. I heard them all. They wanted a response. They didn't get one. I played dumb. I didn't answer their questions. I ignored them. Ha! Why did they have to do that? You want to scream. "Shut up! Knock it off. I don't want to hear it!"

You feel hurt. And confused. It's like overhearing somebody talking about someone you know or care about, and it's not a compliment. It's as if you yourself were attacked. Why can't they act like grownups? A piece of you seems torn away. At that moment, you want to hate them, but you can't. Part of you dies. It can never be replaced.

You begin to learn something from all of this. Something you will need years from your childhood. You learn how to win. I don't mean win like win a race. I mean win like get what you want. You become good at it. You learn the tricks fast. You manipulate. I hate that word. I hate the fact that I did it. I didn't mean it. You know you are doing something, you just don't know what. Control, rule, threaten, no. Handle. I like that much better.

You learn how to handle the situation. I remember those stupid clogs Jen and I wanted. Mom wouldn't let us have them. Dad did. The presents and the trips. The "favorite parent" routine. They didn't try to buy our love, exactly. They already had it. They just tried to show us that no matter what our lives may look like, they were still dedicated, loving parents.

The school functions were the worst. Why couldn't they sit next to each other. Ok, in the same row? After an exceedingly good performance, you have to face it—the praise and congratulations. Who do you go to first? You had to make sure you allotted equal time to each parent. It was your duty. Other kids in grade school didn't have to worry about that. Why did I? It was a pain in the ass for a little kid. You learn that too.

Still, there were benefits. If you got mad at one parent, you could run away—to the other house. Not too many kids have that option. (But they must have talked at some point. We never did escape the clutches of punishment.) Then Christmas and birthdays. Two celebrations, one at each house. How can you beat that? (Now that I think about it, though, I had to make or buy two presents for them instead of one. That's it! They had a master plan all along. Nah!)

Then things changed again. Dr. Jekyll. My parents stopped asking questions and making comments. Probably because as I grew up, I began to tell them I didn't care and didn't want to listen. Now they talk to each other quite a bit. Although I'm sure it's not for fun. Maybe it's because they have finally overcome the anger and the pain.

They have taught me many valuable lessons. They have raised me to be a considerate, intelligent, and responsible adult. One who can stand up for what she believes; one who is not afraid to voice her opinion. (Although when they see this, they may regret it.) They probably regret the mistakes in their marriage. Maybe not. One thing I am certain of—they do not regret the product.

Taylor's Commentary

After rereading my piece, I am pleasantly surprised. I never write in an informal style, so this experience is new to me. I am happy with the voice I produced on the page. I generally don't vary sentence length much or use extremely short sentences, but I think I've succeeded in my experiment with them here.

I read my essay to my parents and to my sister. Their responses tell me I've succeeded at my purpose. I've captured what my sister and I felt. My voice is a new one. It is informal and conversational. I speak to other children of divorce as if they were my friends. I speak to adults from a position of experience. I also back away from my audience, as McEnroe did, when the subject becomes too personal and too painful by shifting to second-person point of view.

Model II: Meagan Schnauffer

The second student model is written by Meagan Schnauffer. I have included excerpts from her prewriting plans and post-writing commentary.

Planning

My essay is aimed first at students applying to college, and second, to those who have been through the process and would be amused by my account of it. My goal is to describe both the frustration and the humor. To imitate Colin McEnroe, I'll need to incorporate more colloquial than formal vocabulary, yet still use analogies that show educational background. I must seem personal, yet distanced. I must also use exaggerated examples to support my ideas, plus a lot of shifts in voice within and between sentences to capture McEnroe's mix of attitudes toward his subject.

The Essay

During the latter half of my junior year, I thought about applying to college. Who didn't? Eight-five percent of the graduating class was accepted to some postsecondary school. It was easy—even my brother did it. Little did I know that I had inadvertently entered a world where acceptance all rested on a piece of paper, a conversation with someone associated with your chosen school (whether it be the dean of students or the guy who trims the bushes), and a ritual involving candles, a mailbox, and thick envelopes.

For a while, I had to subject myself to the incompetency of guidance counselors hidden in some dungeon where they can't advise you about colleges because they haven't seen the sun in thirty years, let alone a Barron's book. The credibility of the guidance department dwindled with each visit. At my last visit, the counselor looked over my transcript and asked if I had considered secretarial school. Not Harvard, Yale, or Brown. Secretarial school. Then I heard this counselor was responsible for missing a student's deadline and the college admissions department withdrew her application.

Unless you pay someone an absurd amount of money to make you look appealing on paper, you really have to take matters into your own hands if you want to get accepted to anything besides Route 10 Tech. I'm talking University of Virginia, William and Mary, and Bucknell—contacting all of the schools, leaving nothing up to guidance. And even that won't do it. My calculus class tried to help matters by making voodoo dolls of our guidance department, placing matches under their feet and poking various metal objects into their stuffy little bodies to "speed things up."

I finally got all my applications. In order to sound appealing, you have to write, trying to sound like you are not the elephant man or Morton Downey, Jr. You, the prospective student, can become more than a little intolerant. After all, a cocaine addict or a stereotypical jock who doesn't know Stonewall Jackson from Bo Jackson can get into college as long as one has the SAT scores, and the other, talent. However, you, who's planted trees for Earth Day and was secretary for the National Honor Society, have to prove to the omniscient admissions evaluator that you are Martin Luther King, Jr., and Plato and Cindy Brady all rolled into one. By the time you complete about seven applications, you're bound to go a little crazy.

Application: "Father's Place of Work"

You: "Oh great! Another trick question. If I put down that my dad's a physical education teacher, you're going to cheat me out of financial aid. Where will I be then? On the street looking for a dry bench to sleep on? In a rehab center? All because I don't have enough money to shell out for college? DON'T YOU HAVE ANY MERCY?"

Application: "Mother's Place of Work" And if the monotonous typing doesn't get to you, admissions decides to throw you a spit ball, dripping with stress, asking you to respond to an essay question. What nerve! Actually asking you to think! Then you have to sound innovative yet conservative; open, yet reserved; and individual yet not socially outcasted to prevent the admissions evaluator from hurling your application into the stack marked "No way, José."

Some of the most mentally taxing questions appear on college applications: If you had the chance to meet anyone in history, living or dead, who would it be? I don't know about you, but I would prefer the person I meet to be living. I thought it would be a great idea to meet Anonymous. Anonymous is learned in many fields. No matter the subject—science, music, poetry— Anonymous has made some mark in it. But, of course, you can't write that because it's too weird. You have to write about something normal like Napoleon or Newton. Beethoven might even be unacceptable. He wouldn't be able to hear you.

And if your essay is on how many ways to sacrifice a goat, you can assume you're out. Seriously, if you are just a plain old American teenager who once in a while considers joining a convent or the military as a means of discipline (whichever is more suitable at the time), you can probably get into college. I did.

One day last spring, I found myself accepted at nine out of the eleven colleges I applied to. . . .

Schnauffer's Commentary

I was generally pleased with the way my essay turned out. I kept the subject light in most places, used more colloquial than Latinate vocabulary, and used sentence fragments where appropriate. I also switched from first person to second but for a different reason than McEnroe. Where he used second person to distance his reader from a too personal subject, I used it to bring my audience closer to me. I incorporated my audience into the essay because they have had this experience and will probably be entertained.

I focused on two aggravations: guidance counselors and college applications themselves. I added some allusions, as McEnroe did (Stonewall Jackson, Plato) as well as some exaggeration (sounding like Martin Luther King, Jr., Plato, and Cindy Brady). I also imitated McEnroe by having a fit when asked a simple question (Father's Place of Work).

Sometimes McEnroe's voice accidently crept into my essay. I would just write and sentences would flow onto the paper without my having to think about them, such as the paragraph about typing applications. My humor turned out better than I anticipated. I didn't sound sarcastic as much as lighthearted. After revising the paragraph about the guidance department, I could really hear McEnroe's voice coming through, especially the sentence about counselors being trapped in the dark both physically and mentally.

MEASURING YOUR SUCCESS

Even if you don't accomplish all your aims in this assignment, you can't fail. Just trying to imitate another voice is an accomplishment. When you practice imitation, you practice another set of relationships to the world at a given time and place. That gives you another view, another way to think about a subject and an audience. Hearing is a way of seeing. The more voices you hear when you write, the more views you have to explore. When you choose a way of speaking about a particular subject to a particular audience, you are also choosing ideas.

CHAPTER EIGHT

The Voice of the Paragraph

The Organizing Power of Intonation Patterns

So far this text has been about the voice of sentences—how writers make graceful and emphatic sentences that indicate by their patterns and progression who is speaking to whom for what reasons. Voice has been discussed as a way of creating particular relationships among subject, speaker, audience, and occasion. And as a way of providing reading pleasure.

By practicing imitations, you've seen the value too, I hope, of voice as an invention tool, a means of discovering ideas. In fact, voice is a lot of what we mean by *thinking* and *narrating*. As I claimed at the end of Chapter 7, we don't think, then find a voice. We find a voice and then think. Put another way, we speak and fill in the voice patterns with subject matter.

In the introductory chapter, I talked about the values of voice—reading pleasure and the sound of sense. It was pleasure that Chapter 1 emphasized. Here I want to focus exclusively on sense, on the organizing power of voice. Information, as discussed in Chapter 1, is carried both by words and by intonation. For example, how we understand "nice party," "search me," even "sure," depends on the intonation pattern. Beyond the single sentence, voice or intonation patterns can hold whole chunks of discourse together. It is the glue that binds not only the words within a given sentence but also the sentences running across an entire paragraph.

This chapter, then, will be about the voice of the paragraph—

the organizing power of intonation patterns. These patterns control the sense. They control both the possibilities and the significance of it. Without voice, in fact, it's hard to hold things together at all. To discover this truth, you'll find several exercises in how to use voice, rather than overly explicit transitions, to connect ideas from sentence to sentence.

THE RELATIONSHIP BETWEEN SOUND AND SENSE: THREE POSSIBILITIES FOR THE PARAGRAPH

We have not only word and meaning expectations but also expectations about intonation patterns. When sentences confound our expectations of the sound of sense, we accuse the writer of incoherence. It could be argued that intonation, or the *sound* of sense, is a stronger organizing device than sense itself. If there is a meaning conflict between sound and sense, sound may not always win, but it's far more likely to. Sense can lie; intonation rarely can.

Let me demonstrate what I mean by illustrating the three possibilities a paragraph can have.

Paragraph Model I

Sense with Little Sound of Sense

For six years I crouched in the mud, breathing marsh gas and fighting leeches and ticks. You know my study. The Yosemite toads, now extinct, lived in the marsh. The albino leopard frogs, really only tadpoles, were what Richard Wassersug studied. Extinction is a slow process. The frogs had mutated.

Sound of Sense without Sense

You all know my study in depth. Six layers I put into it, six layers of mud, of marsh gas and leeches and ticks and all the rest of it, and what did that get me? What did that get the Yosemite toad? A fat blueberry, that's what. They're all gone. Wiped from the face of the earth. And what of Richard Wassersug's elephant trunks in Nova Scotia? Violinists. Exclusively. What kind of study is that? I'll tell you what kind: a gray one. A year later, he flew to Oslo.

Both Sense and Sound of Sense

You all know my study in Yosemite. Six years I put into it, six years of crouching in the mud and breathing marsh gas and fighting leeches and ticks and all the rest of it, and what did it get me? What did it get the Yosemite toad? Extinction, that's what. They're gone. Wiped from the face of the earth. . . . And what of Richard Wassersug's albino leopard frogs in Nova Scotia? White tadpoles. Exclusively. What kind of mutation is that? . . . I'll tell you what kind: a fatal one. A year later they were gone. (T. Coraghessan Boyle, "Hopes Rise")

Paragraph Model II

Sense without the Sound of Sense

In our culture, a woman's youth ends when experience shows on her face. Cher snarls through her video, "If I Could Turn Back Time," because she's spent mega-thousands on rhinoplasty, cheekplasty, riboplasty. A decade can be gained through cosmetic surgery. Cher doesn't look thirty anymore.

Sound of Sense without the Sense

In our culture, once experience shows on a woman's face, she's through. Thanks to the miracle of plastic, you might get a rice bowl. Look at Cher. She's spent mega-thousands on cars, bowling balls, forests. Even so, you can tell Cher's no beekeeper. Maybe that's why she snarls through her video.

Both Sense and Sound of Sense

In our culture, once experience shows on a woman's face, she's through. Thanks to the miracle of plastic, you might get a decade. Look at Cher. She's spent mega-thousands on rhinoplasty, cheekplasty, riboplasty. Even so, you can tell Cher's no thirty. Maybe that's why she snarls through her video, "If I Could Turn Back Time." (Patricia Volk, "Why I'm Glad I Don't Look Like Michelle Pfeiffer")

WHAT THE MODELS SHOW

The paragraphs included in the second and third examples (in both sets of samples) are held together by intonation patterns, by voice. The sound of sense runs across the sentences, linking the ideas. In the first example in both sets, individual sentences make sense, but connections are missing. And sometimes the wrong information is emphasized within a given sentence, further disconnecting one sentence from another. However, in the second set of paragraphs, the intonation pattern binds even insensible ideas together, making the paragraph sound coherent from sentence to sentence. Intonation patterns are so powerful that they can sometimes make sound of sense more persuasive than sense itself.

Here's how the melody of coherence works in Boyle's piece: You all know _____. What did it get me? What did it get _____? _____, that's what. And what of _____? What kind of _____ is that? I'll tell you: _____.

Here's how it works in Volk's: Once _____, (then) _____. Thanks to _____, you might _____. Look at _____, for instance. Even so, _____. Maybe that's why _____.

These cues provide the sound of sense, the melody of coherence. You could almost hum it. The thinking (subject matter) is what fills in the blanks. Once the intonation patterns are fixed, the paragraph will *sound* sensible even if some of the words inside the patterns are nonsense.

But the reverse is not generally true. If the sound of sense is not there, the paragraph, no matter how sensible the filler within individual sentences, will sound disconnected. The less words are strung on recognizable sentence sounds (to use Robert Frost's phrase), the less connected the sense is. We expect sentences to string together in particular ways—the right words get the emphasis, the important words are placed in the important parts of the sentence, and the logical links are either provided or can be easily provided by the listener.

CLASSROOM ACTIVITY: HEARING VOICE CUES

The following two exercises provide you with voice cues. First fill the blanks with several nonsense words. Then fill them with sense.

Exercise 1: **Voices in the Range of Low to Middle Informality**

    1. If I could _____, it would have been different. If _____, it would have been different. But _____.

How _____, I don't know. All I know _____.
What if _____?

2. A _____? It might have been _____. But I _____. Yes, there was/were _____, but I _____. You don't _____. Not _____. But do you see, it wasn't _____. That's what I can't seem to _____. It wasn't just _____. It was _____. It was _____. Enough to _____. And have you ever _____? I thought not. You begin to get the idea?

As a class, you might decide on a particular topic or subject matter that each of you tries to work sensibly into the blanks of the paragraph models. Or you can each choose your own subject matter. Or try both—your own subject matter and a common subject.

An additional exercise is to remove the sound of sense (the cues I've provided), trying to produce disconnected sentences, those I modeled in the first set of paragraphs in the examples. You may find these hardest to write because your own speaking voice immediately tries to make connections. And yet, paradoxically, disconnected paragraphs are often the main problem for inexperienced writers. Teachers, therefore, spend a great deal of time teaching "organization." Developing an ear for spoken sentences, for intonation sense patterns, may be one cure for paragraph incoherence.

The previous models are examples of informal speech intonations, but the same principle of coherence applies to less informal voices. Let's consider a higher range of intonation pattern, one without the sharp pitch and stress changes of colloquial voices.

Exercise 2: Voices in the Range of Middle to High Informality

Try filling in the blanks of the following paragraphs with sense. After you've worked with a few of them, you might construct your own skeletal models by extracting the filler from a paragraph of your own choosing (Chapters 3, 5, 6, and 7 offer many possibilities). You can also make one up in class.

1. It is not enough to _____, having _____ and having _____ and having _____. It is not enough that _____, and that _____. It is not enough that _____ because _____ and because _____. It is only enough to _____. See how _____, when the _____, (they/it) _____.

2. _____ was glad he/she had _____. They were _____ or _____. Other _____ were _____. And his/her _____, although _____, were no less _____. It was not important that _____. What mattered was that _____.

3. After _____, we _____. It is as if we _____. It is difficult even to _____ for (or because, since) _____. Yet _____.

4. When was it that _____ and that _____? It had to be _____, a/an _____. When was it that _____? Was it _____?

5. He could understand _____. And being _____ had helped him when _____. He would be certain to see that, _____, the _____ was not _____ but _____: The _____ was not quite _____; the _____ was wrong. It was curious to _____ and to feel _____.

6. How easily the _____ change to _____. _____ become _____ and yet not _____. The _____ becomes another _____. The _____, the _____, the _____, these are the sources of _____.

Exercise 3: **Creating Your Own Models**

Try constructing your own paragraph example of the second paragraph model (sound of sense without sense). Then take out the nonsense words and fill the paragraph with sense.

AVOIDING A FALSE CURE FOR DISCONNECTEDNESS

Writers who can't hear intonation patterns, and who therefore often write disconnected sentences, tend to solve the incoherence problem either by repeating information from one sentence in the next or by using too many explicit, logical transitions. The apparent problem disappears, but a new one surfaces: wordiness. The fundamental problem, however, the one that gives rise to the others, remains—no strong speech rhythms. Connections, but no voice.

An Illustration

> Given even odds, most people would not gamble. They wouldn't gamble even if gambling meant they would gain much more than they'd lose. The reason they don't gamble is that they don't like big risks. Similarly, businesses don't like to gamble because they want to make safe choices. Consequently, they put off decisions that should be made. Nevertheless, decisions must be made whether they turn out to be good or bad. The best way to learn how to make decisions is by making them.

The simple vocabulary suggests an informal, conversational voice. But it is only a suggestion—there are no musical cues, no strong speech rhythms, to make that sound heard on the page. Yet the paragraph is perfectly coherent; its organization clear, its sentences connected. The paragraph is organized like this: topic, cause, topic (repeated in reference to different incident), cause (repeated), conclusion. Sentences are all linked with transitions. But notice how much overlap exists from one sentence to another.

Now listen to the same paragraph with fewer explicit connections (through logical transitions or repetition) and heavier stresses on important information (underlined).

> Given even odds, most people would not gamble, even to gain much more than they'd lose. They <u>just don't like</u> big risks. Businesses don't like to gamble <u>either</u> because they <u>too</u> want to make safe choices. Consequently, some decisions that <u>should</u> be made are <u>put off.</u> But whether they are good or bad, decisions <u>must</u> be made. And the <u>best</u> way to learn <u>how</u> is by <u>making</u> them.

Better? Listen to the paragraph again, this time with even fewer explicit links, fewer words, fewer steps in argument (organization).

Given even odds, most people would not gamble. Even to
gain much more than they'd lose. They just don't like big risks.
Businesses are not much different. They want to make safe
choices. So some decisions that should be made are put off. But
good or bad, decisions must be made. And the best way to learn
how is by making them. (Julie O'Neill)

In the final sample paragraph, the sound of sense (intonation)
is especially strong; it's heard. What makes it heard is largely
ellipsis, since, as I've explained in earlier chapters, readers make
up for what isn't there by stressing what is. That stress and accompanying change in pitch make sentences sound like speech.
Economy alone can create strong speech rhythms. In the sample
paragraph, it is achieved through ellipsis: the fewest words
necessary, and the fewest steps in argument (short sentences,
fragments). Punctuated sentences (as opposed to grammatical
sentences) emphasize information. They tell the reader, "This is
important enough to earn its own sentence space, so stress it."
    Here is the paragraph again, this time with the omitted ma-
terial in brackets and the stressed words underlined so that you
can hear how your own voice not only connects ideas but also
makes the paragraph sound like spoken conversation,

> Given even odds, most people would not gamble. [They
> wouldn't gamble] _Even_ to gain much more than they'd lose. [The
> reason is that] they just _don't like_ big risks. [new topic here—
> stress] _Businesses_ [don't like to gamble either and so] are not
> _much different_. [Because] _They_ [too] want to make safe choices.
> So [no ellipsis, but the smallest possible connector] _some_ deci-
> sions that _should_ be made are _put off_. But [whether they are]
> _good or bad_, decisions must be made. And the _best_ way to learn
> _how_ [to make decisions] is by _making_ them.

Listen to the rest of this piece. It's short and it illustrates further points about the connecting power of intonation patterns.
(I've numbered the paragraphs for later reference.)

1   Given even odds, most people would not gamble. Even to
gain much more than they'd lose. They just don't like big risks.
Businesses are not much different. They want to make safe
choices. So some decisions that should be made are put off. But
good or bad, decisions much be made. And the best way to learn
how is by making them.

2   What influences our decisions? Experience. Intuition. And advice. They affect our choices. And diminish the risks.

3   Take experience. Knowledge gained from experience is best. We all remember what happened to us the last time we made a choice. If the choice was a good one, we feel ready to make the next decision. If it wasn't so good, we're not so sure. Either way, we rely on experience to help us decide.

4   Then there's intuition. It's not as chancey as it sounds. A hunch is based on experience too. Subconscious information. Just below the surface. Without realizing it, we "know" more about a situation than the facts at hand. Most people won't claim to be clairvoyant. But they will "see" things that defy logic. What they call a hunch is really information from some other level of awareness. They "feel" a decision is right or wrong, even though they can't explain why.

5   Finally, listening to advice can help better the odds. A second opinion can confirm our choice. Or help us see problems we've missed. Without feedback, the risk is greater.

6   It's hard to make a good decision every time. No one can guarantee it. There are no "sure things." Decisions involve risks. Opportunities and profits are the rewards. (Julie O'Neill)

Analysis of Voice Cues

In paragraph 2, speech rhythms are created by typographical cues—questions, short units. When we hear a question, we expect answers and use our "answer" intonation when we get to them. For example, after "What influences our decisions?" we all hear the short answers the same way—the same pitch, stress, and duration of sound. The intonation is formulaic. After "And advice" we expect elaboration. That's the way it is with short answers—writers usually go on a bit about them. And so our expectations about paragraphs influence our intonation of "They affect our choices." Placed as a separate unit, the last punctuated sentence, "And diminish the risks," gets the intonation of parenthesis or afterthought.

In paragraph 3, the very locution "Take experience" is formulaic. We all hear that sentence the same way. It has built-in intonation. The same is true for the if–then sentences that follow. And "either way."

Paragraph 4 begins with "then," but what we supply is "a

second factor that influences our decision making is." Thankfully, the writer does not supply it for us. It's one of those mechanical transitions we have learned to make that does no more than state the obvious, waste space, and turn speech into silent print. Interestingly, the sentence that begins "Most people won't claim," and the one right after it, really belong after the first sentence, "Then there's intuition." The subject matter demands that they occur after sentence 1. But the voice makes it acceptable to keep them where they are. The intonation pattern runs so smoothly across the sentences that we don't hear a snag in the sense. We might, though, if the writer did not have such a well-tuned ear for the rhythms of speech.

The whole piece is written for the ear. It's minimalist art: few pieces, but every one placed in exactly the right spot. It's like a sketch of a duck in which the artist uses only four lines, each suggesting the skeletal shape underlying all fuller renditions of the bird. Or it's like Count Basie's piano playing: one note every couple of beats, sketching in the melody progression and chord changes. As practical prose, it's clear and clean—no noise cluttering the air space.

CLASSROOM ACTIVITIES: DEPENDING ON VOICE MORE, EXPLICIT TRANSITIONS LESS
Paragraph Pattern I: Narrative

Write a paragraph that follows a simple narrative pattern: This happened, then that, then that (and so on), conclusion. As you write, build in lots of overlap from one sentence to another and very explicit transitions.

Next, write two more versions of the same paragraph, each one with fewer repetitions and transitions. Finally, if you haven't already done so, write a version that you think has the fewest possible explicit links without collapsing into disconnection (like those first model paragraphs in the examples: sense without sound of sense).

The following samples should show you how to proceed.

Sample: Version 1

As I walked down the road to the mailbox, a big yellow bird hopped across my path. After the yellow bird hopped across my path, an orange mangy cat took off after the bird. Following the mangy cat that took off after the bird was a pit bull that was the size of a young calf, and it seemed that its day was suddenly made. But its day was not made, because behind the pit bull that was chasing the cat was a wolf running sideways and cleverly disguised as a bush. After I noticed the wolf running sideways, I wondered if a painted train tunnel with disappearing tracks would be next. And after I wondered that, I wondered which of the animals wouldn't make it through the tunnel. The events were so strange that I decided to turn around and go home.

Sample: Version 2

As I walked down the road to the mailbox, a big yellow bird hopped across my path. Then an orange mangy cat took off after the bird. Taking up the rear was a pit bull, the size of a young calf, its day suddenly made. But it only seemed that way because further back, behind the pit bull, was a wolf running sideways, cleverly disguised as a bush. After I saw that, I wondered if a painted train tunnel with disappearing tracks would be next. I didn't want to know which of the animals wouldn't make it through. Events were so strange that I turned back to the house.

Sample: Version 3

As I walked down the road to the mailbox, a big yellow bird hopped across my path. Then, an orange mangy cat. A pit bull, the size of a young calf, suddenly took up the rear. Its day was made. Or so it seemed. Further back, a wolf was running sideways, cleverly disguised as a bush. What's next? A painted train tunnel with disappearing tracks? Who won't make it through? Enough. I turned back to the house.

Paragraph Pattern II: Miniessay in Exposition

Write a paragraph that follows this organization model:

1. Topic sentence
2. Elaboration
3. Illustration
4. Conclusion

As you write, build in massive overlap and explicit connections from one sentence to another. (See my first example of Julie O'Neill's first paragraph.)

Next, write two more versions of that paragraph, each one with fewer repetitions (overlap of material from one sentence to another) and fewer explicit connections between sentences. Finally, if you haven't already done so, try to write a version that operates on the fewest possible explicit connections, or even none, but relies heavily on sound-of-sense connections. That is, try to make connections through intonation patterns rather than through explicit transitions.

Consider the directions for economy that were listed earlier: ellipsis, fewest words necessary, fewest steps in argument (through short sentences or fragments). Consider also built-in formulas for intonation, those you have discovered in this chapter and those you can recall from spoken conversations. For added professional help, reread the essays by Patricia Volk, Colin McEnroe, and others in Chapters 3, 6, and 7. There are plenty of speech melodies to draw from in the professional samples.

Writing Against the Voice

As a final classroom activity, select one paragraph from two different professional writers in Chapters 3, 6, or 7. Each paragraph should make use of ellipsis, short sentences or fragments, and strong conversational rhythms (like the Boyle piece quoted in this chapter).

Rewrite each paragraph, supplying the omitted words and removing the conversational rhythms. Can you still hear two different voices speaking to you? Or do both paragraphs sound the same? How do you account for differences or sameness?

ORGANIZATION AND THE PARAGRAPH

As organizational models, paragraphs are often presented as miniessays: a topic sentence, an elaboration of the topic, an illustration, and a conclusion. That's the most common structure. But paragraphs can follow any pattern of logic. In some cases, blocks of discourse are broken into paragraphs simply for readability. It's visually hard for readers to take in a long, dark page of print. So most writers offer white space by indenting at a logical juncture in the text. Paragraphs are, for the most part, a printer's invention anyway. Readers don't pay a whole lot of attention to paragraphing—unless they suspect disconnectedness, or unless they're having trouble holding ideas together.

The usual way of curing disconnectedness is to send the writer off to a handbook on paragraphing to learn some useful models. The models generally teach writers a logic they already have and preclude the possibility of discovering other means of development. That is, paragraphs can follow as many ways of rational thinking as are imaginable, given what we have to say. And not all those ways are linear. In some of the models I created in this chapter, the paragraphs progress in a nonlinear way. For example, the voice tests an idea, halts, corrects, questions, moves forward, concludes, questions the conclusion, and remains indecisive. Nor are paragraphs necessarily miniessays, as I explained above.

Perhaps a more practical and, ultimately, liberating way of curing disconnectedness is ear-training lessons—listening to the tunes of speech, the intonation patterns we use to connect our thoughts in conversation. The next step is using those patterns as the skeleton of thinking: Find a voice, then think. That sentence brings us full circle, back to the introduction of this chapter.

CHAPTER NINE

Your Voice and Your Audience

WHERE WE'VE BEEN

I want to repeat some information from the beginning of this text because it is important, because you may have lost sight of it by now, and because it has everything to do with thinking about audience.

Voice, as it was defined in the introductory chapter, is the sum effect of our rhetorical and stylistic choices. And it is created by the act of writing itself. We've been discovering how certain combinations of stylistic features might help us make particular speech patterns that reveal our intended relationship to subject, audience, and occasion.

But as we strive to discover and communicate our private relationship to the world, that same world pressures us to conform—to please. Earlier, I claimed we must live with the tension between what pleases the writer and what pleases the audience. It's part of what it means to be an individual and a member of a community. Every day, our voices are spoken and heard, written and read, within that tension. What writers generally attain is an uneasy balance: pleasing themselves in one instance, pleasing audience in another. That can be bad or good, depending on the writer, the subject, the audience, and the occasion. Usually what pleases you will please your audience. But if there's a conflict, you'll simply have to make a choice. Pleasing audiences is part of a writer's skill. Creating voices is how it's done.

Although many professional writers modify their voices to indicate a change in their relationship to audiences, their general stylistic habits tend to remain consistent. So their voices may change, but not wildly from one rhetorical situation to another. They tend to be recognizable. For the most part, only certain qualities change. As you develop and mature as a writer, you will probably notice similarities too, whether you are speaking formally or informally, to one kind of audience or another.

As a later student sample in this chapter shows, William Faulkner's voice is similar in different rhetorical contexts because he doesn't radically change his stylistic habits. He may be literary and eloquent in one, ironic in another, straightforward and funny in a third. These are differences in quality; but because the *general* stylistic patterns are consistent across his writing, they are not differences in nature. And so we recognize the same speaker in all the examples. We don't say to ourselves, here's writer X; here's Y; here's Z. We say that here Faulkner feels this way; here that way. Here he's speaking to this audience; here, that.

In other words, as we modify our voices to the needs of different audiences and occasions, we don't necessarily create entirely new ones. The point is not that we can't or even that we don't want to some times, but that we usually don't have to. Modification may be all that's necessary.

In the preceding chapters, you have been experimenting with various voices, inventing subjects, occasions, and audiences in the process. You have also been practicing different levels of formality. By analyzing the speech characteristics in the examples, by imitating others, and by experimenting on your own, you have begun, I hope, to discover how to create and control a voice on the page.

WHERE WE'RE GOING: A SHIFT IN PERSPECTIVE

This chapter asks you to consider the skills you have been learning from a different perspective. In previous chapters, you discovered how certain sets of style features give rise to a particular kind of voice, and how they evoke certain discourse situations. That is, a particular way of speaking suggests particular relationships: the writer to subject; the writer to language; the writer to occasion; and the writer to audience. But the opposite often happens for experienced writers: certain discourse situations evoke certain sets of style features. Particular relationships suggest a particular way of speaking.

When both of these are clearly conceived, your writing will be persuasive. That is, you will persuade others that a real person is speaking, one with something at stake, who therefore is worthy of interest. When readers believe you take care of your ideas and your audience, they are most likely to give you a hearing, whether they finally agree or disagree with your views. It is this kind of persuasion I am talking about.

GOALS AND MEANS

Let's listen to three writers, each speaking to different audiences on different occasions. The first selections are by Abraham Lincoln: the Gettysburg Address, his Second Inaugural Address, and a letter to Joseph Hooker, appointing him head of the Army of the Potomac. The second set of selections is written by Julie O'Neill, an office manager at a small architectural design firm, for whom writing is a part of her job as well as a pleasure. Included are some self-expressive pieces, personal letters, and business writing (minutes of a meeting, a memo, a letter). The third set is written by Mary Blewett, an English professor. It is a series that explores a problem within different contexts and ends with a letter to a student.

The main purpose of this chapter is to examine the degree to which some writers modify their voices for different audiences and occasions. An unrelated, but interesting, fact about writing also emerges in the samples of Mary Blewett's writing. She shows how the process of invention is often messy and goes through various drafts before a writer discovers what to say in what voice to a particular audience.

As you work through this chapter, you'll have opportunities to discuss the differences you hear in the quality of voice as each writer modifies his or hers in response to a particular audience or occasion. The chapter ends with two suggestions for writing:

a critical analysis in which you discuss three different pieces
by the same author writing to different audiences; and a second piece in which you demonstrate your learning by writing
about the same subject to different audiences and for different
occasions.

ADDRESSING DIFFERENT
AUDIENCES: THREE WRITERS
MAKING CHOICES
Writer 1: Abraham Lincoln

The Gettysburg Address

First, let me set the scene for Lincoln's address delivered at the
dedication of the cemetery at Gettysburg on November 19, 1863.
At 11 a.m., Lincoln rode on horseback across the battlefield in a
procession to the new cemetery just outside of Gettysburg. Dead
horses were still on the field (the battle fought but four months
ago), and the graves near the speakers' stand were only partially
filled. Edward Everett, the main speaker, delayed the ceremony
because he was late. Everett spoke for two hours. Then the Bal-
timore Glee Club sang a dirge. After that, Lincoln was introduced. He had been invited only to make some remarks.

People in the audience became restless and hungry during
Everett's long speech (he talked until 2 p.m.), and many walked
off to look at the battlegrounds. Most people wanted to see Lincoln rather than hear him speak. He spoke for only two minutes. By the time the audience began listening, the president
had stopped. Applause was polite. No journals or newspapers
praised the speech, and Lincoln himself thought it a failure. In
the North, the thrill of victory at Gettysburg was over before
the soldiers who had died there were reinterred in the new cemetery. As far as most in the Atlantic states were concerned, the
important battles were fought in Virginia.

With this background in mind, we can turn to Lincoln's
speech.

> Four score and seven years ago our fathers brought forth on
> this continent, a new nation, conceived in Liberty, and dedicated
> to the proposition that all men are created equal.
> Now we are engaged in a great civil war, testing whether that
> nation, or any nation so conceived and so dedicated, can long

endure. We are met on a great battle-field of that war. We have come to dedicate a portion of that field, as a final resting place for those who here gave their lives that that nation might live. It is altogether fitting and proper that we should do this.

But, in a larger sense, we can not dedicate—we can not consecrate—we can not hallow—this ground. The brave men, living and dead, who struggled here, have consecrated it, far above our poor power to add or detract. The world will little note, nor long remember what we say here, but it can never forget what they did here. It is for us the living, rather, to be dedicated here to the unfinished work which they who fought here have thus far so nobly advanced. It is rather for us to be here dedicated to the great task remaining before us—that from these honored dead we take increased devotion to that cause for which they gave the last full measure of devotion—that we here highly resolve that these dead shall not have died in vain—that this nation, under God, shall have a new birth of freedom—and that government of the people, by the people, for the people, shall not perish from the earth.

Questions for Discussion

1. Lincoln addresses both the past and the future. His theme is twofold: honor for the dead and patriotism. How does Lincoln's use of metaphor unify those themes? And how do elegy and patriotism affect word choice?

2. What does Lincoln's use of the word *proposition* tell us about his relationship to language and to the subject, democracy?

3. What pronouns does Lincoln repeat many times? What is he trying to emphasize, particularly in context with the often repeated *here?* Does he repeat too much?

4. What is the ratio of Anglo-Saxon diction to Latinate diction (not counting repetitions)? What does it tell you about Lincoln's speech habits? Where is each type of diction most effective, given his purpose, the audience, and the occasion?

5. What rhetorical patterns listed in Chapter 4 do you notice in his sentences? Note in particular various uses of repetition, both sound repetitions and grammatical structures. How do these affect his voice? His message?

6. What sentence structure does Lincoln rely on—loose or periodic? How does that affect his voice? His purpose?
7. How many sentences include people rather than abstractions as the grammatical subject? How many sentences have active verbs?

Second Inaugural Address, March 4, 1865

Fellow-countrymen: At this second appearing to take the oath of the presidential office, there is less occasion for an extended address than there was at the first. Then a statement, somewhat in detail, of a course to be pursued, seemed fitting and proper. Now, at the expiration of four years, during which public declarations have been constantly called forth on every point and phase of the great contest which still absorbs the attention, and engrosses the energies of the nation, little that is new could be presented. The progress of our arms, upon which all else chiefly depends, is as well known to the public as to myself; and it is, I trust, reasonably satisfactory and encouraging to all. With high hope for the future, no prediction in regard to it is ventured.

On the occasion corresponding to this four years ago, all thoughts were anxiously directed to an impending civil war. All dreaded it—all sought to avert it. While the inaugural address was being delivered from this place, devoted altogether to *saving* the Union without war, insurgent agents were in the city seeking to destroy it without war—seeking to dissolve the Union, and divide effects, by negotiation. Both parties deprecated war; but one of them would make war rather than let the nation survive; and the other would accept war rather than let it perish. And the war came.

One eighth of the whole population were colored slaves, not distributed generally over the Union, but localized in the Southern part of it. These slaves constituted a peculiar and powerful interest. All knew that this interest was, somehow, the cause of the war. To strengthen, perpetuate, and extend this interest was the object for which the insurgents would rend the Union, even by war; while the government claimed no right to do more than to restrict the territorial enlargement of it. Neither party expected for the war, the magnitude, or the duration, which it has already attained. Neither anticipated that the cause of the conflict might cease with, or even before, the conflict itself should cease. Each looked for an easier triumph, and a result less fundamental and astounding. Both read the same Bible, and pray to the same God; and each invokes His aid against the other. It may seem strange that any men should dare to ask a just God's assistance in wringing their bread from the sweat of other men's faces; but let us judge not that we be not judged. The prayers of both could not be answered; that of neither has been answered fully. The Almighty has his own purposes. "Woe unto the world because of offences! for it must needs be that offences come; but woe to that man by whom the offence cometh!" If we shall suppose that American Slavery is one of those offences which, in the providence of God, must needs come, but which, having continued through His appointed time, He now wills to remove, and that He gives to both North and South, this terrible war, as the woe due to those by whom the offence came, shall we discern therein any departure from those divine attributes which the believers in a Living God always ascribe to Him? Fondly do we hope—fervently do we pray—that this mighty scourge of war may speedily pass away. Yet, if God wills that it continue, until all the wealth piled by the bondman's two hundred and fifty years of unrequited toil shall be sunk, and until every drop of blood drawn with the lash, shall be paid by another drawn with the sword, as was said three thousand years ago, so still it must be said "The judgments of the Lord are true and righteous altogether." With malice toward none; with charity for all; with firmness in the right, as God gives us to see the right, let us strive on to finish the work we are in; to bind up the nation's wounds; to care for him who shall have borne the battle, and for his widow and his orphan—to do all which may achieve and cherish a just and lasting peace, among ourselves, and with all nations.

Questions for Discussion

1. What stylistic similarities do you find between the Gettysburg Address and this inaugural address? Given your answers to the first set of questions, what identifies this speech as Lincoln's?

   To consider the differences between the two speeches and to see how Lincoln modifies his voice to occasion and audience, you need to know the purpose of the Second Inaugural Address: It is primarily a plea for peace. (The question on everyone's mind, remember, is this: What's going to happen after the war? Will the North want revenge?) Lincoln needs to find a way to neutralize blame directed at the South, the North, and himself. That purpose affects his language choices.

2. Contrast the two speeches regarding the use of people versus abstractions as grammatical subjects. Where does Lincoln avoid using human agents as subjects in this speech?
3. How does Lincoln's use of verbs in the first part of this speech differ from that of the Gettysburg Address?
4. How do you account for the stylistic differences you note in your answers for questions 2 and 3? What has Lincoln accomplished in the shift of style?
5. Although Lincoln assigns responsibility for the war to both sides in paragraph 2 and the early sentences of paragraph 3, he has been setting the stage for a new character in the story. Who is it, and how does Lincoln manage the shift, rhetorically and stylistically?

Letter to General Joseph Hooker, January 26, 1863

Again, let me set the scene. After removing McClellan in November of 1862, Lincoln appointed Burnside as commander of the Army of the Potomac. Burnside was defeated at Fredericksburg. In December, Burnside asked to be removed from duty. Lincoln then named Hooker, known as "Fighting Joe." Military morale was very low by then—desertion was high; recruitment, nearly impossible. Hooker disagreed with Lincoln on both army and government administration. While in Burnside's army, Hooker, then a corps commander, conspired to have Burnside relieved from his post. And it was said that Hooker thought the country needed a dictator. Lincoln appointed him as commander of the Army of the Potomac, but he didn't trust him much. As it turned out, Hooker was in charge for only one battle. He was defeated at Chancellorsville, just outside of Fredericksburg. Losses were heavy and the whole Union army retreated.

Here is Lincoln's letter.

Major General Hooker:

I have placed you at the head of the Army of the Potomac. Of course I have done this upon what appear to me to be sufficient reasons. And yet I think it best for you to know that there are some things in regard to which, I am not quite satisfied with you. I believe you to be a brave and a skillful soldier, which, of course I like. I also believe you do not mix politics with your profession, in which you are right. You have confidence in yourself, which is a valuable, if not an indispensable quality. You are ambitious, which, within reasonable bounds, does good rather than harm. But I think that during Gen. Burnside's command of the Army, you have taken counsel of your ambition, and thwarted him as much as you could, in which you did a great wrong to the country, and to a most meritorious and honorable brother officer. I have heard, in such a way as to believe it, of your recently saying that both the Army and the Government needed a Dictator. Of course it was not *for* this but in spite of it, that I have given you the command. Only those generals who gain successes, can set up dictators. What I now ask of you is military success, and I will risk the dictatorship. The government will support you to the utmost of its ability, which is neither more nor less than it has done and will do for all commanders. I much fear that the spirit which you have aided to infuse into the Army, of criticising their Commander, and witholding confidence from him, will now turn upon you. I shall assist you as far as I can, to put it down. Neither you, nor Napoleon, if he were alive again, could get any good out of an army, while such a spirit prevails in it.

And now, beware of rashness. Beware of rashness, but with energy, and sleepless vigilance, go forward, and give us victories.

> *Yours very truly*
> *A. Lincoln*

Questions for Discussion

1. In appointing Joseph Hooker as commander, Lincoln has his reservations. How does he handle the rhetorical problem of expressing both praise and dissatisfaction?
2. Although this discourse is directed to one person instead of an entire nation, it shares some of the stylistic qualities that, in their combined effect, identify the voice as Abraham Lincoln's. What common features of his voice do you recognize in this letter?
3. How does Lincoln's attitude toward Hooker's behavior affect his tone, and how is that tone heard through particular stylistic choices?

Writer 2: Julie O'Neill

Self-Expression

The following selections are written by Julie O'Neill. They are arranged according to audiences—from private to public. The number of samples may strike you at first as too many, but they illustrate what only a few cannot: the often subtle modifications writers make as they switch roles, audiences, and occasions. We rarely have the opportunity to view these habits so closely.

The first example is a collage of set pieces held together by the title: "For Your Information." It is written first for herself, then for a very private audience—one that is particularly attracted to bare, elliptical prose rhythms. In other words, it is directed secondarily to those who share her own aesthetic appreciation for one kind of sentence making.

FOR YOUR INFORMATION

Dear Peg,

Here are the notes from class. You'll see I make two kinds. Let me explain. Right down the center of the page? Those are the facts. You'll need to read them first, to make some sense. Then, when you have the facts, look on the left. The tiny notes? The second kind I make? You don't need those. I do.

*   *   *   *

Closing a door is a signal that something else is going on. Like a whisper—louder than a shout. The trick is not to get the signals crossed.

*   *   *   *

Music is an art which exists in time. Dance moves it through space. Basil picked the music, and Jenny made it move. I never danced; just watched her perfect answers to the tap of Basil's stick on old wood floors. She'd memorize the movements with her hands. I asked about that once. "My hands have movements for the words," she'd said. "Like this," she motioned as she showed me how.

The night she danced a pas de deux with Marc, they must have gestured sultry, windy words.

*   *   *   *

When I was four I got a bike from France. I didn't know where France was, only Sears, and I couldn't ride the bike. I loved it even though it had no brakes. My father held me on the seat and pushed. I wobbled a few feet before I fell.

On Holy Saturday it was quite warm. My mother always

curled our hair that day. With my hair wound up in twenty fat pincurls I slid away and learned to ride that bike. In two weeks I turned five.

Janet rode it too when she was five. We raced around the block, the two of us. I was nine then, so naturally I won. Then I went back, to see what slowed her down. She'd gone too fast, and turning, hit a rock. She didn't know me: I went howling home. She called me from the hospital to say she had her own TV, and that her nurse's name was Julie too.

*   *   *   *

Hal Kemp played hot music to keep from catching cold. Hal had a slow smooth drawl. When the band played "Breezy Rhythm" the crowd approved. Maxine Grey, dressed in sequins and Chanel, stepped up to the baby grand. She sang with a toothy smile. Skinny Inness kept the beat for slide trombones, a clarinet, the trumpets, and three sax. Maxine, all glitter and perfume, smiled "I'm building up to an awful letdown. I'm—falling in love with you."

*   *   *   *

The Pawnees treated colic by massage. They used an ointment made from buffalo fat, mixed with dried seeds from the black rattlepod. And Incas used the ointments of the sea. Dried algae and valerian leaves. The Cherokees, right half the time, applied warmed hands for sprains; the other half for snakebites, with no relief from those. But among the Illinois, said Binneteau, the shamans sang each day to manitous.

*   *   *   *

Dear Mom,
    I lost my key. Please let me in.

The following piece is a personal narrative. It's partially fictionalized. How does it compare with the first piece?

SMOKE AND MIRRORS

When Nick called yesterday I was surprised, since we hadn't parted friends. He owed me money, among other things. He wanted a favor, but then he always did. For awhile we spoke in polite conventions. How have you been; and how is the job; I'm just fine; the kids have grown so. Tapping out all that small talk, remembering a warm night in May, the porch door open and the fragrance of the night prematurely sweet.

Nick used to read Rilke to me. And I, fully conscious, chose to ignore the signs.

Paula Modersohn-Becker died quite suddenly, age thirty-one. She had a daughter, three weeks old. And there was Elsbeth, her husband Otto's child. On Easter Sunday in 1902 she prepared a roast of veal and wrote in her diary: "Marriage removes the illusion, deeply imbedded previously, that somewhere there is a soulmate. . . ."

Every now and then, though less often these days, I am troubled by a certain mystery. I used to be unable to fall asleep if I thought of it at bedtime. Occasionally, I still wake up in the night, trying to arrange my thoughts. Here is what happened, as far as I recall. When Ray wrote from London, it was July of '81. He'd left Manhattan after the fireworks. The letter was from Queen Elizabeth Hall. He sent a sketch of London Tower and a note to meet him there. He signed it with love, and an "X" which meant a kiss. It just so happened that this letter moved me. And it also just so happened that I was broke. But in 1981 the price of gold was sky high, and I had no sentimental ties to precious metals. What I think I did was this. I gathered up a few things of value, two chains, my wedding ring, and thirty francs, Swiss. I remember putting them into an envelope, plain white, and stuffing it into my bag. I had a busy day that day. And the next, and the next after that. Things kept up like that for a while, and I guess a lot of time passed by. It's all so blurry now. I never sold the jewelry, and I never flew to London. Ray wrote from Paris. And from Amsterdam. From Oslo. Hamburg. And Rome. He was home in Melbourne a year after the fireworks.

I found all his letters. All his envelopes. But I seem to have lost mine, the one with the gold. It simply vanished along with my plans. When I wake up at night, trying to work it out, I can't seem to remember the details. Sometimes I dream of a place I haven't searched yet and I get up to look there just in case.

From *The Lady's Guide to Perfect Gentility,* 1856:
"*Sir:*
Surely there must have been something in my behaviour toward you, upon which you have set a misconstruction. Of what it consisted I am wholly unconscious. . . ."

Jody's voice is so lovely. I listen to her speak for the pleasure of the sound. Her eyes are as lovely as her words. They punctuate her phrases. A pause, a glance, a pause. You hardly note the process. It's the effect that knocks you out. At this, she is an artist, though I do not think she'd see it quite that way.

When I put her on the bus to L.A. she had two backpacks and Paco's guitar. She wore one pack in the conventional way; the others she used to balance, sort of, one in the bend of each arm. We hugged goodbye.

She didn't stay long in L.A. She delivered the guitar, and moved on to Leon, slightly less burdened. The truth was, in Leon, Jody was not so free. In Spanish her voice was as lovely as English. But in the small Mexican town, her blue eyes were not understood. It was a little difficult, she wrote, to socialize. I could hear her eyes right there, parenthetically adding the phrase, "Forgive me. I'm lonely." She'd found a job teaching English and a radio station that played "White Christmas." Both had reduced her to tears. The tears I did not hear, but say, splashed in the tiny margin of the page. "Take care. Be happy," she glanced.

For nearly a year after that she did not write. I continued to look for letters until my birthday passed in May, and I finally gave up, seeing it was useless.

Personal Letters

The following piece is a personal letter, dated November 13, 1988. The final paragraph refers to an inside joke. Lila and Nessa are O'Neill's cats. Lila has an extremely heavy coat. The joke was that Lila's long vigils at the window were in anticipation of fur deliveries made while she was alone in the house. How does the voice of the letter compare with the voice in the personal narrative?

Dear ——————,

Twenty years ago tonight I had just given birth to Cindy. Things were tense; RH factors had done their damage and I knew from experience that the next 72 hours were going to be rough. Happily, she thrived. We had a little birthday party tonight at dinner, just me, Jenny and Cindy. We celebrated "20"—the end of the teens. It seems so long ago and so clear at the same time. I feel a little sad. I wish I could go back to when the girls were babies, like Peggy Sue in the movie. We looked at pictures last night. Remember when Collins sold baby picture contracts? And we looked through memorabilia—a first grade "autobiography" and some other grade school stuff. Why don't we know we should take time to enjoy those years? What I remember is that I liked being a mother, but not a wife.

I have attempted that math proficiency test a second time; I needed only two more correct answers in one section and one more correct in the second section the last time. This time I believe I will do worse than the first try. I really knew nothing at all in the calculus, trig, quadratic equation section. And I spent many hours actually studying—something I haven't done since the first class I took at UWM in 1979. I'll have to wait and see, but I clearly am getting too old for this.

This letter is written on my own IBM PS/2-25. I've been able to do writing for school, and for InterPlan, too. It beats going to the office at 9:00 p.m. after class or all weekend long. I have this set up in my room on a big elegant table desk which I made from an expensive discarded desk top. I put 2″ diameter white enameled legs on the top. It takes up a lot of room, but because it is a table, it looks airy enough, not cluttered in the room. The white legs look very contemporary, too. I feel I should do important things at this fancy place. I do not think this will happen.

Lila wants to know if you cancelled the fur deliveries. I told her I did not. She believes that you are the culprit, as she waits in vain for the truck. Nessa sits with a smile on her face, wearing a lovely coat. My own suspicion is that Nessa switched the order, and takes delivery herself. She is lucky if that is the case because, as you may have noted, three inches of snow fell last Sunday. It is melted, of course, but not because we are breaking any heat waves. I have already needed the oil tank filled once. And the electric bill has tripled over the summer rate. I hate not only the inconvenience and physical discomfort of winter, but also the fact that it is so damned expensive. I spent this afternoon raking leaves into the street. I took the clothesline down. That is my surrender, the clothesline. I hardly ever feel more contented than when I am hanging out laundry, or taking it in, smelling the fresh air in the towels and sheets. The life I'd like best would be the one where I could always hang out the clothes. Is that a lot to ask?

Six more months til May.

This next letter was written a week later, November 21, 1988. It is on one topic, a sustained meditative piece. It is written to the same person, but it is not discursive like the first letter. Still, you can see how the first has inspired the second. She is conscious of the need to further explore the subject of nostalgia, to explain it to herself as well as to her audience. How would you compare the voice in both letters? How has purpose affected it?

Dear _____,

I'm still in the grip of nostalgia. Your kind note attempting to put my mood into perspective did help a bit. But do you think we will look back on 1988, its pseudo-politics and politicians, atrocious environmental pollution, materialistic values, and insufferable pace, with nostalgia about the way things were? If so, when will this happen? Will I be too senile to care?

Right now, the world is spinning a bit too fast for me. Oh, true, I like to keep moving. But I don't know, just now, what I'm moving toward. Is it a sense of accomplishment, a feeling of pride, a salary of $50,000, or a total nervous breakdown?

Here's the connection I want to make. I am obsessed with the TV coverage of the Kennedy life and death. I sit mesmerized, exactly as I did in November of 1963, experiencing the same emotions I did then. I watch the two black students attempt to register for classes at the University of Alabama, and I remember when I marched in a picket line at Marquette University against the racist governor of their state. I see the films of Bobby Kennedy, alive then, and know with a sort of dramatic irony, his fate. I see Martin Luther King eloquently unafraid to defy those who oppressed his race, and I know that he, too, will soon be gone. Those were my heroes. They really were. They were important to me then, in a serious way, in spite of the distractions and interferences of life. I had plenty of distractions, too.

Now, looking back, I feel more surprised than anything. I have always felt the values of the '60s were worthwhile. I just forgot about them, and as life went on, so did I. Lately, with Cindy's birthday, and now with the Kennedy films, I remember what I believed in. And with the passing of time, and the process of nostalgia, the memories make me sad.

I'm getting old.

Business Writing

Presented next are the minutes from a departmental meeting. Ms. O'Neill, as explained earlier in this chapter, is an office manager at a small architectural design firm. She wrote these minutes. What do you make of them? And how does the voice here, within a business context, compare with or contrast to the voice you hear in the more private discourse?

DEPARTMENTAL MEETING
MINUTES OF FEBRUARY 13, 1987

Here are the minutes of our meeting of Friday, February 13th.
1. Florence opened the meeting at 7:35 a.m.
2. Florence handed out a pamphlet on telephone skills. The pamphlet suggested ways to answer customer's questions. We all thought it was helpful. We plan to discuss other pamphlets at future meetings.
3. Julie is organizing our supply room. Let Julie know if supplies run low.
4. Susie is taking extra care to check work orders before entering them on the computer. She also includes letters of credit with orders to new vendors. These steps reduce orders being held for clarification or credit approval.
5. Florence showed us a new debit memo she designed. We'll use the form when it comes back from the printer.
6. Barbara is learning the Lotus 123 program. She will use it to develop department budgets and management reports.
7. Spraying carpets with a solution of 4 parts Downy fabric softener and 1 part water solved the static electricity problems around Barbara's word processor. Barbara also enjoys the "April fresh" scent of Downy.
8. The meeting ended at 8:05 a.m.
               Respectfully submitted,

This next piece is a business letter, dated February 7, 1991, written to the general manager of another firm. How would you compare the voice in this letter with the one heard in the personal letters?

Dear _____:

Our computer system is really taking shape. Here is the update I promised you.
• The Autocad programs are finally running! It took two months to convince the Director of Design to invest the time—and money—to train everyone, but it worked. Now all five designers are drawing plans on the computer. And the results are really impressive. Laura did a presentation for B&L yesterday, and today we got the order. I'm convinced that Autocad sold the project. So is Laura.

- I scheduled a DOS training class for my staff and invited the designers to join us. You can sit in if you'll be here March 5th. Karen knows pretty much about the network and DOS now, but she'll be there too. We can all use the training.
- I'm still waiting for the information you promised me. We plan to install the communications satellite in July. If we get the licenses and permits it could be even sooner. I need to order the programs and the computer by the end of March, and I'd like to look over your plans first. Could you send the report by March 15th? I'm counting on you.

Sincerely,

This last piece is an in-house memo.

To:	Sales
From:	Julie O'Neill
Date:	February 5, 1991
Subject:	Service calls

Our computer is fussy about service calls. The way we do our paperwork adds to the problem. Too many loose ends! We need to make some changes. Here's how we'll be doing service calls now.

1. Give your order to your sales assistant, just as you always have.
2. Your sales assistant will make a photocopy of the order. She'll give the copy to the service department right away. That way they can get started on the job.
3. The next day she'll enter your order to the computer. You'll get your copy when the computer prints the orders for the day.
4. Your sales assistant will keep the original order. That way she can check with the service department to see if we need to order parts to finish the job.
5. When the service ticket comes in we'll bill the customer. You'll get a copy of the invoice so you'll know the work is done. No loose ends!

We think this will work better than the way we used to do things, but if you have any other ideas, let me know.

Considering Voice in the O'Neill Selections

Julie O'Neill is not a well-known or published author, but she writes regularly, in a variety of rhetorical contexts, and most importantly, she writes extremely well. Her voice can be heard not only in her creative writing (the self-expressive pieces) and personal letters but also in her public discourse (business communications). As she moves through audiences, occasions, and various roles, she reveals some parts of her speaking personality and edits others. Just as we all do in life, and just as subtly.

Her subtle modifications may suggest to some readers a need to break away from a core voice, from some fixed manner of expression. Some writers play with many kinds of voices, choosing according to mood as well as rhetorical context. Others don't. They change only certain qualities of an essential voice, as I suggested in the beginning of this chapter, when they write to different audiences. For these writers, there's a belief something like this: "I look and feel good in cool colors. Why wear warm for variation? I have enough in the cool spectrum to choose from." All writers modify voice for different occasions, but different writers modify to different degrees, based on their skills, their desires, and the needs of their audiences.

Classroom Activity: Hearing Variations on a Melody

Having read the O'Neill samples, try to list the distinctive features of her voice, those that can be heard across all of the pieces. What stylistic choices appear to give rise to the voice you hear?

Then consider three categories of speech: creative/self-expressive writing, personal letters, and business communications.

1. What changes does she make as she moves from one mode of discourse to another, one audience to another? What features of her voice fade as she shifts from self-expressive to public discourse? Which features seem to become more noticeable, if any?
2. How do you account for those changes? Are they good, bad, or neither?

Writer 3: Mary Blewett

Classroom Journal Excerpts

The final selections are written by Mary Blewett, an English professor at a small liberal arts college in the Midwest. Blewett teaches composition and world literature courses. In both introductory and advanced composition, she requires students to keep a journal. Some of the entries derive from class assignments; some become propositions developed into sustained, revised discourse. Blewett keeps her own journal and, along with students, publicly shares her entries. The following pieces come from that journal. Students listened and offered revision help to Blewett, just as they did for each other.

First, let me give some background. At the time these entries were written, the war in the Persian Gulf had begun. Students wrote journal entries on the following quotations from Natalie Goldberg's *Writing Down the Bones:*

1. "An obsession for peace is good. But then be peaceful. Don't just think about it."
2. "I used to think freedom means doing what you want. It means knowing who you are, what you are supposed to be doing in this life and simply doing it."
3. "Our lives are at once ordinary and mythical."
4. "This is what it is to be a writer, to be the carrier of the details that make up history."
5. "Give things the dignity of their names."
6. "Love this life because it is ours, and in the moment, there is nothing better."

In the class period where this journal assignment had been given, the war came up in discussion. A rather fiery exchange ensued. A student, whom Blewett especially liked, began to cry. Her brother was in the gulf. In the heat of discussion, Blewett had openly decried the war and, in so doing, offended this particular student who was personally committed to defending American involvement. Blewett felt guilty. Here's what she wrote.

IN-CLASS JOURNAL WRITING ON TWO NATALIE GOLDBERG QUOTATIONS

"Our obsession with peace is good. But then be peaceful." One problem is that peace isn't enough of an obsession. I don't and breathe it. It doesn't fill my mind. It remains for me an intellectual topic that I return to out of a sense of duty. Violence may be my real obsession. My fantasies are encounters which are not peaceful because

> a) I express myself to people in my fantasies in the most severe terms. Are my arguments eloquent and would they persuade? If so, I should make them public. Or are they crazy and would terrify (I'm not even talking about the people who would close their ears over anything that's a different opinion). And
> b) I imagine winning.

So I'm not obsessed with peace. I'm obsessed with violence and I'm obsessed with other things that right or wrong fill my mind when I want to escape from thinking about peace. My fantasies about peace are not peaceful. I take a position for Peace but I realize that I don't know where to go next.

"Love this life because it is ours and in the moment there is nothing better." Sister _____ said almost the same thing: these aren't happy times but they're our times. Thoreau says the same thing when he writes that he'll go for the genuine meanness of life if he finds out that meanness is what life's really about. But you get the sense that he hopes—I hope when I read it, anyway—that we'll find out that if we dig deep it isn't mean. His whole book suggests that it doesn't have to be. Of course, it's not meanness that our life is about right now, though James might have said that it's a mean age that led to this war. Now that we're in it, people don't want to hear the truth and let go of the war because it gives them excitement. It gives their lives meaning. For a while their "lives were touched by fire." The *New Republic* talks about giving our kids something to be heroic about other than fighting.

Personal Letter
This piece is a journal entry (dated 1/25/91) addressed to a specific person.

Dear _____,

I tell my students to list their obsessions, according to Goldberg (some obviously too embarrassing to "share") and pick one that they can talk about and write about. . . . I reserve morning time for good coffee and writing or reading, but I see I've wasted an hour going on an imaginary rampage, fighting my own war instead of doing the class prep that started my mind in that direction—the abuse-of-language-in-the-polis obsession. . . .

Peter would say I should write down all that goes through my head—all the reasons to be outraged, to plunk them down in a list the way W. does. But we're all either bored or terrified by W.'s rage. (Lately, she's been screaming about Bush and waving her cane at the TV. Even when you try to talk to her about something else, that cassette of rage clicks on and it's Finger 1, 2, 3, 4, 5: "In the first place. . . .")

When we were at J. and S.'s in France, we met a man who probably is a saint. I know I say that about people, but it's my corollary to my other statement that there's evil in the world. I swear that this man has a nimbus. It's not a gold ring floating behind his head, but light seems to come in a kind of suffused way from his face. It beams, but softly. He's in his 80s. He has a friend who's a hermit. The friend is a Benedictine from Switzerland, maybe, or Strasbourg, and though he's still a B., he asked permission to live as a hermit. So he lives in isolation in a tiny shack in the hills. He has to have some contact with people because he does gardening to support himself (his order can't be expected to support his hermit habit) and more than that, he's apparently very happy to have visitors. His place isn't well heated, and he serves horrible coffee, but likes to talk to people. (I was just reading someplace that the purpose of a hermit is not to get away from people but to have people beat a path to your door.)

I'm interested in this concept of the hermit and wonder if in order to protect myself against rage, I'm going to have to adopt a practice of intellectual hermitage—like studying piano or Greek again or practicing madrigals.

Revised Journal Entry
The following piece is the first journal entry revised with suggestions from an advanced composition class, intended for specific students in that class.

Peace doesn't even count as one of my obsessions. Of course, I want the war to end now; I want a tribunal set up to arbitrate conflicting claims in the region; I want somehow to escape the consequences of our having sown the seeds of lasting enmity in the Middle East; and I want my compatriots to repudiate the foreign policy that led to this war and to the alliance with Hussein and with others like him. But I don't pray for those things to come to pass. Whatever I'm praying to has by definition already forbidden this war. There is no point in praying for the end of actions we willfully continue to take. I can pray for peace in my heart: prayer then is the process by which that kind of peace is achieved.

But it's not even the case that the war is my obsession, though I am dangerously quick to anger when people defend it. What engenders this rage in me, what makes it necessary for me to pray for peace in my heart, is the attack on our democracy which is both a cause and an effect of this war. Even in my calm moments, I sincerely doubt whether people—whether American people—can govern themselves, and I see proofs that they can't in the nation-wide memory loss and hysterical rhetoric that accompany this war. To say that there is nothing better than self-government is not to say that it will succeed, and I am terrified of what life will be like when it fails. My fears about the disintegration of our society and the death of our country, fears caused by the war but also by other things, including some of my teaching experiences, are, if not excessive, certainly obsessive.

If I were obsessed with peace, I'd fantasize about it, and I don't. If our fantasies are where we find our obsessions turned into moving pictures, and if I examine the fantasies about the sermons I'd like to preach to the war supporters whose letters appeared in last Sunday's newspaper, I have to confess that these fantasies feature me as the victor of a verbal battle. When I stand back and consider my rage, I see that my passionate desire is not to be peaceful and loving but to defeat these enemies. What I want is to win. What I want is to win and then to be merciful. But that's another story.

Personal Letter to Student
This is the letter sent to her student.

Dear C.,
When we talked, we each described scenes in which we figured as ranters and ravers—me with our class for not caring about the facts surrounding the war, or about the difference between the facts and their interpretation of them in our reading, or about the uses and abuses of language in political discussions, and you with the television set for showing peace activists whose protests seemed to threaten S. I think we agree that although anger—or rather righteous indignation—might be effective in small, controlled doses, it can frighten or bore people or render

us ridiculous and ineffective. If we want to win peace for the world, we need to nurture it in our hearts and model it in our lives: that's a truism and one manifested as a truth in successful peace movements. But if I fail to achieve that inner peace, my failure doesn't change the reasons I oppose the policies that destroy peace. My loss of credibility doesn't change the truth of the message; it just makes it much harder to communicate it. Well, you've acknowledged both the sincerity of my concern in this matter and the dangers of my anger, and I can see that you need to give your full assent to a venture your brother believed heroic—all for love of him. So here I was with my heart at war with my proclaimed policy and there you were, perhaps, with your heart at war with your mind, a civil war for sure.

I might finally decide that inner peace transcends the need for political and rhetorical power and that the exercise of power might destroy peace too. But I suppose it would always be my duty as a language teacher to condemn language that justifies the destruction of farms and cities and human bodies—the very places which house "inner peace." In any case, your letter and your visit contributed to my heart's peace: they amounted to what a friend of mine calls a mitzvah. I wish, especially now as you prepare for your wedding, that I could confer on you an equal blessing: that in the future you never have to choose between your heart and mind again, that they will remain on civil terms, and that you'll always live in the peace that comes from that accord.

Considering the Selections by Mary Blewett: What Comes to Light

Mary Blewett's pieces illustrate the messy activity of writing, creating a voice and discovering ideas. When emotions are intense, it's hard to separate things, to explain to ourselves, much less to an audience. Sentences run this way, then another, as our voices hurry our feelings along.

Blewett's letter to her student pulls together the themes running across her journal entries. Having turned the subject over and over in a variety of contexts to more than one audience, Blewett begins to take control of her subject; and once she does, she can shape the subject with her real audience in mind. She can find the balance she was seeking for herself as well.

Journals are private places, places to vent our feelings, where we often clumsily explore our thinking. There, our voices can go unchecked by even our own censors. Listening in on those early entries, you, the audience, may have been irritated, dismayed; you may have even disliked the speaker. In the letter (within the journal) another sound emerges, a voice still speaking, however, within a protected zone—to a close friend. The final letter to her student highlights still other qualities of a voice—balanced, sympathetic, carefully talking to a relatively unfamiliar audience, seeking a common ground and recognizing differences with respect.

Questions for Discussion
1. Describe the voice you hear in the first journal entry. How does the genre itself give rise to certain features of voice that might be edited for a different writing occasion? To what extent does the writer seem aware of her students even as she writes a personal journal entry?
2. Do you hear changes in voice when the writer addresses the subject in a personal letter within a journal entry?
3. What specific revisions in voice and arrangement of subject matter do you notice in the journal entry that was edited with the help of her advanced writing class?
4. In the final letter to her student, what ideas and subjects do you see that have been explored in the earlier pieces? How has Blewett modified and added to them as she adjusts her voice to her audience? Consider also the reverse: How may she have adjusted her thinking as she modifies her voice?

WRITING ACTIVITY: ANALYSIS OF VOICE AND AUDIENCE

Find two or three pieces by the same author, each written to a different audience, on a different occasion, for a different purpose. What features of the writer's voice seem similar in all pieces? What features change as the writer changes rhetorical situations? How would you analyze these pieces?

As an example here is a student essay in critical analysis. The

writer is John Nichols; he begins with a few paddlings on the
water before he takes off.

STUDENT ESSAY ON CRITICAL ANALYSIS

Writers reveal their personalities in their sentences. A voice
speaks from each phrase, sentence, and paragraph. As we read,
the voice we hear proclaims that the words were written by a
living, breathing human being. When we hear the voice, the
words become charged with feeling. The phrase lives. Voice also
helps us to understand ideas better. Sense, or logic, is closely
bound to voice. No matter the subject or audience, writers'
voices connect their ideas.

I have selected three pieces from the work of William Faulkner. The subject matter, occasion, and audience are different in
each. The paragraph from *Absalom, Absalom!* leads the reader
from a Mississippi summer to a Harvard winter. Faulkner speaks
with a high literary voice here. His images are complex. His
thoughts expand the sense over one long, complex sentence. The
letter to the editor parodies the reasons why his hometown wants
to ban the selling of beer. Faulkner's voice here is more relaxed
and tinged with irony. The last piece, an interview about his stories, shows Faulkner's words as he spoke them, not after careful
revision. Faulkner's unique voice prevails in each work. Yet he
makes some adjustments to achieve different effects, given his
audience and subject. Whether he's speaking to a sophisticated
reader, the people of Oxford, or to an interviewer, we can identify a consistent personality, a Faulknerian voice.

What exactly is his voice? And how does it permeate his prose,
from the modernistic *Absalom, Absalom!* to a simple interview?
Faulkner's voice reveals a mind constantly testing its own ideas,
clarifying its thoughts as they unfold. The result is a rather convoluted sentence pattern. To unify so many different images requires an intelligent personality with voice to match. Faulkner's
winding sentence structure creates a voice we can identify as
highly literary.

His voice in part derives from sentences in hypotactic, polysyndetic style. Faulkner continually uses conjunctions, adverbs,
and prepositions to stretch the sentence, linking and lending importance to more description and qualification. For example,
here is a sentence from *Absalom, Absalom!*:

The twilight was full of it <u>and</u> of the smell of his father's cigar
<u>as</u> they sat on the front porch <u>after</u> supper <u>until</u> it would be

time for Quentin to start, <u>while</u> in the deep shaggy lawn below the veranda the fireflies flew <u>and</u> drifted in soft random— the odor, the scent, <u>which</u> five months later Mr. Compson's letter would carry up from Mississippi <u>and</u> over the long iron New England snow <u>and</u> into Quentin's sitting-room at Harvard.

Faulkner could have written it this way:

The twilight was full of it and of the smell of his father's cigar. They sat on the front porch. After supper, it would be time for Quentin to start. In the deep shaggy lawn below the veranda the fireflies flew and drifted in soft random. Five months later the odor and scent would carry up from Mississippi, over the long iron New England snow, into Quentin's sitting-room at Harvard.

I tried to eliminate most of the connections in the original passage. The result is a paragraph of seemingly disparate images. It sounds like Faulkner imitating Hemingway. Each sentence flashes a new description. Without the connectors, the flow from the image of the summer porch to the New England winter is broken. In the original, the conjunctions bridge the images smoothly.

The same sentence pattern can be heard in Faulkner's letter to the editor, but with different effect:

Of course, it costs twice as much <u>when</u> it is delivered to your door, <u>and</u> you usually drink too much of it, <u>than</u> if you had to get up <u>and</u> go to town to get it, <u>but</u> better that <u>than</u> to break up the long <u>and</u> happy marriage between dry voters <u>and</u> illicit sellers, <u>for which</u> our fair state supplies one of the last sanctuaries <u>and</u> strongholds.

The subject matter here is quite different. Faulkner is talking about beer, not how the summer scents of Mississippi travel to a wintry Harvard. The letter is also directed to the townfolk, people he knows, not to unknown readers. Still, Faulkner uses a voice that clarifies and qualifies clause to clause. In the *Absalom* selection, the effect was a unified, literary image—from the porch to Harvard. In this letter, the voice is not serious, but ironic. Some of the irony comes from the subject matter, the hypocrisy of the dry voters who would rather go to more trouble to buy beer from the illegal sellers than allow beer to be sold legally. But Faulkner's voice accentuates their ridiculous logic.

In *Absalom,* the structure of the sentence works to clarify and connect the sense. Here, the structure reveals the dry voters' lack of sense. By listing (a Faulkner habit), he uses a rhetorical device that sets up a disparity—the voice is intelligent; the sense the voice describes is not. In *Absalom,* the sense and voice are unified. Here, the voice satirizes the sense.

Lastly, Faulkner uses this same hypotactic sentence structure when he talks to the interviewer. Here is part of it, recorded at the University of Virginia:

Q. Is "A Rose for Emily" all fiction?

A. Yes sir. Yes sir, that's all fiction, for the reason I said, too. If any time a writer writes anything that seems at all familiar to anybody anywhere, he gets a letter about it, and if they think he's got enough money, he's sued too, so he's awful careful not to write anything he ever saw himself, or anybody ever told him.

Even though this interview records Faulkner's words as he spoke them, and not as he would have revised them had they been from a novel or letter, the voice remains essentially his. That mind, constantly thinking, describing, qualifying, can still be heard. In the other selections, the logic is bridged by the voice for a literary effect (*Absalom*), or betrayed by the voice for ironic effect (letter). In the interview, the sense and voice work together for comic effect. The sense is funny: call your writing fiction or you'll get sued. But Faulkner's writing temperament, always modifying, expands the sentence, stretching the humor to the end. When we reach the last clause, the last thought, we laugh as much about the length as the sense. By employing the same sentence patterns as in the other selections, Faulkner here extends the thought as well as the joke.

His voice remains rather consistent in each selection. Granted, in *Absalom,* the voice is more sophisticated than in the others, especially the interview. But that is a novel, a work he labored over. The interview is spur of the moment. Faulkner creates different effects in each piece, from humor to subtle description. But we can still identify the voice as his, despite the change in tone.

Faulkner doesn't change his personality from one rhetorical situation to another. Neither do we. We do not have to spend time searching for completely different voices, alien voices, when we write. We can begin with our own.

WRITING ACTIVITY:
MODIFYING YOUR VOICE
FOR DIFFERENT AUDIENCES

Write two pages on a subject of your choice. Then write three versions of the piece, each one directed to a different audience. Try to make the occasions different, too, if you can. For example, one version may be a journal entry; another, a personal letter; the third, a short essay (or part of an essay). Or you might make one version a formal business report; the second, a personal letter about the information to an insider; and the third, a letter about the information to an outsider.

After you have written drafts of all three, ask members of a small group to read them and to find similarities and differences in your voice from one rhetorical context to another. How do they account for them? How do you?

On another sheet of paper, compare what your audience heard with what you heard yourself in writing the different pieces. What do you conclude from this exercise?

Applications

Practice in Problem Solving

This chapter extends the work of the last chapter. It offers assignments to give you practice in problem-solving skills. Each assignment suggests a rhetorical situation describing your role as speaker, a purpose, an audience, and an occasion. Some assignments include writing for two audiences; occasionally, one of the audiences is yourself. Some rhetorical situations are quite general; others, specific. They have been designed to reflect the varying experience of both traditional and nontraditional students, and to reflect different levels of rhetorical skill.

In choosing, you will need to decide which problems are within the realm of your experience, those not far beyond the range of roles you already play in life. In other words, be careful not to place yourself where you cannot reasonably imagine access. If you do, you will pose unnecessary and even impossible rhetorical and stylistic problems. You want to speak and write with a strong sense of self and place. Your goal all along has been to develop power over your own utterance. Making conscious choices about why this kind of sentence, why this word, gives you that power. It gives you the ability to imagine how to modify your own voice in addressing different audiences on different occasions.

Most of the problem-solving assignments listed in the next section grew out of classroom collaboration. Within your own class, you may choose to modify certain assignments or to design your own in collaboration with your teacher and peers. What is within the range of one writer's experience and abilities may be too far outside the range of another's. The best way to proceed is to begin where you are and to suit the problem to your own particulars. From there, you can move forward, gradually placing yourself in less familiar situations, addressing less familiar audiences. No writer, however, places himself or herself in completely alien situations, for reasons I explained previously.

SUGGESTED PROBLEM-SOLVING ASSIGNMENTS

1. Define a concept or explain an issue you are exploring in another course. Prepare two versions of your essay. The first is for students in that course. In developing your essay for them, try to show the relevance of the concept or issue to the broader questions underlying the course. The second is for students in your English class. In developing your essay for them, try to show the relevance of the concept or issue to their academic study or to their lives.

Test each of your drafts on the appropriate audience. You may want to show version 1 to your professor in the other course. Revise each version in light of audience response.

2. Define or explain something you know very well (a non-academic topic). If you include anecdotal experience, don't let it become the focus of your writing. The focus should be the explanation.

Prepare two versions of it, each one for a different audience. Test both versions on the appropriate audiences. Revise your drafts in light of audience response.

3. You attend a small liberal arts university. You have chosen a major that truly interests and challenges you, but it does not have direct application to a career. Your parents have urged you to choose a more "practical" field, one that will specifically prepare you for a job. They are skeptical about your decision. To be honest, you've had your doubts too. Still, given your interests and abilities, you feel you've made the right choice.

First, assure yourself that you're doing the right thing. Second, assure your parents.

4. You are married and have a full-time job. Last year you decided to return to college and complete your undergraduate degree. Juggling the demands of marriage (family, perhaps), work, and study has not been easy, but you enjoy your courses more now than you did several years ago. You can schedule no more than two courses a semester because of time constraints. This semester you are taking biology of women to fulfill your science requirement. It is a large lecture-designed course in which your grade is determined by performance on three written exams. After the second exam is returned (you have earned an A −), you overhear two young women complaining about their grades:

"Having older women in class really ruins the curve. They only take one or two courses and put all their time in them. If we weren't taking a full load, we could compete. It's so unfair."

This isn't the first time you've been aware of such resentment. You seethe all the way home, constructing different versions of a response to their charges. To put your thoughts to rest, you write a letter to these young women, a letter you do not intend to deliver necessarily, but one that helps you rehearse what you might say should you ever again hear public remarks aimed in your direction.

A variation of this assignment: You are single and juggling the demands of full-time employment and study.

5. You have worked full-time for several years. Your salary pays the bills comfortably and your current position at _____ affords you some measure of satisfaction. You earned your bachelor's degree five years ago, but had always intended to return for a master's. You have recently paid off your student loans and now own your own car. You've begun thinking seriously about graduate school.

Your employer has just implemented an incentive plan, offering to co-pay tuition for ten people in your job class each fall semester. You must write a proposal addressing why further education will benefit you and the company, designating the degree you will pursue and under what time frame you will complete it.

Persuade the five-person committee (who will make the awards) that you should be one of the ten. You are aware that the committee includes your immediate supervisor, who does not want to give you released time from your daily duties. You also have some reason to believe that he or she is personally threatened by your steps toward advancement in the company.

A variation: Assume that the incentive plan is for those who have not earned a bachelor's degree.

6. You attended a private college prep school. Now you are a junior at a large urban university. In the past two years many of your beliefs have been challenged, particularly your sociopolitical beliefs. Several groups on campus have made you aware of and sensitive to cultural diversity and individual freedoms/differences. Some of your friends belong to those groups; they have been actively involved in controversial social and politicial issues. You have wrestled within; some of your values are in conflict, perhaps in transition.

Your best friend from high school attends a local, private college in your hometown where he or she has not had your experiences. Certain issues have been addressed in the classroom, but they have not directly touched your friend's life in the ways they've touched yours. The student population at the local college is very homogeneous.

Your friend is a sensitive, intelligent person. You've wanted for some time to write a letter expressing how your experiences have had a profound effect on certain values/beliefs you once shared.

7. You have been appointed the spokesperson for a group of students, co-workers, or an athletic team of which you are a member. Your task is to present a problem or issue of concern to an immediate supervisor and to offer a possible solution for resolving it.

Although you are on friendly terms with your immediate audience, you do not want to sound too casual. The issue is serious. And your letter most likely will be passed on to a higher authority for review. You'll need to keep that in mind while trying to avoid sounding unnaturally distant. Restrict your topic to a problem and resolution that can be reasonably addressed in the near future.

8. You grew up in a large city, but you have won a scholarship to a private college or university in a small town. Even though you are doing well academically, you feel a cultural and/or social gap that seems unbridgeable. You've tried to adjust, but you can't.

Write a letter to your best friend at home, explaining why you want to transfer.

Write a letter to your parents.

Then explain the reasons to the appropriate authority at the university, if that's expected.

9. As an experienced junior or senior, you have been asked to speak to freshmen during the orientation program next fall. The topic is "Coping with Freedom." You know from your own experience that freshmen hear little that's said during orientation. And yet you also know how difficult freshman year can be without some peer guidance. As an older peer, you could have more credibility than an official authority figure. Write your speech, focusing on a few major problems for freshmen without sounding like yet another parental echo.

10. Your high school is in the process of curricular reform. The curriculum coordinator and the chair of the English department have invited selected graduates to speak about their writing experiences in college. These are the questions you need to address:

What kind of reading/thinking/writing is required in college?

To what degree did high school prepare you for college writing?

Was the transition difficult? If so, how might it have been made easier?

11. Your mother (or father) is a member of Signa Fi Something, a sorority (or fraternity) that has a local chapter at the college you attend. She (or he) has encouraged you to join. Many of your friends on campus are planning to rush or are already members of sororities and fraternities. The pressure increases. Yet you've resisted and have decided not to rush.

Explain your reasons to the appropriate parent.

Explain them to your disbelieving friends.

12. The college or university you attend has been trying to attract students from different cultural and social backgrounds to diversify the community. The goal is to enrich cultural, social, and academic life on campus.

You are one of several students who have been asked to address two committees—recruitment and student affairs—at a meeting both will attend. Your task is to recommend improvements on campus based on your experience. To prepare, you have interviewed many students who, at present, represent a small percentage of the academic community and who are at different levels of experience—freshmen, sophomores, and so on. Write your address to the combined committees.

13. A variation on the assignment in 12: The high school you attended has developed a program called Awareness Week. It focuses on the concerns of graduating seniors. You have been invited as one of several graduates who won scholarships to various colleges and universities that recruit people of color from your high school each year.

In your role as a panel participant, you have been asked to speak to the senior class about your first-year college experience. Your goal is to explain the conditions under which you would recommend or not recommend that students of color enroll at X university or college.

14. You are married and have been primarily attending to your family's needs. You have been active in the community and have served in leadership roles. You have enjoyed that experience, but it has not replaced your desire to return to college and complete your degree.

Your spouse is supportive, but your school-age children seem threatened by your decision. It will mean less flexibility in your schedule and changes in household responsibilities.

Explain your decision and its consequences to your children.

Explain to your friends who have relied on your active support of various issues in your community.

15. In your first year in college, you chose courses based on popularity polls—what other students claim are the easiest courses or required courses that are taught by "easy" professors. Although not all claims were proven true in your experience, you did earn some high grades without much effort, and some by learning precisely how to please your teachers. To put it simply, you took few intellectual risks. And for the most part, it paid off.

This year, you chose according to your developing interests and began to test your own abilities. You didn't throw caution to the wind, exactly, but you took some risks, exploring ideas on exams and papers that were not mere repetition of lecture notes or class consensus. A few of your professors encouraged your efforts and helped you develop your own thinking. Even though your initial grades in their courses were low, they did

improve during the semester. Nevertheless, your g.p.a. was noticeably lower this year than last.
To what degree were your efforts worth the risk? First, evaluate your learning experience for yourself. Then describe your experience to two other audiences—a friend on campus, an advisor, a professor, your parents.

STUDENT SAMPLES

The following essays were written in response to assignment 2: explaining something you know well to two different audiences. The writer is Delbert Rose; his topic, bodybuilding. In the first essay, he addresses those who know little or nothing about the topic; in the second, those who already work at bodybuilding.

Essay I

When most people think of bodybuilding, they usually confuse it with weightlifting. While they want the muscular frame of someone like Arnold Schwarzenegger or football player Hershel Walker, they take the wrong path to achieve those looks. I was one of those people. But I've learned enough to help those who may not know much and who want to achieve the look of a bodybuilder.

Because of my earlier misguided practice, I don't, even now, look like a bodybuilder. When I first started, I trained as a weightlifter. In a nutshell, my training consisted of going to the gym and trying to lift as much as I could. I gained strength but not the appearance I wanted. I looked like a weightlifter, not Schwarzenegger. When people saw me, they may have even thought I was out of shape. But at the age of 16, I was incredibly strong. Luckily, I found out how to train correctly and can pass that knowledge on to you. I must warn you, though, that bodybuilding will be harder than weightlifting because you need more discipline and patience. Results take longer to appear, but they are worth your efforts.

The most important part of training is learning how to lift the weights. Find a weight that is neither too heavy nor too light for you. Then do a high number of repetitions—approximately 8–12. A repetition is each time you flex and unflex the muscle you're working on. A determined number of repetitions makes a set. An example of the terminology is 3 sets of 10 reps.

Although each person wants specific results, there are some basic exercises for everyone. These I'll describe to you. For the upper-body workout (everything above the waist), start with your arms. Do three sets of bicep curls (the muscle that bulges when you flex your arm). Then, to work on the shoulders and the triceps (the muscle that's opposite the biceps), do some shoulder presses. In this exercise, lift the weight above your head and below your chin. Next, work the abdominal muscles. The best exercise is the crunch. Lie on the floor and rest your legs on the bench. Then, tighten your stomach muscles, bending forward, 1/4 to 3/4 of the way up. When you start to tire, complete your sets by going up as much as you can—even if it's only 1/4 of the way.

To work the lower body, use the following machines. The leg curl machine works the hamstrings—the back of the leg. Lie on your chest and curl your legs as high as you comfortably can. Think of this as the legs' version of the biceps curls. The leg extension machine is built like a chair with a bar under it. Place your legs behind the bar and simply extend them. This exercise works the front of the legs—the quads.

The exercises above form the basic workout. For your safety, be sure to go to a weight room with someone who can help you. And be sure to include some aerobic exercise too—swimming, running, bicycling, for example. (Contrary to what some people believe, fat does not turn to muscle.) Proper weight training, aerobics, and diet will help you achieve your goals.

Essay II

For those who are training to achieve the chiseled look with bulging pecs and washboard abs, but are tired of the same basic exercise, try free-weight techniques and variations on your basic machine workout. Remember people were looking like Lee Haney long before machines were used in lifting.

To work your legs, you don't have to confine exercise to the basic leg extension and leg curl machines. Here are three other good exercises. The best is the squat, which is one way to achieve the symmetry you're looking for. Besides, in one good set of squats, you use as much energy as you do running a 100-meter sprint. Be sure to bring your weightbelt, though, so you don't hurt yourself. Next, try the leg press. While the squat gives symmetry and strength, the leg press mainly adds strength. It's especially good if you haven't done much squatting and need to build up strength. The final exercise can be considered a cool-down in the leg workout. It's best to get some comfortable free weights. Let your arms hang while holding them, and find something 6–12 inches high to support your weight. Then do the same number of sets: those where you step up with the right leg first, and those where you step up with the left leg first.

For the upper body, there's not much to add to the basic workout. Mainly, vary it. When you attack those abs with crunches, do them on a decline bench. If that still seems a bit too easy or you feel you're not getting much out of it, hold some weight disks to your chest. For the arms, more specifically, the biceps, use single hand weights instead of the single bar. This exercise helps to build symmetry in the biceps. For your lat pulldowns, instead of the overhand grip, use an underhand for some sets. The underhand puts more emphasis on the biceps.

Now it's time to hit those pecs. The oldest and best workout for the entire pectoral is the push-up. Push-ups force the body to balance itself and add mass to muscle. For the upper pecs, use two free weights and an incline bench. Once on the bench, simply do whatever number of sets that feel comfortable.

These exercises will add variety to your workout and help you achieve your goals. As you advance, you may find your own versions and variations of the basic workout. Just remember to do your best and work out safely.

SOLVING AUDIENCE PROBLEMS

In the following chapter from *Tough, Sweet, and Stuffy*, Walker Gibson describes three different voices speaking about the same general topic. The exercises that follow focus on particular kinds of audience problems.

HEARING VOICES:
Tough Talk, Sweet Talk, Stuffy Talk

> It ain't what ya do,
> Hit's the way that ya do it,
> That's what gets results.

Suppose we begin to read—to expose ourselves to an introduction.

Suppose we pick up, for instance, a magazine, the *Saturday Review*. We riffle its pages. Already we are taking on some attributes of an assumed reader: we have some experience of this magazine and its general personality, and we know vaguely the sort of person we are expected to be as we read it. We are not, at any rate, at this moment, the assumed reader of *The Hudson Review,* or *The New Yorker,* or *House Beautiful,* or *Frisky Stories.* The eye lights on a title. Just our subject. Who's speaking here?

The Private World of a Man with a Book

The temptation of the educator is to explain and describe, to organize a body of knowledge for the student, leaving the student with nothing to do. I have never been able to understand why educators do this so often, especially where books are concerned. Much of this time they force their students to read the wrong books at the wrong time, and insist that they read them in the wrong way. That is, they lecture to the students about what is in the books, reduce the content to a series of points that can be remembered, and, if there are discussions, arrange them to deal with the points.

Schools and colleges thus empty books of their true meaning, and addict their students to habits of thought that often last for the rest of their lives. Everything must be reduced to a summary, ideas are topic sentences, to read is to prepare for a distant test. This is why so many people do not know how to read. They have been taught to turn books into abstractions.

Everything depends on the *personality* to whom we have just been introduced. His message can never be divorced from that personality, that speaking voice—or at least not without becoming essentially another message. The question I am asking is not "What is he saying?" but "Who is he? What sort of person am I being asked to *be,* as I experience these words?" A difficulty immediately arises. We can hardly describe with justice the fellow talking except by quoting his own words. He is what he says, precisely. The minute we lift an assumed "I" out of the text and start to describe or reproduce his personality in *our* language, or in language that we infer might be his, we are admittedly altering him, mangling him, killing him perhaps. But it is the only way. The biologist studying cellular structure has to dye his specimen under the microscope so he can see its parts, but the dye kills the living tissue, and what he sees is dead and gone. It is a familiar intellectual dilemma, and there is nothing to do but be cheerful about it, applying one's dye as liberally as necessary while recognizing its poisonous possibilities.

With that proviso, then, who's talking, in the first two paragraphs of "The Private World of a Man with a Book"? What assumptions is he sharing with his ideal reader? What follows is, as I hear it, a between-the-lines communication between the assumed author and the assumed reader:

> You and I know all about the shoddy academic situation, where lazy and wrongheaded teachers do so much harm to the true meaning of books. You and I share a true knowledge of true meanings, and can recognize instantly when wrong books are taught at the wrong time in the wrong way. I am a rugged no-nonsense character, for all my academic connections, and you, thrusting out your jaw, couldn't agree more.

Now it is clear from this effort that I (the assumed author of this essay) do not very successfully engage myself as the ideal assumed reader of these two paragraphs. It is clear that when I have the speaker saying "You and I share a true knowledge of true meanings" I am not writing a paraphrase at all, but a parody. I am exaggerating what I take to be a sort of arrogance in the speaker, with a view to ridicule. How did I reach this curious position?

I reached it because, as I read the two paragraphs, I suffered a conflict. I was aware, on the one hand, of the person I was supposed to be (one who knows what "true meanings" are, for instance). But I was also aware, much too aware, that I was *not* that person, and, more important, didn't want to pretend to be. This is not a question of changing one's beliefs for the sake of a literary experience—that is easy enough. One can "become" a Hindu or a Hottentot if the speaker is sufficiently persuasive and attractive. But that's the rub: the speaker must be attractive to us. And in this case, because of qualities I have called "arrogance" and "rugged no-nonsense," I have become not the assumed reader at all, but a hostile reader. Consider one moment where hostility, at least in this reader, was aroused. It is the second sentence—"I have never been able to understand why educators do this. . . ." The difficulty here is that we sense hypocrisy in that remark. Just how is the assumed reader being addressed? Is it this?

> I've tried and tried to understand why teachers go at books this way, but I just can't get it.

Or is it this?

> The trouble with teachers is that they're either too dim-witted or too lazy to teach books the right way. Oh I understand it all right!

Now which is it? Let's admit it could be either (a fault in itself?), but insofar as we may strongly suspect it's the second, then the actual phrasing ("I have never been able to understand") seems falsely prevaricating in its covert antagonism.

I have used such expressions as "rugged no-nonsense," "covert antagonism," and "thrusting out your jaw." In the next-to-last sentence of our passage we can illustrate one rhetorical technique by which impressions like these are conveyed. "This is why so many people do not know how to read." We have here, to anticipate, some rhetoric of Tough Talk. The phrasing does not allow the possibility that not so many people are so benighted after all. No doubts are permitted. By placing its "many people do not know how to read" in a subordinate clause, the voice assumes a *fact* from what is at best an extreme statement of an arguable position. The independent clause ("This is why") merely speculates on the cause of the "fact." The reader is pushed around by a tough-talking voice.

But insofar as we can divorce the utterance here from the utterer—and I have said that this is strictly impossible—then what is being said in this paragraph seems to me both true and important. Indeed, I would personally agree, books *are* too often taught as abstractions, and in any vote in any faculty meeting, the assumed author and this reader would vote together on this issue. But we do not take pleasure in reading for such reasons as that. In fact it may have been this very agreement, this sense that I personally did not need persuading, that led me to read no further in the article than the two paragraphs I have quoted. But surely it was not only that. I read no more because I felt that the assumed author was browbeating me, and changing me over in ways I did not like. I don't care how "right" he is: he's got to be *nice* to me!

But unfortunately, it is not enough to be nice. Life is very hard. Let us consider now another assumed author—same magazine, a few years earlier, same general subject—and listen to a voice that goes out of its way to be nice.

Unrequired Reading

The title of this essay may strike you as a typographical error. You may be saying to yourself that the writer really means required reading, and the phrase conjures up for you, I suspect, lists distributed on the first days of college courses: Volume One of this distinguished scholar's work on the Byzantine empire in the fourth century, that brochure on the economic interpretation of the Constitution, this pundit's principles of economics, that pedant's source book.

Or, perhaps, still under the apprehension that I mean required reading, you are reminded of what by now is one of the more maddening insolences of criticism, or at any rate of book reviewing. "This," says Mr. Notability, "is a *must* book." This in the atomic age is compulsory reading. In a world of anxiety this uneasy novel is not to be passed by.

I beg of you to forget such obligations and responsibilities. To this day you have to forget that you *had* to read "Macbeth" in order to begin to remember how perturbingly moving a play it is. Hardly anyone would reread Burke's "Speech on Conciliation" if he recalled how he had to make an abstract of it in high school.

Once again let us try to assess the sort of person addressing us here, remembering that this person bears no necessary connection with its author. In listening to this voice, we become aware as always of an ideal listener, a "you," whose characteristics we are expected to adopt as we read.

I am a sweet professorish sort of fellow, full of big words but simple at heart—you are younger than I, and though you have of course been through college, you are by no means an academic professional like me. My charm is based on an old-fashioned sort of formality ("I beg of you") combined with a direct conversational approach that I trust you find attractive. I wear my learning lightly, occasionally even offering you a tricky phrasing (*pundit's principles, pedant's source book*) or a modern cliché (*world of anxiety*) to show you I'm human. But we share, you and I, a knowledgeable experience of literature; we both recognize for example how "perturbingly moving" *Macbeth* really is.

It is easy to identify at least one rhetorical device by which the professorial voice is often dramatized. It is the device of parallel structure. A pattern of balanced phrasings suggests a world similarly balanced, well ordered, academic. The first paragraph's list is an example: *this distinguished scholar, that brochure, this pundit, that pedant*. A somewhat similar effect occurs later: *this a must book, this is compulsory reading, this is not to be passed by*. Triplets like that are characteristic of the fancier tones. In the last two sentences we have the balanced device of chiasmus, a criss-cross relation of parallel ideas. The clauses there are arranged in an order of time past, time present, time present, time past.

You have to forget that you *had* to read to remember how perturbingly moving it *is*.

Hardly anyone *would reread* Burke (now) if he recalled how he *had* to make an abstract.

Very neat, literary, elegant. Parallel structure alone, of course, could not produce a sweet-professorish voice. But it can support the meanings of the words, as it does here.

The assumed reader, here as always, is a sympathetic yes man, responding uncritically (yet of course intelligently) to the speaker's invitations. When a reader responds critically, in the negative sense, and begins to disagree, he forsakes his role as assumed reader and lets his Real-Life Self take over. If this goes on very long, he will simply stop reading, unless he has some strong motive for swallowing his irritation and continuing.

We can imagine a sympathetic conversation going on between speaker and assumed reader in our passage, something like this:

> The title of this essay may strike you as a typographical error. [Why, yes, as a matter of fact it did.] You may be saying to yourself that the writer really means required reading [I did rather think that, yes], and the phrase conjures up for you, I suspect, lists distributed on the first days of college courses [Oh yes, those dreadful things]: Volume one of this etc. [You certainly have it down pat! And I do appreciate your gentle scorn of pundits and pedants.]

But suppose, once again, that one does not enjoy playing the part of this particular assumed reader. Suppose one is uncomfortably aware of an insupportable gap between one's Own True Self and the role one is here being asked to adopt. Again it is probably obvious that I (still the assumed author of this essay) suffer from just such an uncomfortable awareness. The mechanical and prissy straight man that I have constructed out of the assumed reader reveals my own antagonism, both to him and to the sweet talk of the speaker. Suppose we were to play it my way, and invent a conversation between the speaking voice and a hostile reader who refused to take on the required qualities:

> The title of this essay may strike you as a typographical error. [Why, no, as a matter fact that never occurred to me.] You may be saying to yourself that the writer really means required reading [Don't be silly. I would be more surprised to see a title so trite. In fact your title embodies just the sort of cute phrase I have learned to expect from this middlebrow

magazine.] and the phrase conjures up for you, I suspect, lists distributed on the first days of college courses [That's a dim memory at best. How old do you think I am?]: Volume one of this distinguished etc. etc. [You bore me with this lengthy list and your affected effects of sound-play.]

Or, perhaps, still under the apprehension that I mean required reading ["Perhaps" is good. How *could* I be "still" under such an apprehension?'], you are reminded of what by now is one of the more maddening insolences of criticism [You're maddened, not I. Calm down.], or at any rate of book reviewing. "This," says Mr. Notability, "is a *must* book." [Do even book reviewers use such language?] This in the atomic age is compulsory reading. In a world of anxiety this uneasy novel is not to be passed by. [I appreciate you are ironically repeating these tired phrases, but they're still tired.]

Now of course this mean trick can be worked by anybody against almost anything. The assumed reader of this essay, for example, may so far forget himself as to try it on *me*, though I deeply hope he doesn't. Again it is important to emphasize that the argument here is not between two people disagreeing about an issue. I agree with the educational stand taken here about reading, just as I did with the similar stand taken in our first passage. *The argument is between two people disagreeing about one another.* And this time it is not a case of the Tough Talker pushing the reader around, but a case of the Sweet Talker who condescends and irritates in a totally different way.

The general subject our two writers have been discussing comes down to something we could call The Teaching of Reading. It is a subject that can easily be confronted in some other voice, of course; in fact it seems to me doubtful that there can be *any* subject which by definition *requires* any particular voice. To illustrate the third of my triumvirate of styles, and to exhibit The Teaching of Reading as attacked with a very different voice, I offer the passage that follows. Again it presents a thesis with which I am quite in agreement—as who is not?

Teaching Literature

Rapid and coherent development of programs in modern literature has led to the production of excellent materials for study from the earliest years of secondary education through the last of undergraduate study. The sole danger—if it be one, in the opinion of others—lies in easy acceptance of what is well done. The mechanics of mass production can overpower and drive out native creativeness in reflecting on literature and so stop individual interpretation in teaching. We hear a good deal of the dangers to imaginative experience in youth from excesses of visual exposure, and we know that they therefore read much less, in quantity, from longer works of prose and poetry. It may prove to be true, therefore, that in the study of literature the critical authority of the printed page will seem an easy substitute for individual analysis of original texts, first for the teacher and next inevitably for students who have never learned to read, with conscious effort in thinking, through verbal symbols.

After making necessary allowances for a passage ripped from context (for I have had to choose this time a paragraph from inside a work rather than an introduction), the fact remains that this is a Stuffy voice. It is by no means an extreme example of Stuffy Talk, but it is Stuffy enough to be marked off as distinct from the Toughness of "Private World" and the Sweetness of "Unrequired Reading." We become, as we read, solemn; the brow furrows; perhaps we are a little Stuffy ourselves. This transformation is the direct result of certain habits of vocabulary and sentence structure by which the Stuffiness is conveyed. I put off identification of these habits until we have examined the Tough Talker and Sweet Talker more thoroughly. Meanwhile, my point is that a *style* is not simply a response to a particular kind of subject-matter, nor is it entirely a matter of the writer's situation and his presumed audience. It is partly a matter of sheer individual will, a desire for a particular kind of self-definition no matter what the circumstances.

The point can be further illuminated by trying just one more introduction, asking ourselves what sort of voice this is:

On Teaching the Appreciation of Poetry

I hold no diploma, certificate, or other academic document to show that I am qualified to discuss this subject. I have never taught anybody of any age how to enjoy, understand, appreciate poetry, or how to speak it. I have known a great many poets, and innumerable people who wanted to be told that they were poets. I have done some teaching, but I have never "taught poetry." My excuse for taking up this subject is of a wholly different origin. I know that not only young people in colleges and universities, but secondary school children also, have to study, or at least acquaint themselves with, poems by living poets; and I know that my poems are among those studied, by two kinds of evidence. My play *Murder in the Cathedral* is a set book in some schools: there is an edition of the English text published in Germany with notes in German, and an edition published in Canada with notes in English. The fact that this play, and some of my other poems, are used in schools brings some welcome supplement to my income; and it also brings an increase in my correspondence, which is more or less welcome, though not all letters get answered. These are letters from the children themselves or more precisely, the teenagers. They live mostly in Britain, the United States, and Germany, with a sprinkling from the nations of Asia. It is in a spirit of curiosity, therefore, that I approach the subject of the teaching of poetry: I should like to know more about these young people and about their teachers and the methods of teaching.

This is an interesting case, unlike our other three passages but not uncommon in expository prose, where the assumed reader simply has to know who the real author *is* if he is to understand the message at all. In this instance, he is the late T. S. Eliot. Implicit in the speaker's words is the knowledge, on the part of both his reader and himself, that he is speaking for one specific human being, and that the most distinguished literary figure of his time. How pleasant to meet Mr. Eliot. This knowledge is modest (or is it smug?) on the speaker's part, deferential on the reader's part—but it is *there*. We may imagine messages going out from speaker to assumed reader something like this:

> How pleasant it is for me to acknowledge my academic deficiencies when you know exactly who I am! (Besides, *are* they deficiencies? You and I know better, don't we?) When I start in to attack an educational method, my own method can assume the mild forms of amateurishness, good humor, and mere "spirit of curiosity." My words can be so light because my reputation is so weighty. You, surely an admirer of my long career, can smile knowingly when I say that I "should like to know more about" these teachers and this method. *You* know that I'm going to tear them apart, but gently, deftly, without losing an ounce of my urbanity. They are scarcely worth my heavier weapons.

The assumed author of this essay finds that voice very hard to deny. This is not Tough Talk at all, nor is it exactly Sweet Talk, nor is it Stuffy. Some readers may find it overly self-conscious, possibly condescending, possibly banking too much on the reader's swooning before this great reputation. But I do not find it so. The spectacle offered here, of the great man unbending, seems to me not unattractive, and I am won more than lost by such carefully human touches as the reference to his income, or the amused use of the slight vulgarism "teenagers." The blunt repetition of "I" and the simple structure of the opening sentences seem candid and there is some deliberately comic hypocrisy in the modest admissions. (I hold no diploma, true, but you know I don't need to!)

We have—or at least I have—a trust in this speaker. Why? Is it because of his overpowering reputation? In large measure, probably. This is a speaker with an enormous advantage, and he takes advantage of his advantage. But it is more than that. The personality that emerges here, with his wit, his urbanity, his refusal to be ruffled, is simply a personality I am willing to go on listening to. The fact that he is about to take a general stand about teaching that is more or less in agreement with all three of our previous voices, and myself, is neither here nor there. The fact that he may also tread on some educational methods I myself espouse (or have been guilty of) is mildly disturbing, but not seriously. It is the character I meet here that makes the difference. He is not pushing me around, like the Tough Talker. He is not cuddling up to me, like the Sweet Talker. He is not holding me off, like the Stuffy Talker. He respects me. I return the compliment.

This is the case of the speaker as famous man. It is, as I say, not uncommon in argumentative prose, though it is seldom so graceful. But it is impossible in fiction, and for most of us it is impossible anyway. You have to be very famous indeed to get away with it. It does show us a respectable voice in operation, but it tells us only a little about how rhetoric can produce a respectable voice without the Real Author looming in the wings. Our questions remain. How are words selected and arranged so that a particular speaking voice is dramatized and identified for us? (15–27)

Exercise: Tough, Sweet, and Stuffy

1. Find a short passage from your own reading that illustrates a tough, sweet, or stuffy voice. Try to describe

why you are unwilling to play the role of the assumed reader. (You could, as Gibson does, invent a conversation between the speaking voice and an unsympathetic reader.) Rewrite the passage, eliminating the qualities that evoke your negative response. If the passage is too tough, make it sweeter; stuffy, make it unstuffy; too sweet, make it tougher. You are trying to modify the voice so that you are more inclined to be a sympathetic reader.

2. Write two versions of the same piece on a subject of your choice. Make one an example of sweet talk; the other, tough talk. Ask members of your group to respond critically to both versions—what in each interferes with their willingness to play the role of assumed reader? Remember, as Gibson says, that "the argument . . . is not between two people disagreeing about an issue." Your reader may accept your position. "The argument," Gibson emphasizes, "is between two people disagreeing about each other."

Now rewrite the paragraph in a voice that is not dominated by either quality. Ask the group to respond again. To what degree are they closer to becoming your ideal readers? Are their responses similar or varied? From their responses, what and how much would you change, if anything? How have you decided to balance pleasing yourself and pleasing your audience?

3. Find a passage that seems written directly to you as a reader. What in the writer's voice accounts for your positive response? What has the writer assumed about you that makes you an ideal audience? Ask members of your group to read the passage too. To what degree do they respond as you do? If there are noticeable differences, how do you account for them?

Reading List

The following selected bibliography is a short list of works on style and voice that you may find useful and interesting. The list, of course, reflects my own tastes and experience as a developing writer.

Anderson, Chris. *Free/Style.* Boston: Houghton, 1992.

In an informal and inviting voice, Anderson covers approaches to style, the sound of words, the shape of content, sentence structure, some "tricks of the trade," and the achievement of special effects. All chapters show how revision shapes style. The text includes examples and analysis of both professional and student writers.

Belenky, Mary, et al. *Women's Ways of Knowing: The Development of Self, Voices, and Mind.* New York: Basic, 1986.

"Voice" in this text is a metaphor describing women's "intellectual and ethical development." According to the authors, one's senses of voice, knowledge, and self are inextricably connected.

Elbow, Peter. *Writing with Power, Techniques for Mastering the Writing Process.* New York: Oxford, 1981.

This text addresses the whole writing process. Of particular interest are Chapters IV ("Audience") and VI ("Power in Writing"). These address matters of voice directly.

———. "The Pleasures of Voice in the Literary Essay." *Literary Nonfiction: Theory, Criticism, Pedagogy.* Ed. Chris Anderson. Carbondale: Southern Illinois Press, 1989.

Peter Elbow argues that voice is a "useful critical concept for the study of texts," and in his essay he distinguishes among "audible voice" (what we hear as we read), "dramatic voice" (implied speaker or writer), and "one's own voice" (relationship of text to actual writer). He illustrates these with examples from the work of Gretel Ehrlich and Richard Selzer.

Gass, William H. *The World within the Word.* New York: Knopf, 1978.
William Gass, philosopher and fiction writer, examines literature, culture and writers (their lives and works), and the nature and uses of language. His own critical prose is an example of voice as literary art.

———. *Habitations of the Word.* New York: Simon, 1985.
In this collection of essays that range from literature to philosophy to the theory of language, William Gass considers the relationship between word and event, word and writer, word and reader. See, especially, "Culture, Self and Style," "The Soul Inside the Sentence," "On Talking to Oneself," and "On Reading to Oneself."

Gibson, Walker. *Tough, Sweet, and Stuffy: An Essay on Modern American Prose Styles.* Bloomington: Indiana UP, 1966.
This book is a "must read" for anyone interested in how voice is produced through attention to various stylistic features. Gibson draws examples from a variety of prose genres. Exceptionally helpful is the analysis of voice styles relative to their effects on audience.

Hugo, Richard. *Triggering Town, Lectures and Essays on Poetry and Writing.* New York: Norton, 1979.
Although the text is intended for poetry writers, there are some real gems tucked inside several lectures and essays, advice that would help all writers who attend to the sound words make on the page.

Lanham, Richard A. *Analyzing Prose.* New York: Scribner's, 1983.
This book is an introduction to rhetorical analysis of prose styles, intended for the advanced student. Lanham describes and analyzes a variety of prose styles, drawing examples from business, technical, political, psychological, and literary prose. To study style, according to Lanham, is to study human behavior and motives. Our motives affect our prose styles.

———. *Revising Prose.* 2nd ed. New York: Macmillan, 1987.
In this text, Lanham offers a quick cure, the "paramedic method," for bureaucratic prose. Bureaucratic style is formulaic writing based on the habit of shunting the action of verbs into nouns, using weak or passive verbs, and stringing together prepositional phrases. Because the writing is formulaic, it can be cured by formula. Although *Revising Prose* focuses on one kind of writing problem, it is a central problem for many writers across disciplines and professions.

Williams, Joseph M. *Style, Ten Lessons in Clarity and Grace.* 3rd ed. Glenview, Ill.: Scott, 1988. Paperbound.
For advanced writers, this book is a sophisticated discussion of

stylistic features that improve the coherence, rhythm, "clarity and grace" of individual sentences and paragraphs. Each lesson includes exercises for application.

Zinsser, William. *On Writing Well, An Informal Guide to Writing Nonfiction.* 3rd ed. New York: Harper, 1976.

Zinsser talks directly and informally to writers about craft. He addresses a variety of subjects, including general principles of style, various genres of nonfiction, word processing, attitudes toward language (matters of taste, tone, and eloquence) and toward one's work (matters of confidence, ego, and pride). Voice is implicitly an integral part of the text.

List of Works Cited

Chapter 1

Bechet, Sidney. *Treat It Gentle.* New York: Da Capo, 1975.

Hugo, Richard. *Triggering Town.* New York: Norton, 1979.

Lanham, Richard. *Analyzing Prose.* New York: Scribner's, 1983.

Moore, Marianne. *Complete Prose of Marianne Moore.* New York: Viking, 1986.

Thompson, Lawrance. *Robert Frost, Selected Letters.* New York: Holt, 1964.

Chapter 2

Britt, Suzanne. "That Lean and Hungry Look." *Newsweek* 9 October 1978.

Gass, William. *On Being Blue, a Philosophical Inquiry.* Boston: Godine, 1976.

Ghiselin, Brewster. *Against the Circle.* New York: Dutton, 1946.

Hickey, Dona J. "Not for the Best." *Carolina Quarterly* Fall 1982.

Hugo, Richard. *Triggering Town.* New York: Norton, 1979.

McEnroe, Colin, "How to Get a Baby." *Mirabella* Mar. 1990.

Robinson, Michael. "A Classy Joint Called Benjamin's: Lights Are Low, Waiters Know." *Richmond News Leader* 14 June 1990.

Volk, Patricia. "Why I'm Glad I Don't Look Like Michelle Pfeiffer." *Mirabella* Mar. 1990.

Chapter 3

Britt, Suzanne. "That Lean and Hungry Look." *My Turn* column. *Newsweek* 9 October 1978.

Cochran, Connor Freff. "For God's Sake—Do Something!" *Keyboard* July 1987.

Robinson, Michael. "A Classy Joint Called Benjamin's: Lights Are Low, Waiters Know." *Richmond News Leader* 14 June 1990.

Volk, Patricia. "Why I'm Glad I Don't Look Like Michelle Pfeiffer." *Mirabella* Mar. 1990.

Chapter 4

Cochran, Connor Freff. "Going Too Far." *Keyboard* Sept. 1987.

Corbett, Edward P. J. *Classical Rhetoric for the Modern Student.* 2nd ed. New York: Oxford UP, 1971.

Gass, William. *On Being Blue, a Philosophical Inquiry.* Boston: Godine, 1976.

Lanham, Richard. *Analyzing Prose.* New York: Scribner's, 1983.

Volk, Patricia. "Why I'm Glad I Don't Look Like Michelle Pfeiffer." *Mirabella* Mar. 1990.

Chapter 5

Corbett, Edward P. J. *Classical Rhetoric for the Modern Student.* 2nd ed. New York: Oxford UP, 1971.

Gibson, Walker. *Tough, Sweet, and Stuffy, An Essay on Modern American Prose Styles.* Bloomington: Indiana UP, 1966.

Lanham, Richard. *Revising Prose.* 2nd ed. New York: Macmillan, 1987.

Turner, Frederick W., ed. *The North American Indian Reader.* New York: Penguin, 1978.

Williams, Joseph. *Style, Ten Lessons in Clarity and Grace.* 3rd ed. Glenview, Ill.: Scott, 1988. Paperbound.

Woolf, Virginia. *To the Lighthouse.* New York: Harcourt Brace Jovanovich, Inc., 1927.

Chapter 6

Beattie, Ann. *Picturing Will.* New York: Random, 1989.

Dillard, Annie. "Living with Weasels." *Teaching a Stone to Talk.* New York: Harper, 1982.

Ettinger, Austen A. "Mum's the Word." *New York Times Magazine* 3 Feb. 1991.

Frith, Simon. "Rock and Sexuality." *Sound Effects.* New York: Random, 1981.

Hurston, Zora Neale. "How It Feels to Be the Colored Me." *The World Tomorrow* 11 May 1982.

Styron, William. *Darkness Visible.* New York: Random, 1990.

Chapter 7

Barthelme, Donald. "The Sandman." *Sadness.* New York: Farrar, 1970.

Elkin, Stanley. "The Future of the Novel: A View from the Eight-Seated Spaceship." *New York Times Book Review* 17 Feb. 1991, sec. 7.

McEnroe, Colin, "How to Get a Baby." *Mirabella* Mar. 1990.

Chapter 8

Volk, Patricia. "Why I'm Glad I Don't Look Like Michelle Pfeiffer." *Mirabella* Mar. 1990.

Appendix

Gibson, Walker. *Tough, Sweet, and Stuffy, An Essay on Modern American Prose Styles.* Bloomington: Indiana UP, 1966.

Index

Acknowledgments

Donald Barthelme, "The Sandman," from *Sadness*. Copyright © 1970, 1971, 1972 by Donald Barthelme, reprinted with the permission of Wylie, Aitken & Sons, Inc.

Ann Beattie, *Picturing Will*. Copyright © 1989 by Irony and Pity, Inc. Reprinted by permission of Random House, Inc.

Sidney Bechet, excerpts from *Treat It Gentle*. Copyright © 1960 by Farrar, Straus and Giroux, Inc. Reprinted by permission of Hill and Wang, a division of Farrar, Straus and Giroux, Inc.

Suzanne Britt, "That Lean and Hungry Look," *Newsweek*, October 9, 1978. Copyright © 1978 by Suzanne Britt. Reprinted by permission of the author.

Connor Freff Cochran, "For God's Sake—Do Something!" *Keyboard*, July 1987, Miller Freeman Publications, Inc. "Going Too Far," *Keyboard*, September 1987, Miller Freeman Publications, Inc. Copyright © 1987 by Connor Freff Cochran. Reprinted by permission from *Keyboard* magazine.

Edward P. J. Corbett, *Classical Rhetoric for the Modern Student*, 2nd edition, reprinted by permission of Oxford University Press.

Annie Dillard, "Living with Weasels," from *Teaching a Stone to Talk*. Copyright © 1982 by Annie Dillard. Reprinted by permission from HarperCollins Publishers.

Stanley Elkin, "The Future of the Novel: A View from the Eight-Seated Spaceship," from *The New York Times*, February 17, 1991. Copyright © 1991 by The New York Times Company. Reprinted by permission.

Austen A. Ettinger, "Mum's the Word," from *The New York Times*, February 3, 1991. Copyright © 1991 by The New York Times Company. Reprinted by permission.

259